Contributions to Economics

For further volumes:
http://www.springer.com/series/1262

Mainak Mazumdar

Performance of Pharmaceutical Companies in India

A Critical Analysis of Industrial Structure, Firm Specific Resources, and Emerging Strategies

Physica-Verlag
A Springer Company

Mainak Mazumdar
Centre De Sciences Humaines (CSH)
New Delhi
India

ISSN 1431-1933
ISBN 978-3-7908-2875-7 ISBN 978-3-7908-2876-4 (eBook)
DOI 10.1007/978-3-7908-2876-4
Springer Heidelberg New York Dordrecht London

Library of Congress Control Number: 2012948155

Printed on acid-free paper

Physica is a brand of Springer
Springer is part of Springer Science+Business Media (www.springer.com)

Acknowledgements

I am happy to place on record my gratitude towards numerous persons who helped make this work possible.

First and foremost, I am deeply indebted to my supervisor, Professor Meenakshi Rajeev, for her incredible guidance and support. As a teacher, she taught me how to understand seemingly incredible and complex problems in a simple way and motivated me to think about the "economics" of research problems, whenever I was in doubt.

I had the good fortune of being advised by Professor Subhash Ray from the University of Connecticut with the fascinating technique of DataEnvelopment Analysis that I have extensively used in my dissertation. I am indebted to Professor Ray for being so generous with his time.

I am indebted to Ms. B.P. Vani, Assistant Professor, CESP, ISEC, for her generous help in econometric analysis throughout my work and for always having an answer to every possible question on econometric-related problems that a graduate student may have.

I also thank Dr. Gopal Tribedy, my teacher during college days, and Swami Supernanda, a monk of the Ramakrishna Mission, who introduced me to this fascinating subject.

I am grateful to the Institute for Social and Economic Change (ISEC), Bangalore, for providing me with an opportunity to pursue my Ph.D. I thank the present director, Professor R.S. Deshpande, for all his support and encouragement during this period. I am also thankful to him for teaching me to consider even the most minute research problems seriously, which helped me in my research. I thank the former director, Professor Gopal K. Kadekodi, for all his affection towards me and for teaching me to always keep the big picture in mind. I also want to thank Professor N. Jayaram, the former director of ISEC, for his support. It would have been impossible for me to complete this study without the inspiration and encouragement that I received from him.

I am thankful to late Professor Hemalatha Rao, Economics Unit; Dr. Devendra Babu; and Dr. M.R. Narayana, CESP, ISEC, for their valuable suggestions as members of my Doctoral Committee. I also express my gratitude to Professor

S. Madheswaran; Dr. K. Gayathri; Dr. C. Nanjundaiya, CESP; Mrs. Vasantha Kumari, ISEC; and Dr. Thippaiah, ADRT, for their valuable inputs as panelists of various works-in-progress and seminars of my doctoral work.

Thanks are also due to the former Ph.D. co-ordinators, Professor M.D. Ushadevi, Professor A. Inbanathan, Dr. N. Sivanna, and the present Ph.D. course co-ordinator Dr. C. Nanjundaiah, for their support and help. I am also thankful to the pre-Ph.D. course work co-ordinators, Professors, G.K. Karanth, Rajasekhar, Supriya Roy Chaudhuri, and Ramachandra, for their valuable teaching.

I wish to express my special thanks to Mr. K. S. Narayana, the present registrar (AR), for his administrative support. I would also like to thank Mr. Satish Kamath and Mr. Krishna Chandran for their help in solving all problems related to informatics. I also want to thank Mr. Jadgish for his help in accounts-related matters. I express my gratitude to Mr. B.S. Krishnamurthy, Mr. Kalyanappa, Mr. Venkatesh, Mr. Rajanna, Mr. T. R. B. Sharma, Mrs. Leela, Mrs. Naaz, Mr. Suresh, Mrs. Akhila, Mr. Venkatesh, Mrs. Margaret Dawson, Mr. Prakash, Mr. Amarnath, Mr. Chandrashekar, Mr. Sudarshan, Mr. Shivananda, Mr. Shashi, Mr Jagdish, and Ms. Vimala for the efficient and friendly support they rendered at different times. I specially want to acknowledge the love and help I received from Mrs. Shantakumari during my stay at ISEC.

I was extremely lucky to be surrounded by friends, old and new, whose love and affection made leaving ISEC much harder. I thank Krushna Mohan Pattnaik for being part of many happy memories. I specially thank Monojit Bhattacharya for being a very supportive friend throughout. My sincere thanks also go to my batch mates at ISEC, Skylab, Srikanth, Pradeep, Naveen, and Sachi, and specially Durba for her good company. I also thank Sukumar, Poulomi, Badri, Nisha, Lija, Emil, Subir, Sarala, Anand, Santosh, Architesh, Benson, Nitin Khalid, Sabyasachi (boss), and Jaga for their friendship during my stay at ISEC. I want to thank Prashob (*anna*) for his brotherly advice and support. I still miss the warmth of my friendship with the late Deepak Bishoy. I want to thank specially Avinandan, Amrita, Biplab, Rajdeep, Kaushik, Sabuj, Indrajit, Malini, and Tunga for all their love and concern for me.

I want to acknowledge all the support and help I received from the Centre de Sciences Humaines (CSH) team in New Delhi to finish my Ph.D. Without the sponsorship of CSH, finalizing this book would have been difficult. I am especially grateful to Dr. Basudeb Chaudhuri, Director of CSH, for patiently going through the final draft of the book and for giving me the valuable time and space that was required for finalizing my work. I want to thank Dr. Loraine Kennedy, CNRS France, for her support and valuable guidance and Jean-Luc Gourmelen for administrative support. I had a wonderful time in CSH due to the companionship of Mallika, Shelly, Ridima, Remi, Dalel, and Pushpa. I am grateful to Arpita for editing the book in spite of her busy schedule. I thank them wholeheartedly.

I received constant support and encouragement from my friends, Munna and Pratyusha. I also received immense support and encouragement from my brother Mayukh and my Sister in Law Godhuli Chakraborty. I thank them all.

I am also thankful to the managing directors and scientists of various pharmaceutical companies for sharing their valuable information with me, which was invaluable for understanding various interesting features of this industry.

It has been a pleasure to be able to work with the editorial team at Springer Press. Tumele Frank, my main person of contact, has been an amazing source of advice and help. I likewise appreciate contribution of Bethke, Barbara.

I am equally grateful to Dadamani, who showed me that man is born not just for pursuing self-interest but also to serve humanity. He stayed with me through-and-through, showered unconditional love and affection on me, and inspired me to follow my heart and pursue this path. I owe much to my grandmothers, late Mrs. Sandhya Mitra and Mrs. Saraswati Mitra, for their unconditional care and concern. Lastly, without the continuous support, inspiration, and blessings of my parents I would not have been able to start and finally complete my research. It is my duty to mention my heartfelt thanks to them, and I dedicate this book to them.

Mainak Mazumdar

Contents

List of Figures

List of Tables

Abbreviations

AC	Average cost
ACP	Average cost of production
API	Active pharmaceutical ingredients
ASI	Annual survey of industries
BCC	Banker Charnes and Cooper
BCPW	Bengal chemical and pharmaceutical work
CCR	Charnes Cooper Rhodes
CDR	Cost disadvantage ratio
CDRI	Central drug research institute
CMIE	Centre for monitoring of Indian enterprises
CPI	Consumer price index
CRS	Constant returns to scale
CSIR	Council of scientific and industrial research
DEA	Data envelopment analysis
DGP	Data-generating process
DGTD	Director general of technical development
DNA	Deoxyriboneucleic acid
DRS	Decreasing returns to scale
EC	Efficiency change
EU	European union
FDA	Food and drug administration
FDI	Foreign direct investment
FERA	Foreign exchange regulation act
FICCI	Federation of Indian chambers of commerce and industry
GEM	Global efficiency measure
GLS	Generalised least square
GMP	Good manufacturing practices
GMPI	Global Malmquist productivity index
HAL	Hindustan antibiotics Ltd
H_D	Herfindahl index
ICMR	Indian council of medical research

IDPL	Indian drugs and pharmaceuticals Ltd
IICT	Indian institute of chemical technology
IID	Identically and independently distributed
IO	Industrial organisation
IPR	Intellectual property right
IRS	Increasing returns to scale
LMPI	Local Malmquist productivity index
LP	Linear programming
MEP	Measure of efficiency proportion
MES	Minimum efficient scale
MES	Minimum efficient scale
MNC	Multi national companies
MNE	Multinational enterprises
NCE	New chemical entities
NCL	National chemical laboratory
NDP	New drug policy
NERA	National economic research associates
NIHCM	National institute for health care management
OLS	Ordinary least square technique
OPPI	Organization of pharmaceutical producer of India
PCM	Price cost margin
PPR	Production possibility ratio
PRS	Pastor Ruiz and sirvent
PSU	Public sector units
R&D	Research and development
RAM	Range adjusted measure
RBI	Reserve bank of India
ROA	Rate on asset
ROE	Return on equity
ROS	Returns on sale
RRL	Regional research laboratories
SCP	Structure conduct performance
SVF	Sales volume of firms
TC	Technical change
TCR	Technology closeness ratio
TFP	Total factor productivity change
TGR	Technology gap ratio
TRIPS	Trade related aspects of intellectual property rights
UK	United Kingdom
UNICEF	United nations children fund
USA	United States of America
VRS	Variable returns to scale
WHO	World health organization
WTO	World trade organization

Chapter 1
Introduction

1.1 Background and Motivation for the Study

The Indian pharmaceutical sector is a knowledge driven high technology industry. It is also considered as a 'Life-Line' industry because of the pivotal role it plays in mitigating human disease by producing drugs. The importance of the industry therefore cannot be judged merely by its contribution to the manufacturing sector alone. One also has to take into account the vital role it plays in the formation of human capital in the long run through a disease-free world.

The comparative advantage of Indian pharmaceutical firms lies mainly in imitative technology and in reverse engineering, whereby the industry can produce over 90 % medicine consumed in India. The industry manufactures almost the entire range of therapeutic products from its basic stage. With its exports destined to about 100 countries around the globe (which also includes the highly regulated markets of the US, Europe, Japan, and Australia), it is one of the top 20 exporters of bulk drugs and dosage forms and also the largest producer in the global generic market placing it in the fourth position in the international market.[1] The country can supply high quality drugs at a very low price in the international market and is a major supplier of essential drugs to the World Health Organization (WHO) and other developing and underdeveloped countries.[2]

The rapid growth of this sector is largely an outcome of the patent regime that the Government of India has pursued since 1970. The Patent Act of 1970 was in force for more than three decades and recognized only process patents for inventions related to medicines, drugs, or chemical substances for a period of only 5–7 years. Well equipped with technological expertise (that was acquired mostly due to government patronage), Indian firms availed of opportunities in the

[1] Ernst and Young Report (2005)

[2] It has the highest number of US approved plants outside the USA, which indicates a good manufacturing practice at par with global standards among domestic players.

M. Mazumdar, *Performance of Pharmaceutical Companies in India*, Contributions to Economics, DOI 10.1007/978-3-7908-2876-4_1,

Patent Act of 1970. They 'reverse-engineered' patented innovative products of foreign firms, mastered the technique of manufacturing and in most cases could eventually come out with better process technology for the same product. The comparative advantage of the industry is, therefore, an outcome of the earlier Patent Act of 1970, which has helped Indian producers create a niche for themselves[3] (Chaudhuri 1997, 1999; Kumar and Pradhan 2004; Watal 2000; Raizada 2002).

However, a major intervention in the policy system was noticed in 1994 when India along with other developing countries agreed to comply with Trade Related Aspects of Intellectual Property Rights (TRIPS) requirement of the World Trade Organization (WTO) agenda. The TRIPS Agreement compels its member countries to recognize and enforce product patents in their Patent Agreement in all fields of technology including the pharmaceutical sector. Because of WTO compulsions India was forced to amend its Patent Act of 1970 first in 1995 and subsequently in 2005, thereby paving the way for product patenting in the area of pharmaceutical and other chemical inventions. Apart from changes in Patent Law, as a part of the liberalization policy of 1991, there have also been some salient changes in the domestic regulation pertaining to this sector. In particular, the Drugs and Cosmetics Act, 1940 was amended in the years 1995, 2002, and 2003. It emphasized more on competition by abolishing industrial licensing requirements for all varieties of drugs[4]; by removing restrictions on imported bulk drugs; by limiting the scope of price control; and by automatically approving foreign ownership of up to 100% with foreign technology arrangements. Also concerned with the extent of spurious drugs in the domestic market, the Indian government incorporated Schedule M in the Drugs and the Cosmetic Act of 1995 which laid down the rules and regulations for strict quality control and good manufacturing practices amongst domestic players.

Changes in policy have evoked considerable debate, much of which is centered on the impact of policy changes on future prospects and the fate of the Indian pharmaceutical sector and in turn on the question of the availability and affordability of patented drugs for Indian consumers. With the TRIPS Agreement in force, it is expected that, compared to the past, there will be a fall in the total number of new products that Indian firms launch by re-engineering innovative products of foreign firms. Indian firms will therefore try to survive the market by focusing more on the production of off-patented products. However, the enforcement of the product patent may also induce the return of global pharmaceutical

[3] The industry now accounts for about 8 % of the world's production by volume, placing it in fourth place in the international market (Ernst and Young Report 2005). It is the largest producer in the global generic market with its exports destined to around 175 countries including the highly regulated markets of the US, Europe, Japan, and Australia. The country can supply drugs at a very low price in the international market and is an important source of essential drugs to the World Health Organization (WHO) and other underdeveloped countries. It has the highest number of US-approved plants outside the USA (FICCI Report 2005) which indicates good manufacturing practice at par with global standards among domestic players.

[4] Except for those produced by the recombinant DNA technology, those requiring in-vivo uses of nucleic acid and specific cell/tissue targeted formulations.

firms to the domestic market. This indeed implies that Indian pharmaceutical firms have to face increased competition in the domestic market even for off-patented products from foreign MNCs. The growing competition among players in the domestic market is also evident when we find that there has been an entry of about 150 new firms in the market between the years 1990–2003. As documented by a number of business reports (see Ernst and Young Report 2005; KPMG Report 2006; Pharma Guide 2005), the total number of firms operating in India stands at around 2000 in the year 2005, (many of which are small-sized firms) competing fiercely with each other to grab a share of the market.

Given the regulatory changes that had taken place pertaining to the lifeline industry, in this book we wish to analyze the performance of Indian pharmaceutical firms. In particular, we wish to examine the factors that are responsible for good or poor performance of firms in terms of efficient management of resources or in improving the productivity and profitability of firms. Such an analysis is necessary to address certain research questions that arise regarding the future performance of Indian pharmaceutical firms. Specifically questions that we want to address in our research are as follows:

First, *have increased competition and the resulting changes in the strategies of firms led only a section of firms that have adopted strategies like innovation and trans-nationalization to perform better? Have the rest, which consists of a large set of small and medium sized firms that have not adopted the above strategies, been left behind in the competition?* If not, the revelation of this fact through a formal exercise itself is a value addition and throws light on the behavior of firms.

Second, *what are the main features of the frontier or the best performing firms in this industry? Have increased liberalization and competition enabled frontier firms to perform better?* Progress of frontier firms implies a shift in the technological frontier or a technological change in the Indian pharmaceutical industry.

Third, *if we see a technological improvement then what are the sources of technological change in this industry? Does increased competition or adoption of strategies by firms have any relation with technological changes in the industry?* Such strategies may include R&D, modernization of plant and machinery to meet export norms and so on and so forth. These activities involve heavy investment but the returns may not be immediate.

Finally, we also wish to investigate *how firms that are not at the realm of the technological frontier perform compared to the best performing ones in the sampl*e?

It is evident from research questions that we have implicitly hypothesized large-scale persistent variations in the performance of firms. Such variations among firms may persist due to their size of operation or investment decisions and so on. Such assumption also stands against the traditional Industrial Organization (IO) theory by Mason (1939) and Bain (1951; 1956). The traditional IO theory neglects the importance of firm specific factors for their persistently higher performance. On the contrary the proponents of the IO theory argue that firms can persistently perform better only when they can successfully collude and behave like a monopoly firm. Such moves on the part of firms is possible if they are adequately protected by entry barriers like scale economies or degree of product differentiation. Popularly known as structure conduct performance (SCP) theory, scholars from this school of thought argue that firm performance depends solely on the structure of the industry in which it operates. Here the Industrial structure is measured in terms of *concentration level, barrier to entry*, and *degree of product differentiation* (see Scherer and Ross 1990; for more on SCP theory).

While the SCP framework has been successfully utilized to explain the impact of the structure of industry on the performance of firms, a major limitation of this paradigm is the neglect of firm specific factors in explaining their persistent differences in profitability. The role of the firm's conduct has been downplayed by pioneers of the SCP theory like Bain (1956) and Mason (1939), on the ground that is determined mainly by structural parameters of the Industry. The SCP theorist therefore considers the heterogeneity of firms (and hence by implication differences in the profitability of firms) to be a temporary phenomenon that is ultimately followed by the convergence of firms in the conduct and performance as a result of competition in the same industry. Later economists, however, disagreed with this generalized view (see Barney 1991) and argued that firms are not homogenous in terms of strategically relevant resources (as assumed by the SCP theorists) and that all resources in a firm are not tradeable. Thus, resource heterogeneity may exist among firms. Pioneering studies of firms in the US, by Mueller (1986) reported long-lived differences in profitability within industries, while studies of firms in the UK (Cubbin and Geroski 1987) and in several other countries (Mueller 1990) corroborate earlier findings. The recent evidence gathered about the performance of firms in developed nations also document large and persistent heterogeneity among firms even in a narrowly defined industry[5] (Robert and Tybout 1996; Tybout 2000).

The common observation of the persistent heterogeneity of firms within an industry has also stimulated several studies seeking to identify and describe the factors that block the convergence of the conduct and performance of firms over time. After the seminal paper by Demsetz (1973a) who pointed out that a superior competitive performance might be specific to the firm that has developed a differential advantage in producing and marketing its products, further studies identified technological, industry-based, historical and organizational considerations as leading factors in firm performance (Röller and Sinclair-Desgagn´e 1996). Recent theories of firms also suggest that asymmetric information and incomplete contracting, organization of firms and governance structures are also important drivers of firm specific persistent heterogeneity.

In this book, we also wish to examine the 'performance-differential' of Indian pharmaceutical firms. Given the regulatory changes that have taken place in this industry, we would like to examine and locate the sources of such differences in the

---

[5] Industrial organization literature explains profitability differences by factors external to the firm, such as the demand and technology characteristics of the product market, see e.g. Church and Ware (2000)

strategies and size of firms. *Additionally, we also wish to address the problem of availability of drugs that might arise due to changing strategies of domestic and foreign multi-national firms in the face of policy changes.*

1.2 Studies on the Pharmaceutical Sector

The global pharmaceutical industry, in general, has some unique features, which have attracted the attention of scholars for research. The industry[6] is known for its high thrust on R&D (Di Masi et al. 1991, 2003a,b), marketing tactics to sell its products (Hurwitz and Caves 1988) and high degree of regulation (Peltzman 1973, 1974). While R&D and marketing related activities in general enable firms to come out with new innovative products, they simultaneously charge high prices and maintain a competitive edge. Therefore, the concern for accessibility and availability of medicinal products at affordable prices also prompts the government to regulate prices for pharmaceutical products. The industry is also regulated to ensure good manufacturing practices and quality R&D among producers.

1.2.1 R&D in the Global Pharmaceutical Industry

While discussing R&D in the context of the pharmaceutical industry, a number of issues come to the fore, which has been examined by different authors. The issues related to R&D in the pharmaceutical industry can be broadly classified as follows:

1. Extent and productivity
2. Nature; and
3. Financing

1.2.2 Extent and Productivity of R&D

R&D involves heavy investment with uncertain returns. Therefore, it appears to be affordable only to large firms. Consequently, a number of studies have been conducted to examine whether 'large-sized' firms do more R&D. The end result is however, mixed. Two earlier studies that have examined this issue are by Comanor, (1967), and by Mansfield (1968). These studies, however, found a less than proportionate increase in R&D expenditure with firm size. However, studies by Schwartzman (1976a, b), Grabowski and Vernon (1981) and Wiggins (1981) indicate a more than proportionate rise in R&D expenditure with an increase in the

[6] See Schweitzer S O (1997) for a detailed discussion on various issues of the pharmaceutical industry.

size of the firm. Differences in the conclusion arise because compared to earlier studies the relationship between firm size and research expenditure differed significantly in the later period on account of changes in various government regulation.

An increase in R&D productivity with the size of the firm also puts large- sized firms at an advantageous position. The presence of economies of scale and scope in R&D activities also implies that large sized firms can sustain multiple projects and can also benefit from external and internal knowledge spill-over (Henderson and Cockburn 1996a). In recent times the biotech revolution has also brought about certain changes in the R&D productivity of firms. The study by Mariani (2007, 2004) examined the impact of biotechnology on the productivity of R&D. It supports the view that, in the traditional pharmaceutical sector, large sized R&D-intensive firms are more likely to produce important chemical innovations. However, when biotechnology is separated from traditional pharmaceutical sectors the co-location and geographical clustering of firms becomes an important determinant of R&D of firms. With technological specialization and knowledge spill-over in the area of biotechnology, small sized firms are also important drivers of innovation and can co-exist with large sized firms.

Apart from 'firm specific factors', the innovation decisions of firms are also propelled by the future market size and the expected revenue generated from the product invented (Scott-Morton 1999; Reiffen and Ward 2005). Using a dynamic model of R&D investment Acemoglu and Linn, (2004) estimated that a unit increase in the expected market leads to a 4–6 % increase in innovative products. They also noticed a positive relationship between the introduction of innovative drugs and expected revenues in the target market.

1.2.3 The Nature or Type of R&D

The nature of R&D also varies across firms. Bottazzi et al. (2002) observes the coexistence of two basic types of firms in the international pharmaceutical industry. The first group closely corresponds to the core and undertakes what is sometimes called 'pioneering R&D' (Grabowski and Vernon 1987). They generally generate the overwhelming majority of new chemical entities (NCEs) when successfully enjoying big, albeit not very long-lasting, first-mover advantages. They also charge premium prices. The second group undertakes primarily imitative R&D, generates incremental innovations and more competitively priced 'me-too' drugs. They take up licenses from the core, and are present in different degrees in generic markets, after patent expiration.

1.2.4 Financing of R&D

While the propensity to undertake R&D depends on a number of important factors, the ever-increasing expenditure on R&D necessitates some amount of cost sharing.

Cost sharing can be of various kinds, of which the importance of private–public partnership has generated a lot of study. The paper by Cockburn and Henderson (2000) has dealt with the research program of the 21 most important drugs discovered in the USA from 1965 to 1992 and concluded that only 24% (6) were developed without public support. Cockburn and Henderson (1998), Gambardella (1992), also studied the different forms of associations between public research institutes and the private sector in terms of research collaboration, exchange of knowledge etc. Their study strongly supports the hypothesis that the ability to access and interact with public research institutes is important in determining the productivity of downstream private sector research.

While R&D is an expensive affair, the cost of imitation is extremely low. The study by Mansfield (1985, 1986) shows that the cost of imitation, as against innovation, is less than 60 % for the pharmaceutical industry while the time taken for imitating the new drug is less than 70% per cent of the time taken for successfully launching the product. Firms, therefore, must have some means to recoup high costs incurred on R&D. Patent is a form of arrangement whereby innovative firms get monopoly rights to market the product developed for some stipulated period of time. With patent expiry, competing firms, however, enter the market with generic products to grab a share of the market for the innovated product.

1.2.5 The Role of Pricing and Marketing in the Pharmaceutical Industry

The trade mark or the brand names of patented products built during the patented life act as a means of maintaining the good name of the innovative company. The demand for pharmaceuticals is shrouded with agency problems (Ellison et al. 1997; Coscelli 2000). The patient who is the end consumer, does not select the drug he or she consumes; instead, the physician selects the drug therapy and also chooses either the brand or generic form of the medicine (Scott M 2000; Hurwitz and Caves 1988). Due to these agency problems, price does not have as much influence on the pharmaceutical market as in the case of other product markets. Instead, advertising is the instrument with which innovator firms can create switching costs and move future demand from generic to branded product. Thus, because of asymmetric information and imperfect information, it is noticed that even after the entry of generic substitutes, the price difference between the original drugs and the substitute remains the same or in some cases it even rises. Following Scherer (1993), this is popularly known as generic price paradox in the pharmaceutical market.

To maintain the brand name and market share for innovative products, pharmaceutical companies heavily pursue marketing or promotional activities for their products (see Leffler 1981). Pharmaceutical firms spend as much on promotion of brands (much of it directed at physicians) as on R&D (Hurwitz and Caves 1988). A recent study by Sachverständigenrat (2005) also confirms that in 2004 the ten major innovative pharmaceutical firms spent between 29–36% of sales on marketing and administration as compared to between 13 % and 19% per cent on R&D.

While there has been much complaint against the marketing effort of pharmaceutical firms to keep the anti-competitive effect alive (in spite of the presence of cheaper generic products after the patent life of the product), advertisement or detailing activities also play some positive role. They emphasize the brand's therapeutic advances, disseminate valuable information and also enable the consumer to make rational choices (see Leffler 1981). Thus, while on the one hand, (informative) advertisement provides valuable information to consumers (Findlay 2001); on the other hand, it might also act as a barrier to entry by merely persuading the consumer of product differentiation (Calfee 2002). Thus, it is difficult to know how marketing or advertisement affects generic product entry because the role of advertisement is not known apriori (Kwong and Norton 2007). Whether advertisement acts as a barrier to entry or provides valuable information is a matter of intense debate and has generated a large volume of theoretical and empirical literature (see Leffler 1981; Hurwitz and Caves 1988; Rizzo 1999; Grabowski and Vernon 1992; Scott Morton 2000; Kwong and Norton 2007). On the whole, results from empirical findings support the view that 'informative advertisement' encourages generic entry and allows competition, while persuasive advertisement thwarts competition in the sector.

1.2.6 Regulation of the Pharmaceutical Industry

From a policy perspective, the large market share of higher priced brand-names relative to their generic versions is an unsatisfactory outcome in the pharmaceutical industry. To curb excessive profit and ensure steady access to its product, price control is a common feature for this industry (see Danzon 1997; Kanavos 2001). One important concern that has been raised by several quarters is the effects of price regulation on lags in new drug launches. Danzon et al. (2005) studied the launch experience of 85 new drugs in 25 leading markets in the 1990s, focusing on drugs that had met registration requirements of one of the two strictest agencies the US Food and Drug Administration, (FDA) and the UK Medicines Agency and hence could potentially meet registration requirements in other countries. It concluded that price regulation that leads to low prices deters launch and that the potential for price spillovers to higher-price markets exacerbates launch lags in low price markets. Other studies by Kyle (2003, 2004) and Lanjouw (2005) also confirm the above facts. Another argument against price regulation is that price regulation drives out competition. Danzon and Chao (2000) argue that regulation drives out competition and is thus counter-productive to obtaining cost-savings. They base their conclusion on a cross-national study using data for 1992, showing that price competition between generic competitors is stronger in unregulated or less regulated markets (United States, United Kingdom, Canada, and Germany) than in countries with strict price or reimbursement regulations (France, Italy, and Japan).

1.2.7 Studies Relating to Indian Pharmaceutical Industry

The studies mentioned above unveil a number of important features relating to the global pharmaceutical industry. While previous studies are useful for understanding certain basic features of the pharmaceutical industry, the case of India also stands out as being different from the global pharmaceutical industry. In India, firms evolved around the soft process of patent regime that the government pursued for decades. Therefore, R&D was not an important activity and most companies were engaged in production and process engineering related activities. The primary thrust of activity among pharmaceutical firms lies in production related activities, process technology and reverse engineering (Narayana 1984; Kumar and Pradhan 2004; Chaudhuri 1999; Govindaraj and Chellaraj 2002; Lalitha 2002).

With the recent amendment of patent law, a large number of Indian firms started undertaking R&D related activities. However, the nature of R&D activities also differs between pharmaceutical firms of developed and developing countries like India. Thus, while pharmaceutical firms in the developed country do mostly product R&D, most Indian pharmaceutical firms do absorptive and adaptive R&D through the assimilation of imported technology, quality control, improved plant layout and reverse engineering (Bhadhuri and Ray 2001).

To understand what propels firms to undertake R&D, Pradhan (2002a) studied the extent of R&D activities in pharmaceutical companies in India, using a Tobit model. The study indicated that the market pressure and increased competition has worked effectively in pushing firms for increased R&D activities. The study also indicated a U–shaped relationship between R&D intensity and firm size for the pharmaceutical sector of India.

Other than market and firm size, for a developing country like India, the extent of R&D activities also depends on foreign direct investment (FDI). An attempt to understand the impact of FDI on local R&D activities of the pharmaceutical sector of India was made by Feinberg and Majumder (2001) using the data from 1980 to 1994. Their result showed that due to weak Intellectual Property Rights (IPR) and government regulation for FDI flow, the only significant R&D spillovers were between multinational companies (MNCs). Pradhan (2002b) has also tested the impact of the FDI spill over in drug and pharmaceutical R&D activities. The study confirms that the FDI flow by itself may not be an important factor for the productivity growth of the domestic firm unless the firm does more R&D on its own or it increases its size. The relationship between R&D expenditure intensity, firm size, and foreign collaboration for the emerging bio-pharmaceutical sector of India has been studied by Ramani (2002). The study indicates that R&D expenditure for the biotech sector decreases with the size of the firm with the medium and large sized firms enjoying the comparative advantage of diversification in this new field.

Since expenses for R&D is an imperfect measure of R&D of a firm, Dutta (2006) examines the factors that determine new product launches due to R&D in the Indian pharmaceutical industry and noticed that it is mainly driven by the size of the market for the new product and the age of the drug. The study also investigated the possibility of new products launched by Indian pharmaceutical firms being an outcome of the strategic response of firms due to product patents. The study, however, could not conclusively prove the above assertion but also did not rule out the possibility of strategic behaviors of domestic firms.

1.2.8 Marketing and Entry Barrier in the Indian Pharmaceutical Industry

Compared to developed nations the absence of legal barriers in India provides a different setting in which a firm can enter the market after incurring the cost for 'process technology or process R&D' and the cost of marketing and distribution of the product. In a recent study on the entry decision of foreign firms in the Indian pharmaceutical industry due to policy changes, Dutta (2006) revealed that a 'large component of the entry cost in the Indian Pharmaceutical industry can be attributed to marketing and distribution as opposed to R&D cost and this therefore puts foreign firms in a comparative disadvantage. Further, the study also proved the first-mover advantage of Indian pharmaceutical firms in terms of higher price and higher revenue. Such advantage may arise due to the brand name acquired by firms that enter early in the market.

1.2.9 Trans-nationalization Activity of Indian Pharmaceutical Firms

Apart from increased expenses for R&D and marketing related activities, a large number of Indian pharmaceutical firms are also becoming global in recent years. To identify the factors that enable firms to gain international competitiveness and become global leaders, Pradhan and Kumar (2007) and Aradhana (2007) regressed the export intensity of firms on a set of firm specific variables. The study indicates that their own R&D effort, foreign technology import and outward investment of firms are significant factors for them to gain international competitiveness. Pradhan (2007a) also studied the impact of product patents on India's pharmaceutical export using a gravity model. His study indicates that the higher the strength of patent protection, the higher is the export performance of firms.

1.2.10 Pricing of Pharmaceutical Products and Welfare Related Issues

Finally, the pharmaceutical industry, being a lifeline industry, the question of the welfare of individuals is intimately related to the pricing of its product. Therefore, a number of studies have also examined the impact of product patents on the prices of its product, particularly for a developing country like India. In particular, the study by Lanjouw (1997) identified an advanced chemical industry, cheap labour and raw material, the absence of product patents and fierce competition among firms as the possible reasons for the low price of the pharmaceutical product.

However, concern has also been voiced in a number of studies regarding the problem of availability of patented drugs and the possible rise in price due to the recognition of the product patent in 2005. The question of the availability of patented drugs in the context of developing countries was first analyzed using proper economic modeling by Marjit and Beladi (1998) under the assumption of a uniform price charged by firms. The study indicates that the mere presence of product patent or even the low cost of production may not be a sufficient condition to ensure a patented product for developing nations if a firm charges uniform prices for its product.

Fink (2002) has stimulated the effect of a product patent by estimating the demand and supply functions for the pharmaceutical product. The result indicates that because of availability of off-patented therapeutic substitutes there will be no price rise and, hence, no loss in welfare in the case of existing products. However, for newly discovered products, price will be above the competitive level. The controversy around the decline of consumer welfare and the imposition of patent has also been studied in detail in the paper of Chaudhuri et al. (2006) and Watal (2000). Stimulating the estimated demand and supply function for the pharmaceutical industry of India the paper predicted a rise of the price of the product with the imposition of patent. It is estimated that even if there is price control, welfare may fall due to loss in the product variety due to product patent. However, the study emphasizes that, with the provision of compulsory licensing and the drug price control mechanism the government can successfully control price rise.

1.3 Research Issues and Gaps

It is evident from the above review of literature that the performance of Indian pharmaceutical companies measured either in terms of efficiency or productivity or profitability has not been adequately analyzed in previous studies. While the existing literature has identified the factors that induce firms to do more R&D,[7] or be more global, how effective these strategies are has not been evaluated in terms of their performance. Therefore, what is more important is not just to see whether the larger or smaller firms are more innovative or more global but also to see the viability of these strategies by examining their impact on performance. If a firm's performance deteriorates due to the lagged effects of R&D investment, a question arises about the feasibility of such efforts on the part of firms. We also find that research questions that we have made in the context of the Indian pharmaceutical sector (see Sect. 1.1) have not been addressed comprehensibly in the previous literature. There is thus a need for a detailed study of the performance of Indian pharmaceutical firms, particularly in the post-reform scenario.

---

[7] Pradhan (2002b); Bhadhuri and Ray (2001).

An important objective of firms to perform better in this competitive environment is to use their resources efficiently. In efficiency analysis, it is possible to examine how far a firm is managing its resources in the best possible way to produce the maximum possible output compared to similar firms in the sample. In a sense, the efficiency analysis therefore looks at the production aspect of firms and provides a reason or guidance for firms to introspect on their own performance. In case a firm is inefficient it has to think why it is so. This can be answered by identifying the determinants of the inefficiency of firms. Here, one can examine the effectiveness of its strategies like R&D or marketing pursued by firms. The efficiency analysis as mentioned above therefore examines the production performance of firms in a relative sense and also examines whether in a competitive environment the performance differential of firms has aggravated or not. While a volume of research has been conducted across the globe and also in the context of India to examine the efficiency of manufacturing firms,[8] relatively fewer studies are there that have examined the efficiency of firms rigorously for an emerging sector like the pharmaceutical sector. The present research therefore attempts to examine the efficiency of Indian pharmaceutical firms that are undergoing a phase of transition due to regulatory changes and the consequent adoption of new technology and strategies by firms.

Efficiency analysis gives exclusive focus to an inefficient firm. However, for a better understanding of the performance of firms, it is also necessary to understand the performance of 'efficient firms' or the frontier firms in this industry. Better performance of 'efficient firms' that remains at the realm of technological frontier also implies an outward shift in the technological frontier for the sector. An outward shift in the technological frontier indicates a rise in the distance between efficient and inefficient firms unless the inefficient firms also improve technologically. In productivity analysis it is possible to analyze such changes. Examining the productivity change of a firm therefore addresses the basic question as to what part of change in the productivity of firms is due to its efficiency changes and what part can be accounted for by the change in the technological frontier. While a large volume of empirical literature also exists that has studied in detail the productivity of manufacturing firms across the globe, there is a dearth of studies that have examined this issue in the context of Indian manufacturing firms. Further, to the best of my knowledge there is hardly any study that has examined the productivity of Indian pharmaceutical firms in a comprehensive manner. Thus, the present study is an attempt to bridge this gap.

After computing the efficiency and productivity of manufacturing firms, existing studies have also identified its determinants. However, very little is known about the characteristics of frontier firms in an industry. Which are the frontier firms in this industry? What is their role in the technological change for this industry? To which strategic group do they belong? How do the frontier firms from a group perform when the canvas of comparison is increased by considering all other firms

[8] See Chap. 3 for a detailed discussion on the review of literature on the efficiency of firms.

in the sample? Are there any differences in the production opportunities of frontier firms from one group to another? One can answer such questions rigorously by employing the recently developed technique of Meta-Frontier analysis for efficiency and productivity analysis. In this book, an attempt has also been made to explore this issue in detail.[9]

Maintaining higher efficiency and productivity, however, does not necessarily imply that a firm also earns maximum profit. To maximize profit a firm must be able to bag an appropriate price for its products. In other words, for an inefficient firm to maximize its level of output production by overcoming its inefficiency does not necessarily imply that a firm will also maximize its level of profit. In a differentiated market for profit maximization it is indeed necessary for a firm to channelize its level of output production in proper market to get an appropriate price for its product. At the same time it must also take into consideration the cost of its production while it maximizes its level of profit. Thus a profit maximizing firm takes into consideration factors on both the demand and supply sides and also the market condition while it maximizes its profit. In view of the importance one has to move beyond the efficiency and the productivity framework and consider the important questions of profitability of a firm. Profitability of the Indian pharmaceutical firms has also not been adequately examined. In this book, we therefore wish to address this issue in detail. Regarding the relationship between efficiency and profitability of firms, results from the empirical and theoretical literature are mixed. Thus, while examining the profitability of firms we would also like to explore this issue further and see whether the most efficient firms are also the most profitable ones. Additionally, we would also like to examine if factors that influence the efficient functioning of a firm in terms of technical parameters also have similar influence on the prime objective of a firm, namely, maximizing its 'profitability'.

Finally, the pharmaceutical industry produces drugs that have a high social value. Consequently, the welfare of the country is directly related to the question of the availability of drugs that are supplied by private firms. An important concern that arises in the post-patenting regime is whether there will be any problem of availability of patented drug. Such a problem may arise in the future because Indian firms still do not have enough resources and capabilities to undertake product R&D and come out with innovative products. Thus, one may have to rely on foreign multinational companies for the supply of patented products. Under what conditions a foreign firm will supply its patented product is a highly relevant question at this juncture. Such questions being futuristic in nature cannot be resolved using existing data. It is, therefore, necessary to address these questions theoretically.

Given the relevance of the issues discussed and the existing research gaps, in this book attempts have been made to address some of these questions theoretically and empirically. The objectives of the study are as follows:

---

[9] Being a relatively recent technique the empirical application of Meta-Frontier approach to efficiency analysis is, however, limited (see Das et al. 2007; Bhandari and Ray 2007 for the application of such a method in the Indian case).

1.4 Objectives of the Study

1. To present an overview of the growth and structure of the Indian pharmaceutical industry and the current changes that are taking place in this industry.
2. To investigate the output and input efficiencies of firms and to identify factors that would explain such differences.
3. To classify firms into various groups considering their R&D, export and other such efforts and examine the efficiency of firms within and between groups.
4. To examine the productivity of firms over time and decompose it into different components like productivity change due to growth in input, efficiency change of firms and technological progress.
5. To examine the determinants of the profitability of firms.
6. To address the problem of the availability of patented drugs due to product patents.

1.5 Methodology for the Study

The methodology of the study is guided by its objectives. While the detailed methodology is discussed in the respective chapters, a brief discussion of the same is presented here.

The growth and the structure of the industry have been examined based on different secondary sources of data and reports relating to regulation and policy changes. To examine the changes in the structure of the industry like the concentration ratio, scale economies, capital-labor ratio, degree of diversification, etc., data from the annual balance sheet of companies have been employed. A cross-comparison of certain basic features of the industry will also be made with the manufacturing and the chemical sector to understand the relative importance of Indian drugs and pharmaceutical sector on various counts.

To study the efficiency and productivity of firms, frontier technique and Malmquist productivity index (Ray 2004) are used. To estimate the best practice frontier and the efficiency and productivity of firms, the present study uses the non-parametric technique of Data Envelopment Analysis (DEA). Details about the methodology are illustrated in the respective chapters.

For profitability analysis, we have measured the profitability of firms as the rate of return on revenue. The profitability ratio is regressed on a set of industry and firm specific factors. Since we have a cross section of firms repeated over time, that is, a panel data, we have used standard panel data techniques for estimating the profitability equation.

Since product patents are of recent origin, it is not possible to empirically test the problem of availability of patented drugs caused by product patents. The issue has therefore been addressed theoretically by developing a tractable economic model.

Additionally, a field survey with 20 companies has also been conducted to gain certain insights about the behavior of firms in this sector. As the sample is of limited size, the present dissertation has not undertaken any quantitative analysis.

1.6 Database Used

For the empirical analysis, secondary sources of data have been used. The Capital-online and the Prowess databases provide the financial sources of data and the annual balance sheets for the registered companies for 15 years (1991–2005) out of a total of 280 companies. Data on policy changes and major aggregates of the pharmaceutical sector are collected from reports and documents published by the Indian Drug Manufacturing Association, Drug Controller of India, Ministry of Chemical and Petro-Chemical and Org Marg Ims retail survey data for the Indian pharmaceutical sector. The deflators used for the analysis are gathered from the various issues of the RBI monthly Bulletin. A general understanding about the industry and in-sights for theoretical modeling are gathered from the primary survey of around 20 pharmaceutical companies.

1.7 Organization of the Book

The book contains seven chapters. Chapter 1 discusses the motivation for the study, various research issues, methodology, time framework and data description, and finally the significance/relevance of the study. Chapter 2 traces the growth and development of the Indian pharmaceutical sector starting from 1970 to the present day. It also examines the present structure of the Indian pharmaceutical sector and the emerging new opportunities for Indian pharmaceutical companies. Chapter 3 takes up the second objective, which includes the review of literature related to the efficiency analysis, the model used to measure the output and the input in measuring the efficiency of firms, the broad finding from the efficiency analysis and also the factors that determine the efficiency of firms. Chapter 4 concentrates on the third objective. It includes a brief discussion of the Meta-frontier or the group-grand approach to efficiency analysis and the review of literature relating to this methodology, its empirical application in the context of the Indian pharmaceutical industry and finally the estimated results. Productivity analysis and the framework to measure Malmquist productivity index for global frontier and group frontier is taken up in Chap. 5. The determinants of profitability of the firms are analyzed in Chap. 6. The problem of the availability of patented drugs due to product patent is analyzed theoretically in Chap. 7. Finally, Chap. 8 provides concluding remarks and policy suggestions.

Chapter 2
An Overview of the Indian Pharmaceutical Sector

2.1 Introduction

Over the past 40 years or so the Indian pharmaceutical sector witnessed rapid growth and transformation. From a mere volume of just Rs. 10 core in 1947, the industry registered a sales turnover of about US $ 5.5 billion in 2004 with an annual growth rate of about 17%. The flexible provisions of the Patent Act of 1970 and other supportive policies of the Government of India played an instrumental role in the growth and development of this industry. Given the importance of public policies in influencing the present structure of the industry this chapter, reviews in brief the important policy changes that have taken place in this sector and also examines the current changes in the structure of the industry and the changing behavior of firms in responding to policy changes.

2.2 The Evolution of the Indian Drug and Pharmaceutical Industry

The history of the evolution of the Indian pharmaceutical industry can be divided into four principal epochs. The first epoch is from 1850 to 1945. The second epoch spans from 1945 to the late 1970s. The third epoch for development is from the early 1980s to the early 1990s, and the fourth epoch spans from the early 1990s to the present time.

2.2.1 The Early Stage of Pharmaceutical Evolution

For convenience, the early stage of Pharmaceutical evolution has been divided into two distinct phases viz., the pre-independence and the post independence scenarios.

M. Mazumdar, *Performance of Pharmaceutical Companies in India*,
Contributions to Economics, DOI 10.1007/978-3-7908-2876-4_2,

2.2.1.1 Pre-independence Scenario

Before the advent of British Rule, the indigenous forms of medicine were in use (Ayurrvedic or Unani) in India. The Central Government of British India first introduced the allopathic form of medicine in the country. However, there were no production units in the country. Instead, the foreign companies exported raw materials from India, transformed it into finished products, and imported it back to India (Chaudhuri 1984). In spite of sincere efforts by a handful number of entrepreneurs[1] to establish indigenous companies, drug production in the country was low and could hardly meet only 13% of the total medicinal requirement of the country.[2] The indigenous industry, however, received impetus during the Second World War due to the fall in the supply of drugs from foreign companies and many more Indian companies like Unichem, Chemo Pharma, Zandu Pharmaceutical Works, Calcutta Chemicals, Standard Chemicals, Chemical Industrial and Pharmaceutical Laboratories (now known as Cipla), East India Pharmaceutical Works and others were established. With the entry of new firms in the market the production of drugs increased rapidly and indigenous firms were able to satisfy about 70% of the country's medicinal requirement.[3] During this period, foreign companies across the globe as well as Indian companies were engaged in production related activities and the importance of R&D was unknown to them (Temin 1979). Whichever new inventions of drugs were made were mainly due to the individual efforts of scientists and the drug companies were not involved in it (Chaudhuri 2005).

2.2.1.2 Post Independence Scenario

The period spans from 1945 to approximately the mid 1970s. A major breakthrough known as therapeutic revolution marked the beginning of this period and resulted in a phenomenal growth of the global pharmaceutical industry located mainly in Germany, Switzerland, the UK and also to some extent in the US (Gambardella 1992, 1995). A noteworthy achievement during this period was a shift in drug therapy from treating the symptoms to treating the disease itself (Temin 1979). At the same time there was a significant shift in the structure of the industry mainly because the global pharmaceutical industry instead of being mere production units

---

[1] Concerned about the lack of domestic manufacturing facilities and the unequal pattern of trade, few scientists like Prafulla Chandra Ray, TK Gajjar and AS Kotibhaskar laid the foundation of Bengal Chemical and Pharmaceutical Work in Calcutta (BCPW) in 1892 (see, BCPW 1941 for its activities in the early days) and Alembic Chemical Works by in 1907 in Baroda. The establishment of the Bengal Immunity in 1919 by a group of notable scientists and physicians, namely Nilratan Sircar, Kailash Chandra Bose, Bidhan Chandra Ray etc was yet another landmark in the history of the evolution of the Indian pharmaceutical industry. The company was established with the sole objective of attaining self-sufficiency of the production of synthetic medicine and of sera and vaccines.

[2] See Pharmaceutical Enquiry Committee 1954, pp 17–18.

[3] See Pharmaceutical Enquiry Committee 1954, p 75.

Table 2.1 Selected indicators of the pharmaceutical industry in 1952

				Employment	
Sector	No. of units	Investments	Sales value (Rs Cores)	Technical	Non technical
Public	11	1.48	1.16	181	1,492
Foreign	28	6.9	13.14	354	3,126
Large	54	9.26	13.38	1,076	15,896
Small	1,550	6.00	7.00	1,700	8,300
Total	1,643	23.64	34.68	3,311	28,814

Source: Narayana P.L. (1984)

also embarked on the path of massive investment in R&D (Temin 1979). The commercialization of newly invented pharmaceutical products like penicillin and other synthetic drugs also turned out to be a lucrative business. As noted by Statman (1983), the accounting rate of returns from a newly invented drug between 1954 and 1978 averaged at around 20.9 for global pharmaceutical companies. This encouraged firms to conduct more R&D to tap the potential emerging markets by inventing new drugs in a scientific manner. Further, the public sector also extended its unprecedented support for health related research (see Cockburn and Henderson 1996). In comparison Indian companies were however, not influenced by the wave of therapeutic revolution. The lack of technology, capital and support from the government were the principal hindrances for Indian companies to embark on the new trajectory of drug development.

Concerned about the lack of manufacturing facilities and guided by the perception that 'foreign technology' was an important component for the growth of the pharmaceutical sector, the Government of India in its Industrial Policy Statement of 1948 decided to take a liberal attitude towards MNCs and allowed them to establish plants without facing the hurdle of licensing agreements. Such liberal attitude of the government towards MNCs led to a free flow of foreign capital and the sector witnessed rapid growth. As noted by the Pharmaceutical Enquiry Committee of 1954, the drug production of India witnessed a 3.5 times growth in the production from just Rs. 10 core in 1947 to about Rs. 35 core by the end of 1952 (see Table 2.1).

However, in spite of the progress made by the sector, it was observed that foreign companies did not establish any production unit in India, but were engaged in assembling bulk drugs[4] (imported from their country) for manufacturing the final product (Pharmaceutical Enquiry Committee 1954). MNCs were not keen to establish production units in the country because the production of bulk drugs required investment in plant and machinery whereas importing bulk drugs and

[4] Drug manufacturing in India has two important vertically linked processes: (1) production of bulk drug; and (2) the production of formulation. The Bulk drug production is essentially the production for the raw material or active pharmaceutical ingredients (API) for drugs, whereas production for formulation is achieved by synthesizing the bulk drug into final products like tablets, ointments, capsules etc.

processing them into the formulation was an easier and more profitable business (Pharmaceutical Enquiry Committee 1954).

To overcome the structural weakness that the sector was suffering from, the government in its industrial licensing policy of 1956 made it mandatory for foreign multinational companies to establish their production unit in the country and produce drugs from the basic stage. The pharmaceutical industry was also included in the core group of industries for the purposes of licensing because of the 'high social value' content of medicinal products. Accordingly, the license was granted under the supervision of the Director General of Technical Development (DGTD) for setting up a new unit or expansion of the existing units keeping into account the medicinal need for the country.

In order to fulfill regulatory requirements many foreign companies started their production in India. During this period, a large number of domestic companies also entered the market mainly due to government support under the Industrial Licensing Act and started producing a wide range of products. Between 1952 and 1962, drug productions in the industry increased from Rs. 35 crore to about Rs. 100 crore. Besides, the capital investment for the sector was about Rs. 56 crore in 1962 as compared to its value of Rs. 23 crore in 1952.

2.2.1.3 Role of Public Sector Units and Research Institutes

Another note-worthy achievement of this period was the establishment of two public sector units (PSUs) the Hindustan Antibiotics Ltd (HAL) in 1954 and the Indian Drugs and Pharmaceuticals Ltd (IDPL) in 1961 to start the production of drugs from its basic stage. HAL was established to produce antibiotic with the assistance of WHO and UNICEF. It was the first company in India to manufacture a number of antibiotic drugs like penicillin, streptomycin, Sulfate, ampicillin, anhydrous, gentaminin from the basic stage (Sahu 1998). The technology required to produce these drugs were imported mainly from a large number of foreign companies which were then adapted to the local condition assisted by the in-house R&D wing of the company (see Sahu 1998 for details). The IDPL was established with the support and assistance of the Soviet Union to produce antibiotics, synthetic drugs, and surgical instruments. The technology acquired for the production of drugs was transferred to IDPL by the Soviet Government and was upgraded and adapted to local conditions by Indian scientists.[5]

Apart from PSUs, the public funded research institute also played a pivotal role in the growth of the sector. The government created a number of research institutes under the guidance of the Indian Council of Medical Research (ICMR) and the

[5] IDPL has three major plants – the Rishikesh plant, which was established to produce a majority of the basic drugs and their product mix. The Hyderabad unit was established to produce 16 synthetic vitamins, analgesics, antipyretics and other varieties of drugs, and the Madras unit produced the surgical instruments. Subsequently, two more plants were established at Gurgaon and Muzaffarpur to produce nicotinamide and acetic acid manufacturing (Chaudhuri 2005).

Council of Scientific and Industrial Research (CSIR) to promote the technological advancement of the country. Some of the CSIR institutes, which have played a significant role in boosting up the knowledge base in the pharmaceutical sector of India, are the Central Drug Research Institute (CDRI) of Lucknow, the Indian Institute of Chemical Technology (IICT) of Hyderabad, the National Chemical Laboratory (NCL) of Pune and the Regional Research Laboratories (RRL) of Jammu and Jorhat. Among the few innovative drugs developed in India, the CDRI has made a major contribution (Chaudhuri 2005). However, in spite of the achievement, what was really missing among the research institutes was commercial orientation. Therefore, most of the new and 'Novel Drugs' developed could not be profitably introduced in the market. However, CDRI[6] had invented more than 100 new process technologies, which were successfully commercialized. Besides CDRI, the technologies developed by NCL and other RRL were also transferred effectively from laboratories to industries. The success of the CSIR laboratories in fostering the technological environment of the Indian pharmaceutical sector is also evident when we find that almost all the top pharmaceutical companies like Lupin, Ranbaxy, Cipla, Nicholas Primal, Wockhardt, Unichem, Torrent, J.B chemical, Neuland, Sun Pharmaceutical, Orchid, S O L Pharmaceuticals Ltd and Aurobindo Pharma Ltd have benefited from the services of the research institutes in India in some way or the other (Chaudhuri 1997a).

The Public enterprises and research institutes also played a key role in enriching the human capital endowment that was necessary for the pharmaceutical sector of the country to flourish. Almost all the entrepreneurs of the big companies (about one-third of the 200 large companies) have worked in IDPL production or the R&D wing at some point of time or the other (Chaudhuri 1997). The necessary skill that is required for reverse engineering was acquired by entrepreneurs of the pharmaceutical industry through their long-term associations with public sector units, which is fundamental to the product and process development for this industry.

By early 1970s due to favorable government policies, the domestic industry had grown considerably from a state of non-existence. In 1952, the total turnover for the sector was around Rs. 32 crore. This increased to approximately Rs. 75 crore for bulk drugs and Rs. 370 crore for formulation production in 1970. However, the industry was still dominated mostly by foreign MNCs with a share of about 68% (see Tables A.1 and A.2 in Appendix A). It is interesting to note that during this period the public sector and indigenous companies contributed to a significant share of the bulk drug production, whereas the contribution of MNCs was less than 12% of the total bulk drug production in India. It was also noted that out of the 66 foreign companies that operated in India, only 19 were engaged in bulk drug production (Hathi Committee Report 1974). Most of the companies were engaged in high-payoff formulation production in which they had monopolistic position for certain life saving drugs like Metholdopa, Indomethacin, etc. MNCs even misused the

[6] Source CDRI website: www.cdriindia.org

provision of Product Patent in the Patent Act of 1911 to maintain their monopolistic position in India,[7] which resulted in prices for formulations in India becoming as high as in developed nations (Tariff Commission Report 1968).[8] In contrast, the prices for bulk drugs were the lowest because of the significant presence and contribution of public sector units and indigenous players (see Tariff Commission Report 1968).

2.2.2 *The Amendment of Patent Law and the Implementation of the New Drug Policy (The Second Epoch of Development)*

Concerned by the high price of medicines and the lack of domestic infrastructure, the government constituted the Hathi Committee in 1974 'to probe into the problems and suggest a rational drug policy that would meet the medicinal needs of the country'. Recommended by the Committee's report, the government amended the Patent Act of 1970 and enacted the Foreign Exchange Regulation Act (FERA) 1973 in its New Drug Policy (NDP) of 1978.

The Patent Act of 1970 recognized only process patents. The life of the patent was also reduced significantly from 16 to 5 years from the date of sealing or 7 years from the date of filling a complete application, whichever is shorter; in other words, the maximum period of patent was 7 years. Further, in the amended Act an MNC could patent only one process. FERA was implemented to compel MNCs to manufacture high technology bulk drugs. It was laid down in Section 29 that FERA companies, i.e., foreign companies with an equity holding of more than 40% and engaged in the production of only formulation products or bulk drugs not involving 'high-technology', should reduce their equity holding to 40% or below. For FERA companies licenses would be granted only when the companies provide 50% of bulk drugs to non-associated formulators, and the ratio of value of bulk drugs used in own manufacture to the value of total formulation production would not exceed 1:5. The corresponding figures for domestic firms were about 1:10. In addition, the NDP of 1978 had reservation for the domestic manufacturer for the production of various categories of drugs. Economies of scale, technology and pricing of products are the deciding factors for the production of drugs. The Patent Act of 1970 and the changes in domestic regulation virtually curbed the monopoly of MNCs. Adopting the flexible provisions of the amended patent act, indigenous companies started imitating the patented product and could eventually come out with better processes for the same product. The FERA and the NDP of 1978 also restricted the activities of MNCs. It is, therefore, not surprising to find that the share of MNCs dropped from 70% to about 50% by the late 1980s (see Table A.1

[7] For further details, see Chaudhuri (1999, 1997).

[8] The Kefauver Committee of US in 1950 (see Jordan 1999), also noted that India was among the high priced nations in the world.

in Appendix A). The industry also embarked on the path of high growth during this period. The other significant outcomes were fall in the prices of the medicines and the introduction of a large number of generic versions of patented products.

The drug policy of 1978 was, however, revised in 1986 to dilute the mechanism of check and control with respect to the production of certain categories of drugs. NDP 1986 also regularized the production of a large number of drugs that were earlier questionable on regulatory grounds. This was done to encourage greater participation of private players in the production of drugs, because the public sector started to suffer from industrial sickness due to the lack of proper commercial orientation (See Sahu 1998).

2.2.3 *The Phase of Liberalization, De-Control and Product Patent (The Third Epoch of Development)*

The growth impetus that the sector received during the 1980s continued even in the 1990s. The pharmaceutical sector witnessed a consistent growth of around 16% from 1995 onward. The bulk drug and the formulation sector also experienced a growth rate of between 15% and 20% during this period (see Table A.3 in Appendix A). Because of the competence gained by the Indian pharmaceutical companies in process engineering, the Indian companies also emerged as the major players in the domestic market. This resulted in a further fall in the share of MNCs in the country (see Table A.1 in Appendix A). The country also gained reputation in the international market as low cost producer.[9] The number of production units in the Indian pharmaceutical sector also increased from 1,752 in 1952–1953 to 20,053 in the year 2000–2001(see Table A.2 in Appendix A).

However, there was a shift in the regulatory framework under which the sector was operating. As part of the liberalization policy, the Government of India in the New Drug Policy of 1994 and 2002 abolished the licensing requirement for entry and expansion of firms. Further, 100% inward foreign direct investment has been allowed under the automatic approval of RBI and automatic approval for technological collaboration has been approved. Further, free import of formulations, bulk drugs and intermediaries are allowed.

The government also implemented certain rules in its New Drug Policy for producers to follow good manufacturing practices and produce quality products. Concern about quality medicine was high on the agenda of the government, because the WHO study reported (2007)[10] that about 35% of fake drugs produced in the

[9] India has gained fame as a low-cost producer and supplier of anti-retroviral and supplier to international organizations and to needy patients in Africa. In a recent case of supplying anti-retroviral drugs to South Africa, the price quoted by Indian firm was the lowest at US $ 350 per year per person compared to $ 1679 quoted by US MNCs.

[10] See *The Hindu*, September 2007.

world come from India, which also had a spurious drug market worth Rs. 4,000 crore.[11] Thus, while, on the one hand, India has shown its competence in manufacturing high quality products that also have demand in the international market, paradoxically, the Indian market is also flooded with spurious drugs to a large extent. To control spurious drugs, the government incorporated Schedule M in the Drugs and Cosmetic Act in 1995 that lays down Good Manufacturing Practices (GMP) at par with WHO standards.[12]

Apart from the changes in domestic policies, perhaps the most controversial and debated regulatory changes relate to the amendment of the Patent Act of 1970. To recall the Patent Law was amended under the WTO compulsion to recognize product patent from 2005 onward. This was implemented in three successions. The first version of it was implemented in 1995 in which the 'mail-box' system was recognized. On January 1, 2000, a Second Amendment was introduced. Its key issues re-defined patentable subject matter, extended the term of patent protection to 20 years and amended the compulsory licensing system. A third amendment of patent law was made on January 1, 2005 to introduce product patent regime in areas, including pharmaceuticals that were hitherto covered by process patents only.

To summarize, we notice that there is a gradual shift in public policy from the regime of control and process patents to a regime of decontrol and product patents. It is expected that such changes in policy will have a far-reaching effect on the industry. In the following section, we, therefore, discuss certain indicators pertaining to the industry.

2.3 Market Structure and Firm Behavior

Market structure of an industry is determined by the degree of competition and the collusive behavior among firms.[13] This, in turn, is determined by the number of firms in an industry and by their relative size distribution. A crude way of

---

[11] About 20% of medicines in the country are fake or substandard, of these, 60% does not contain any active ingredient, 19% contain wrong ingredients and 16% have harmful and inappropriate ingredients.

[12] It is worth mentioning here that many small scale units in India do not have adequate resources to upgrade their facilities at par with the GMP standard which requires investment worth 25 million for plants and machinery. Consequently, these companies might have to exit the market or may merge and grow in size.

[13] The data relevant for the analysis has been collected from the financial balance sheets of the companies provided by the Prowess and the Capital-online data sources. The other sources of data are the ORG-MARG data on the pharmaceutical sector of India, the Annual Survey of Industries (ASI) and the annual balance sheets of the Bulk Drug association of India, Organization of Pharmaceutical Producer of India (OPPI), Ministry of Chemical and Petro-Chemical of India.

Table 2.2 Concentration index over the years

Year	C4	C25	H-Index
1991	0.32	0.80	0.041
1992	0.27	0.71	0.032
1993	0.25	0.87	0.029
1994	0.29	0.76	0.037
1995	0.27	0.70	0.033
1996	0.22	0.86	0.024
1997	0.23	0.85	0.027
1998	0.22	0.87	0.028
1999	0.24	0.85	0.030
2000	0.23	0.86	0.030
2001	0.27	0.90	0.036
2002	0.32	0.84	0.046
2003	0.31	0.85	0.044
2004	0.30	0.86	0.042
2005	0.29	0.89	0.049

Source: Calculated from the annual balance sheet of companies

measuring the degree of competition in an industry is its four firm concentration ratios[14] and the Herfindahl index of concentration.[15] Table 2.2 summarizes the concentration level computed for the Indian pharmaceutical sector from the year 1991 to 2005.[16]

Whether calculated in terms of the C (4) or Herfindahl index, it is observed that the extent of concentration is low. This also implies that the level of competition is high for the Indian pharmaceutical sector. Figures in Table 2.2 also indicate that on an average the top four firms capture about 30% of the total market for the industry. Since there is no reason to believe that one has to consider only four firms to

[14] The four firm concentration ratio C4 is computed by ranking firms with respect to their market share in the industry. It is the industry sale accounted for by the four largest firms in the industry. Values of the C4 may range from Zero (0) to the limit, to one (1). The selection criteria of "Four – firm" in determining the concentration of the industry is done on an ad hoc basis and there is no reason to believe that one has to consider only four firms to determine the concentration in the industry. A better measure of concentration is the Herfindahl index for concentration.

[15] The Herfindahl index (H) is measured as the sum of the square of each firm's market share; thus $H = \sum_{i=1}^{n} s_i^2$ where $S_i =$ share of the ith firm. H index utilizes the size distribution as well as the total number of firms in the industry and is therefore a more appropriate measure of concentration. Moreover, the H Index is constructed from a theoretical framework under the assumption of the Cournot – Nash equilibrium (see Stigler 1964, pp 201–220) and satisfies all the criteria of the good measure of concentration (see Stephen 1979, pp 67–75). The range of the value of H is from 1 (monopoly case) to 1/n (for n equal sized firm).With perfect competition when n $\rightarrow \infty$ the value of H is zero. The general norm is that the H-index with a value of less than 0.1, between 0.1 and 0.18 and above. Eighteen indicates an un-concentrated to moderately concentrated to highly concentrated market structure.

[16] These ratios are computed using information about firms as per CMIE data base.

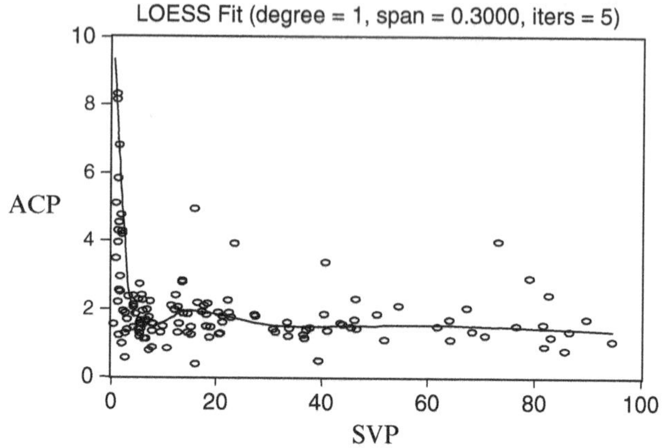

Fig. 2.1 Average cost of production (ACP) by sales volume of firms (SVF) (Source: Computed from the information provided by CMIE data base)

determine the concentration in an industry, the concentration among the top 25 companies has also been calculated for the Indian Pharmaceutical industry. The figures for C (25) also indicate that about 85% of the total pharmaceutical market is captured by the top 25 companies.

The figures for C (4) or the H-Index calculated over the years indicate some degree of fluctuation. It is noticed that from 1991 to 2000 the level of concentration has reduced in the Pharmaceutical industry by around 26%[17] which is, relatively, a large change for such a short time period. However, from 2001 to 2005 the level of concentration has increased by about 8 per centage points for an even shorter period of just 4 years. On the whole, it can be inferred that the top 25 companies, dominate the Indian pharmaceutical industry, which captures about 85% of the total market, and the rest of the firms (the total number of small to tiny firms are around 200–250) operate at a very low level of output. In recent years, the concentration in the industry has increased to some extent.

2.3.1 Economies of Scale in the Indian Pharmaceutical Industry

Economies of scale capture the effect of increased production on the average cost of production of a firm. To get an idea about the extent of the scale economies in the

[17] The figure is arrived at by calculating the percentage change in the concentration indices from 1991 to 2000.

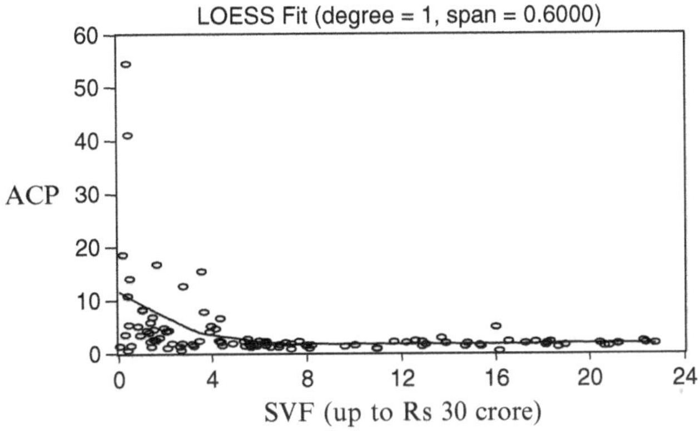

Fig. 2.2 Average cost of production (ACP) by the sales volume of firms (SVF)

Indian pharmaceutical industry the average cost of production[18] is plotted against the *sales volume* for a sample of 280 firms for the year 2002.[19] In the presence of scale economies, the average cost of production exhibits a non-linear relationship with the level of output. Ideally, it initially falls and then rises exhibiting a U-shaped relationship. To capture the non-linear relationship between the output and the cost of production, the nonparametric local curve fitting technique has been applied (loess fit, see Cleveland 1979). The loess fit is shown in the diagram below (Fig. 2.1).

The vertical axis measures the average cost of production and the horizontal axis the total revenue of the firms. The diagram indicates the presence of scale economies for the industry within a range of about Rs. 10 crore of sales volume, beyond which the average cost curve takes a flat shape. This indicates the industry cost curve to be L shaped which implies that there are no significant *diseconomies of scale* for large sized firms. To get a clear idea about the approximate size of the Minimum Efficient Scale (MES)[20] in the industry the loess fit is also done separately for firm size up to the sales volume of Rs. 30 crore. This is illustrated in Fig. 2.2.

Figure 2.2 indicates the presence of scale economies at a Minimum Efficient Scale size (M.E.S) of Rs. 8 crore. The above diagrammatic representation indicates that the industry exhibits a certain degree of economies of scale at a low level of

---

[18] The average cost is measured by the total expenses for production which is the sum of the cost of labor, capital, raw material and fuel and also the total operating expenses, which includes the administration and selling cost, and other manufacturing expenses divided by the sales volume of the companies (all units measured in Rs crore).

[19] Scale economies is a phenomenon that is observed for a cross-section of firms. Hence, the analysis is done for the year 2002, which has the maximum number of observation (280 firms) for all the years considered in the study.

[20] M.E.S is defined as the output level at which the average cost curve attains the minimum value. If M.E.S is achieved for a large plant size or larger value of output then a company can enter the market only after investing heavily in plant and machinery.

Table 2.3 Estimate of n for the industry, large, medium and small sized firms in 2002

	a	n	R-Square Adjusted R Square	t-Statistics for a	t-Statistics for n
Industry	1.104[a]	0.850[a]	0.897, .895	8.332	26.947
Size wise top 25% of the firms	0.219	1.021[a]	0.843, .835	0.219	1.021
Size wise middle 25% of the firms	0.277	1.031[a]	0.432, .417	0.389	7.718
Size wise bottom 50% of the firms	1.203[a]	0.777[a]	0.762, .760	11.673	20.979

[a]Significant at 1% level
White Heteroskedasticity-Consistent Standard Errors & Covariance

output value of Rs. 8 crore. We next estimated the magnitude of scale economics using the following functional form[21]

$$C = aq^n \tag{2.1}$$

Here C is the total cost of production, q is the total output and ***a*** is the technological parameter. Suppose q increases t times, if now n is greater than unity we have decreasing returns to scale (DRS), if n is less than unity we have increasing returns to scale (IRS) and for n equal to unity we have constant returns to scale (CRS). Taking the log form of the above equation we get

$$LnC = lna + nlnq \tag{2.2}$$

$dlnc/dlnq = n,$ is the measure of the elasticity of cost with respect to output and captures the economies of scale in the industry. The above equation is estimated using the simple ordinary least square technique (OLS) taking into consideration all the observation in the sample to get the industry wise measure of economies of scale. Further, firms are also classified into different groups based on their size[22] and the equation is re-estimated for each group of firms to capture the variation in the scale economies for different firm size. The main findings from the estimation are summarized in Table 2.3.

The above table indicates the presence of scale economies for the overall industry as well as for all groups of firms. The estimated value of the scale

[21]The following functional form was used by **Silberston Aubrey** (1972) to measure scale economies of the industry in the U.K. We have also applied the same form to measure scale economies for a cross-section of 280 pharmaceutical firms in 2002. We have conceptualized the size of the firms in terms of the sales volume (value of output).

[22]Firms with a sales volume of Rs. 8 crore is defined as: tiny firm, firm within the range of Rs. 9–100 crore as small sized firm, firm within the range of Rs. 100 crore to 300 crore as medium sized firms and firms with sales volume of more than Rs. 300 crore as large firms. The classification of firms as tiny, small, medium and large-sized is arrived at by dividing the sales distribution into four groups: firms with sales up to 25th percentile are taken as tiny firms, firms having sales greater than 25th percentile and up to 50th percentile are classified as small firms, firms having sales greater than 50th percentile and up to 75th percentile are classified as medium sized firms and those having sales greater than 75th percentile are designated as large-sized firms.

parameter ***n*** is 0.85 for the industry and .77 for the small sized firm. This implies that if output rises by one unit then cost rises by 0.85 units for the industry and .77 for the small – sized firms, indicating the presence of IRS in the industry as well as for the small sized firm. The magnitude for ***n*** is 1.02(>1) and 1.03 (>1) for large and medium sized firm, which implies the presence of DRS for both these groups of firms. However, the magnitude is close to one. In order to test the robustness of the above results Wald[23] test has been conducted for the estimated scale parameter ***n*** by imposing the restriction that $n = 1$ for the industry as well as for the other groups of firms. The result indicate the presence of IRS in the industry with a magnitude of $n = .85$ and for small sized firms the magnitude of $n = .77$. The Wald Test however, accepts the null hypothesis (Ho) that $n = 1$ for large and medium sized firms.

The pattern and the estimate of scale economies in the pharmaceutical sector exhibit certain interesting phenomenon. First, simple computation of scale economies shows that for reasonably small-sized firm (size of Rs 8 core in sales volume) economies of scale exists. Since there has been a dense clustering of small firms with a sale volume of less than Rs .1 core on the falling part of the AC curve (see Figs. 2.1 and 2.2) it is advisable that firms enlarge in size and reap the benefit of scale economics. It is easy to calculate that small firms can save on their cost front by around 29% by increasing their scale of operation. The near presence of CRS type production structure for large scale of production, however, indicates that medium and large firms do not gain additional benefit by simply enlarging their size of operation. Scale economies also achieved a low level of sales volume of Rs. 8 crore. This implies that the Minimum Efficient Scale (MES) size is achieved at about Rs. 8 crore and thus it does not pose entry barrier in the pharmaceutical industry from the production point of view. This explains to an extent the presence of such a large number of firms (approx. 10,000) in this industry.

2.3.2 Capital Intensity of the Indian Pharmaceutical Sector

To understand the extent of capital intensity in the Indian pharmaceutical industry a cross comparison of capital intensity of pharmaceutical firms reported in the CMIE database is made with the total manufacturing and chemical firms.

Table 2.4 summarizes the mean capital intensity of the pharmaceutical, chemical and manufacturing sectors. Table 2.4 suggests that the trend in capital intensity is rising after 1995. On an average, the capital to sales ratio is around 55 % for the

[23] The Wald test computes the test statistic by estimating the unrestricted regression without imposing the coefficient restrictions specified by the null hypothesis. The Wald statistic measures how close the unrestricted estimates come to satisfying the restrictions under the null hypothesis. If the restrictions are in fact true, then the unrestricted estimates should come close to satisfying the restrictions.

Table 2.4 Cross comparison of capital intensity across industries[a]

Year	Pharmaceutical	Chemical	Manufacturing
1989	0.28	0.39	0.53
1990	0.28	0.40	0.52
1991	0.35	0.41	0.54
1992	0.33	0.41	0.55
1993	0.35	0.44	0.57
1994	0.36	0.47	0.59
1995	0.41	0.43	0.56
1996	0.47	0.45	0.56
1997	0.50	0.47	0.60
1998	0.56	0.54	0.66
1999	0.55	0.52	0.68
2000	0.57	0.51	0.66
2001	0.57	0.46	0.60
2002	0.55	0.52	0.66
2003	0.55	0.49	0.62
2004	0.55	0.46	0.58
2005	0.64	0.43	0.52

Source: Compiled from the annual balance sheet prowess data base
[a]Capital intensity = Total value for pant and machinery and building/total revenue

pharmaceutical sector. This implies that as the market size of the pharmaceutical industry is increasing due to growth in this sector by about 16 % in recent years, the capital investment is also rising over the years. However, on the whole the sector is less capital intensive compared to the manufacturing sector.

2.3.3 *Labor Intensity in the Pharmaceutical Sector*

After measuring capital intensity, the labor intensity in the Indian pharmaceutical sector is also computed and compared with the chemical and the manufacturing sector to get an idea about the employment potential of the sector. Table 2.5 summarizes the mean labor intensity for the pharmaceutical, chemical and manufacturing sectors.

It is observed from the figures in Table 2.6 that the pharmaceutical sector (on an average) spends more on wages and salaries compared to the chemical and manufacturing sectors. However, there has been a marginal fall in the potential to absorb labor in the pharmaceutical sector in the early 1990s though it again picked up from 1997. Since the industry is growing at an annual rate of 16%, it can be inferred that the potential to absorb labor and generate employment in the pharmaceutical sector is also rising over the years.

Table 2.5 Cross comparison of labor intensity accross industries[a]

Year	Manufacturing	Chemical	Pharmaceutical
1989	0.075	0.036	0.121
1990	0.073	0.036	0.115
1991	0.071	0.036	0.110
1992	0.068	0.036	0.102
1993	0.069	0.036	0.096
1994	0.066	0.037	0.090
1995	0.061	0.034	0.093
1996	0.062	0.038	0.088
1997	0.060	0.034	0.089
1998	0.062	0.035	0.092
1999	0.064	0.035	0.088
2000	0.059	0.032	0.092
2001	0.055	0.028	0.094
2002	0.055	0.030	0.091
2003	0.052	0.028	0.093
2004	0.048	0.026	0.096
2005	0.043	0.024	0.101

Source: Computed from the CMIE data base
[a]Labor intensity = Industry expenses for wages and salaries/total revenue

Table 2.6 Profitability[a] and productivity[b] of large and small sized firms

	Large firms		Small firms	
Year	Profitability	Productivity	Profitability	Productivity
1991–1995	0.514	2.298	0.368	1.977
1996–2000	0.440	2.175	0.274	1.824
2001–2005	0.543	3.232	0.398	2.545

[a]Profitability = Total Revenue – (expenses for wages and salaries + for raw-material + for power and fuel + rental rate of capital)/total Revenue
[b]Productivity = Total revenue/(Total expenses for wages and salaries + raw-material + power and fuel + rental rate of capital)
See Chap. 6 for details about the construction of the rental rate of firms

2.3.4 *Extent of Diversification in the Pharmaceutical Industry*

The pharmaceutical industry is also diversified and most of the firms produce multiple products. The degree of differentiation in the pharmaceutical industry is measured in terms of the Herfindahl Index of Diversification.[24] Table A.4 in

[24] The Herfindahl index (H_D) for diversification for a firm is measured as the sum of square of the share for the *i*th commodity in the total revenue earned by a firm. Thus, $H = \sum_{i=1}^{n} s_i^2$ where s_i = share of the *ith* commodity in the total revenue earned by a firm. The Herfindahl index takes a value of one (1) for firms producing single output and for a highly diversified firm the value of H-Index of Diversification falls.

Appendix A summarizes the mean H-index of diversification.[25] The figures in the Table suggest that instead of producing too many products, pharmaceutical firms in India are gradually becoming specialized over the years. To confirm the above statement firms are also classified into different groups based on their degree of diversification. A close look at the figures in Table A.4 indicate that there is a fall in the proportion of highly diversified firms (with a value of less than .25) from 37% to around 12–11%. A rise in the proportion of firms in the highly specialized to specialized group (1 to .75) is also evident from figures in Table A.4. On the whole, it thus appears that instead of producing too many products, pharmaceutical firms are gradually specializing in certain core product groups.

There can be few possible reasons for such a rise in the proportion of specialized firms in the industry. First, in recent years a large number of new firms have entered the industry with new technology. Generally, the new firms bring in specialized products in which they have competence. Second, there has been a spurt in R&D activities of the pharmaceutical firms. If firms have a focused product basket, chances of success will be high for its R&D effort. Finally, if firms are more specialized in their production, it is easier to differentiate its product and establish a good brand name in the domestic as well as the international market.

2.4 Examining the Performance of Indian Pharmaceutical Firms

The analysis of the data reveals that the pharmaceutical industry is one of the most profitable industries in India. The average profit earning (profit as a percentage of sales) of the pharmaceutical industry stands at around 8.8% in the year 1995 as against the 5.8% of the chemical industry, 4.8% of the food and the beverage industry, 5.5% of the machinery industry and 5.8 % of the transport and equipment industry.[26] Further, there has been a rise in the profitability of firms from 8.8% to about 15.4 % in a short span of only 10 years from 1995 to 2005. In the pharmaceutical industry the extent of concentration is low. However, the co-existence of low levels of concentration and ever-increasing rise in profit earning stands against the conventional economic wisdom and a feature which is peculiar to this industry.[27]

We next compare the performance of firms on the basis of their R&D, marketing and export related activities as well as size. We first take up the case of the size of firms. We have classified the firms into two groups based on their size

[25] H_D is estimated for registered pharmaceutical companies based on the information provided by the CMIE database.

[26] Computed from the prowess database using the aggregated data of the industries.

[27] The co-existence of high profit and low concentration for the pharmaceutical industry is also observed in other parts of the globe see for example the studies by Santerre and Stephen 2004, p 467; Viscusi et al. 2000, p 820; Schweitzer 1997, p 25.

Table 2.7 Profitability and productivity of firms with and without R&D units

	Firms with R&D units		Firms without R&D units	
Year	Profitability	Productivity	Profitability	Productivity
1991–1995	0.435	2.054	0.350	2.096
1996–2000	0.401	2.069	0.247	1.773
2001–2005	0.492	2.871	0.305	1.487

Companies that have reported positive outlays for R&D have been clubbed together as firms with R&D units and the rests as firms without any R&D units

distribution. Thus, firms that jointly capture sevent 5% of the sales volume of the industry are classified as large sized firms and the rest as small-sized firms. Table 2.6 summarizes the performance differences for large and small-sized firms.

It is evident from the figures in the Table that large sized firms have earned higher profit and also have higher productivity compared to small firms. In the pharmaceutical industry, the benefits of higher profitability accrue to large sized firms not because of economies of scale in production but because of other factors like ability to undertake R&D or do more of marketing activity at large scale (Santerre and Stephen 2004; Viscusi et al. 2000; Schweitzer 1997). Consider now the case of firms with R&D related outlays.

It is noticed from Table 2.7 that, on an average, firms with R&D units have earned higher profit compared to firms without any R&D unit. The productivity difference also reveals similar trends. This indicates that investment in R&D is an effective action for firms to perform better. Since most of the firms in India have embarked on R&D related activity quite recently, we also explain in brief the emerging R&D trends of the Indian pharmaceutical industry.

2.4.1 *Patterns of R&D Investment in the Indian Pharmaceutical Industry*

Research and Development (R&D) is a comparatively recent phenomenon for Indian pharmaceutical firms, which gained momentum only after 1995. R&D spending by the pharmaceutical industry has increased from a mere 1.5% of the total sales turnover in 1981–1982 to almost 4% in 2004. A rise in the total actual R&D expenditure in the Indian pharmaceutical sector is also evident from Fig. 2.3, which plots the aggregate actual R&D expenditure by the Indian Pharmaceutical industry over the years.

A cross comparison of R&D (see Fig. 2.4a) spending by the Indian pharmaceutical sector with respect to other industry groups also indicates a rise in the share of R&D expenditure by the drugs and pharmaceutical sector of India.

Figure 2.4b, which plots the contribution of R&D by the Indian pharmaceutical sector in the total R&D pool of the manufacturing and the chemical sectors shows two noticeable trends: (1) the pharmaceutical industry is one of the major

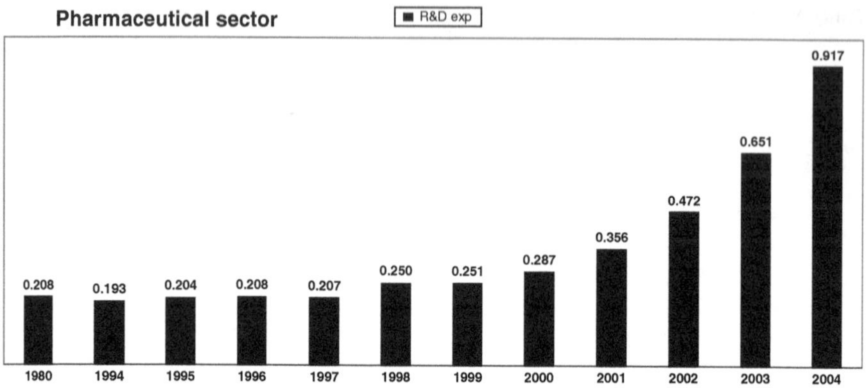

Fig. 2.3 Real R&D expenditure (Crores and dollars) in the Indian pharmaceutical sector (Source: Computed from the Bulk Drug Association of India)

contributors of R&D in the chemical and manufacturing sector; and (2) the share of pharmaceutical R&D in the total manufacturing and chemical sectors is rising over the years. This indicates that the pharmaceutical industry plays a leading role in R&D activities in the country.

Figure 2.5 indicates that from 1995 onwards, the total number of new generic products introduced in the Indian pharmaceutical market has increased substantially. This is an outcome of R&D initiatives of the Indian pharmaceutical firms and could be an important strategic move of firms to deter the entry of foreign firms into various product groups.

However, in spite of its investment in R&D, the mean R&D-sales ratio of the Indian pharmaceutical companies is only 4% in 2005, which is far below the global figures of around 10–15%. R&D spending in India is low because most of the firms either do process R&D or the thrust for R&D is targeted mainly for minor product improvement. The thrust of R&D activities of firms also differs according to the size of firms.

Size-wise differences in the R&D intensity (R&D by sales ratio of firms (see Table 2.9)) reveal that on an average, large sized firms spend more on R&D activities, followed by medium and small sized firms.[28] The trend in R&D also indicates that R&D intensity has also been steadily rising for all groups of firms though the rise is much higher for large and medium sized firms.

[28] Presentation of such data cannot establish a causal relation. However, such data no doubt provides certain indicators. Relations have been examined in subsequent chapters in a statistically rigorous manner.

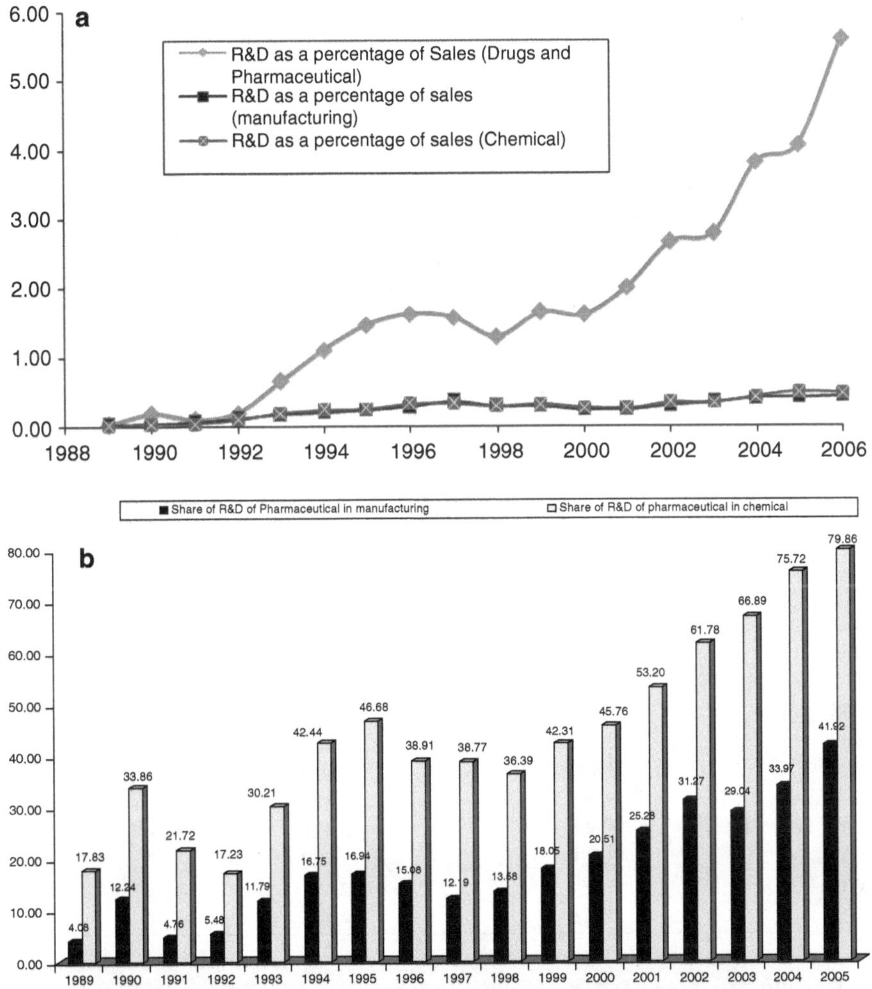

Fig. 2.4 (a) R&D intensity in the manufacturing, chemical and pharmaceutical sectors. (b) Share of Pharmaceutical in Total Manufacturing and Chemical Sector R&D spending (Source: Computed on the basis of information provided by CMIE prowess data base)

2.4.2 *Pattern of R&D Spending in the Indian Pharmaceutical Industry and the Emerging R&D Models*

In recent years, there has been a shift in the R&D emphasis of firms from imitative to innovative R&D. Further, even in imitative R&D the transition is towards advanced process R&D. With respect to the product and process R&D, Indian pharmaceutical companies are gradually adopting different models depending upon their capability and long-term vision. Some of the important models followed by Indian pharmaceutical companies are as follows (see Fig. 2.6).

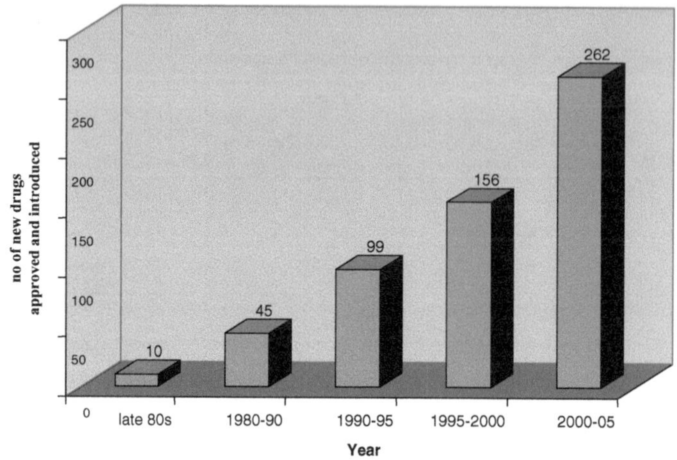

Fig. 2.5 New drug introduced by R&D (Source: Constructed form the Pharmabiz data base)

Table 2.8 R&D intensity for different sizes of firms

Year	Large	Medium	Small
1995	2.224	0.988	0.663
1996	2.314	1.053	0.585
1997	3.309	2.993	0.617
1998	1.628	0.900	0.979
1999	2.191	0.953	0.639
2000	2.478	1.099	0.850
2001	3.065	1.374	0.877
2002	3.606	2.021	0.694
2003	3.879	2.020	0.608
2004	5.364	2.881	0.859
2005	7.776	4.157	1.718

Broadly speaking, R&D activities adopted by the Indian Pharmaceutical companies are of two types: in-house R&D effort and contract R&D. Let us first take the case of the in-house R&D effort of firms.

The in-house R&D effort of firms can be for (1) novel product (2) advanced process and (3) bio-pharmaceutical products. Firms following the above strategies are mainly large sized firms with sales turnover of more than Rs. 300 crore (at least from the years 1995) and earn about 50–60 % of their revenue from the international market of the US, Europe, Japan, and Australia.

2.4.2.1 Product R&D

Few firms from these groups have also ventured into product R&D. It was first started by Dr. Reddy's laboratory and Ranbaxy as early as 1995 and today there are almost 15 companies engaged in product R&D and many of them have also

Table 2.9 Profitability and productivity of firms pursuing marketing

Year	Marketing high ≥ 25%		Marketing low <25%	
1991–1995	0.553	2.547	0.386	1.980
1996–2000	0.468	2.516	0.297	1.816
2001–2005	0.538	3.587	0.402	2.468

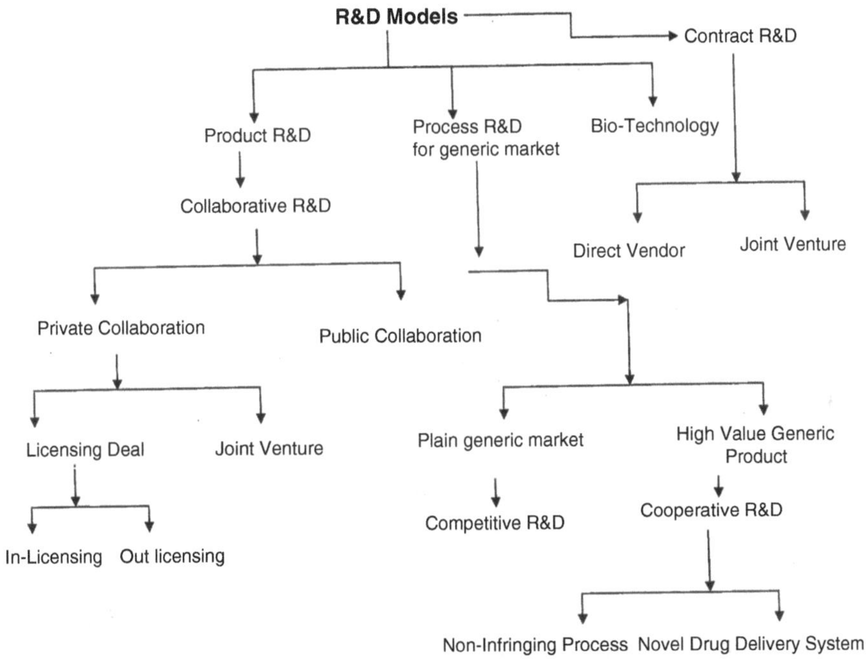

Fig. 2.6 Alternative R&D models followed by Indian pharmaceutical companies (Source: Author's own classification from the balance sheet of the companies)

reported some success (see Table A.5, Appendix A). However, none of these firms is fully engaged in the whole process of R&D for product innovation because of the lack of appropriate skills. Since most of these firms have competence in the manufacturing stage of drug development, but lack the necessary skills for the initial stage of drug discovery, they are adopting various forms of collaborative strategies to make up for their deficiency in resources and skills. Two most important forms of collaborative activity noticed in the context of the Indian pharmaceutical industry are (1) Joint Venture (JV), and (2) Licensing Deal. In JV schemes, the risk is shared with foreign MNCs and in licensing arrangements, a firm licenses out the molecule to foreign MNCs, and gets a royalty from the deal.

Apart from private collaboration, Indian companies are also availing of the benefit from research institutes of CSIR, ICMR, and around 30 universities funded by the government in their endeavor for product R&D. However, compared to the global level the extent of public spending in India is still low. Internationally, the public sector has played a significant role in the development of new drugs. An investigation of the 21 block buster and top 50 drugs from 1965 to 92 and 1992–1997 respectively indicate that almost all the drugs (almost 95%) received government funding at some stage or the other (Cockburn and Henderson 1997, 2000; NIHCM 2000, 2002[29], p 2). In contrast, public spending of the Indian drug and pharmaceutical sector was only Rs. 559.78 lakh or US dollars 1.24 million in 1998. Though the situation has improved in recent years, it is not adequate compared to the global level. The need of the hour is to enhance public spending to boost up the R&D environment for pharmaceutical companies.

R&D targeted for process development: Very few companies have ventured into the business of product R&D because of the high costs and risks involved therein. Instead, most of them are targeting the ever-emerging generic market because of their age long competence in process engineering.

The global generic market is of two types (1) the plain generic market and (2) the niche generic market. The R&D endeavor of medium and small sized firms is mainly targeted for the plain generic market. A few ambitious medium sized firms and large firms are also targeting the niche generic market of developed nations. The entry barrier in the niche segment of the generic market is high because of strict regulatory requirements, but the returns are also high.

Two forms of strategies are adopted by the Indian pharmaceutical companies to enter the generic market viz., the competitive and the cooperative strategy. The competitive strategy is adopted mainly for the plain generic market. There are almost no entry barriers for such a market and a firm's R&D is targeted for product improvement. Generally, the small or medium sized firms follow this strategy.

Few large firms also target the high-end generic market by following co-operative strategies. Since the cost of entry is high, because of strict regulatory requirements, firms enter into various forms of collaboration with foreign multi-nationals. To cite a few examples, Glenmark Pharmaceutical has entered into various forms of partnership with Merk Generics to capture the Dermatology market of Europe. Zydus Cadila has entered into partnership with Mayne Pharma to market their anti-cancer product in Australia. To capture the high-end generic market, firms either come out with a non-infringing process or a novel drug delivery system (NDDS). In non-infringing processes,[30] companies come out with a new process which does not infringe upon the existing process patent of the innovative company and enjoy the benefit of early mover advantage with the patent expiry of

[29] Available at http://www.nihcm.org/~nihcmor/pdf/innovations.pdf

[30] Generally, innovating companies not only obtain patent on the NCE in the drug invented but also "ring-fence" their product with other secondary sources of patent. These secondary sources of patent are obtained (1) on specific formulation (2) for methods to cure the diseases and (3) process of manufacturing the product. The presence of the secondary sources of patent assists the company to extend the monopoly period of the product even after its patent expiry (Chaudhuri 2005). In such cases, generic companies cannot enter the market even with patent expiry.

the product. Another route for capturing the generic market is by inventing a new delivery system for the familiar drug.[31]

Indian pharmaceutical companies are also leveraging themselves to tap the potential emerging market of contract research.[32] It is estimated (Grace 2004) that the overall cost of clinical trials in India is 46 % lower than that in developed countries. Hence, foreign innovative firms are also outsourcing their clinical trial activities in India an opportunity which many Indian firms are availing.

2.4.3 The Role of 'Detailing' or Marketing for Indian Pharmaceutical Companies

The pharmaceutical industry also spends a large proportion of its revenue on marketing or detailing activities. As compared to the manufacturing and chemical industry, which spends around 4% of its revenue (in the year 2000–2005) on marketing, the pharmaceutical industry spends 7% of its revenue on it. In recent years, there has been a spurt in such activities because of an increased focus of companies on sales for formulations, which requires investment in setting up sales infrastructure. Further, the domestic market is over saturated with a large number of branded products, with similar therapeutic benefits.[33] Consequently, companies spend heavily on marketing activities to maintain brand loyalty for its products and keep its market share.

How effective is the marketing effort of firms? To examine this question we have classified firms into two groups: (1) firms that spend 25% or more of their revenue on marketing related activities and (2) firms that spend less than 25% of their revenue on marketing. Figures in Table 2.9 indicate that spending more on marketing enables firms to earn a higher profit and maintain higher productivity.

In this regard, we have also examined whether the extent of marketing expenditure of a firm has any relation to its size. A simple computation reveals that in the early 1990s large sized firms spent around 7–8% of their revenue on detailing

[31] In NDDS a commonly quoted example is the noteworthy success of Ranbaxy. The firm has come up with an improved version of antibiotic ciprofloxacin which is developed by the American company Bayer AG. The Ranbaxy formulation proved to be much more effective with better patient – compliance. Recognizing the potential benefit of the product, Bayer entered into a licensing agreement with Ranbaxy and agreed to market the product world-wide against a payment of US $ 65 million. Other Indian companies like Dr.Reddys Laboratory, JB Chemicals, Cadila Healthcare, Zydus Cadila, Morepen Labratories, FDC Limited are also in this NDDS business.

[32] The Boston Consulting Group estimated that the contract research market for global companies in India would touch US$ 900 million by 2010 and industry estimates suggest that the Indian companies bagged contract research worth US$ 75 million in 2004.

[33] For example, the Amoxicillin groups have 100 and 36 brands in the market. But this is available at different prices and the price differences can be as high as Rs. 308.50 through use of brand name and advertising.

activities; whereas, medium and small sized firms spent around 5% of their sales on marketing related outlays. The differences in the average marketing to sales ratio among the different group of firms, however, dropped significantly in the late 1990s or early 1920s and the average marketing to sales shot up to 7% for the years 1997–2005. However, the average marketing to sales ratio remained constant at around 7% for all those years. A possible reason for such change could be as follows. Large sized firms were already spending a substantial amount of their revenue on establishing a brand name for their products. Given the large scale of operation, it is expected that by spending heavily on marketing activities from the early days of its operation, large sized firms have already contributed to the stock of goodwill of the company (Nerlove and Arrow 1962a). However, with the rise in the total number of players in the mid of 1990s many medium and small sized firms faced difficulties in maintaining their competitiveness. Thus, they have also started spending on marketing related activities to maintain competitiveness. Besides the new entrants (which are mainly medium sized firms) also have to spend heavily on marketing activity to get a share of the market. On the whole, we, therefore find that the average spending for marketing expenditure has increased for all firms including small and medium sized firms in the recent year.

2.4.4 Exploring the Global Market

The wave of globalization and the liberalization policy[34] of the government have opened up new opportunities for the industry and large numbers of firms[35] are also competing at the global level. Evidence of increased internationalization is noticed among Indian pharmaceutical companies from Fig. 2.7, which plots the average export and import intensity[36] of the Indian pharmaceutical sector.

With respect to outward orientation, figures in Table 2.10, reveal that firms exposed to international market perform better compared to firms that target the domestic market alone.

Pharmaceutical exports are destined for around 175 countries which include the highly regulated markets of the US, the European Union and Australia, the semi-regulated markets of Singapore, Taiwan, Brazil etc to markets of lower regulation such as that of Sri-Lanka and African countries. The bulk of India's export of pharmaceutical products are however, destined toward the US and other European

---

[34] Apart from removing the trade barrier for the free flow of medicinal products the Government of India also relaxed the limit for outward investment from a meager US $ 4 million in 1993–1994 to any amount up to the net worth of US $ 199 million in 2003–2004. In other words, firms have more flexibility to export their product and also to establish any overseas production unit.

[35] There has been a phenomenal rise in the number of firms exporting their products in the international market.

[36] $\text{Export Intensity} = \frac{\text{Export earning in the Year}}{\text{Total revenue in the th Year}}$

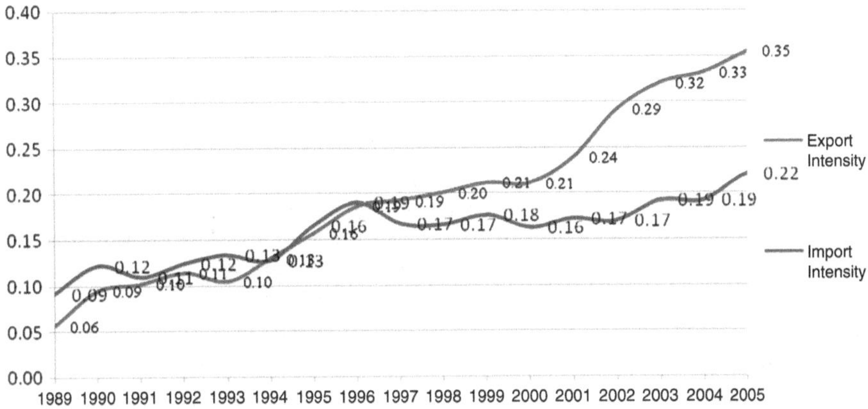

Fig. 2.7 Exports and import intensity of the Indian pharmaceutical sector (Source: Computed from the aggregated Prowess Data base)

Table 2.10 Profitability and productivity for firms with export earning

	Firms targeting the international market		Firms targeting the domestic market	
Year	Profitability	Productivity	Profitability	Productivity
1991–1995	0.5155	2.506	0.412	2.437
1996–2000	0.422	2.4825	0.271	1.966
2001–2005	0.6145	3.762	0.379	2.481

Source: Computed from the aggregated data of the Prowess Data base

nations. This shows the relative strength of Indian Pharmaceutical firms in producing high quality generic products.[37] Further, because of stringent regulatory barriers in the global regulated market, the numbers of players in the regulated market are less and therefore there is a higher price realization. However, exporting in the regulated market is not easy because it involves high cost in maintaining good manufacturing practices and quality standards at par with global norms. Very few pharmaceutical companies have adequate resources[38] to undertake such activity; we, therefore, find that only top domestic players like Ranbaxy, Dr. Reddys Laboratory, Cadila, Cipla, Lupin Laboratory and few medium sized companies like Ipca Labratories, Neuland Laboratory, Alembic Limited and a few others have targeted the global regulated market.

Large proportions (about 40%) of the companies are, however, exporting their products in the semi-regulated or unregulated market. The process of exporting products in the unregulated market started as early as the 1980s. The advantage of exporting in the unregulated market is that there is lesser of anentry barrier and

[37] Presently, India has about 75 U.S. FDA approved plants. This is the highest number of U.S. FDA approved plants outside the U.S.

[38] The cost of establishing a dedicated bulk drug facility for a simple bulk drug can be as high as US $ 3–5 million in India; most of the Indian companies have, however, invested up to US $ 10 million for bulk drug facilities (Chaudhuri 2005).

production can be started with a very low technological base. The disadvantages are low price realization and intense competition, which may result in lower profit realization as well. In recent years, for certain categories of bulk drugs the prices of the product have slashed by more than 30% and for certain cases prices have come down even below domestic market prices. (see Chaudhuri 2005, pp 188).

To pursue internalization strategy, firms are following two different routes: Direct Investment and Merger & Acquisition. Indian pharmaceutical firms embarked on the route for direct investment in the late 70s.[39] Direct investments in global market (also known as Greenfield investment) are undertaken either with production motive or with marketing motive (Pradhan 2006a). Overseas merger and acquisition is another attractive route, which has lately gained ground among Indian pharmaceutical companies. In a short spell of 6 years from 2000 to 2006 the total number of trans-border acquisition stands at around 49, which is worth US $ 1.3 billion of financial deal (Pradhan and Abhinav 2006b). Apart from the usual market share gain, access to firm-specific assets like new product portfolio with an established brand name, internationally accredited manufacturing units, R&D infrastructure, marketing synergies are some of the other motives for firms to follow the route of merger and acquisition (Pradhan and Abhinav 2006b).

2.5 Conclusions

In this chapter, we have reviewed some of the important policy changes pertaining to the pharmaceutical sector of India. We noticed that government policies played a pivotal role for the growth and development of this sector over time. Particularly, the absence of product patents, assured the market for life saving drugs, and protection from foreign competition, helped the growth of this industry. We also notice that positive externalities from the public sector and the research units enabled firms to gain competence in process engineering and maintain a competitive edge in the international market.

The recent changes in government policy from protection to competition are also evident from the review of policies. Aggregate indicators like concentration ratio, scale economies etc. also suggest that the industry is highly competitive with a low level of concentration. However, in spite of high competition, the pharmaceutical industry is one of the most profitable industries. We traced the largeness in the size of the firm, R&D, marketing and export intensity as the possible main sources for better performance of firms. However, the analyses are not statistically rigorous. In the subsequent chapters of this book, we have done an in-depth analysis of the performance of firms by examining their efficiency, productivity and profitability and the factors that influence performance.

[39] The first case of overseas investment was undertaken by Sarabhai M. Chemicals in Indonesia and Malaysia in 1976 followed by Ranbaxy. A total of 15 Greenfield investments took place by 11 companies from the late 70s to the early 1980s.

Appendix A

Table A.1 Market share of MNCs and Indian companies

Year	MNC (%)	Indian companies (%)
1952	38	62
1970	68	32
1978	60	40
1980	50	50
1991	40	60
1998	32	68
2004	23	77

Source: Chaudhuri (2005)

Table A.2 Production units in the pharma sector

Years	No. of units
1952–1953	1,752
1969–1970	2,257
1977–1978	5,201
1979–1980	5,126
1980–1981	6,417
1982–1983	6,631
1983–1984	9,000
1984–1985	9,234
1985–1986	9,540
1989–1990	16,000
2000–1901	20,053

Source: Organisation of pharmaceutical producers in India

Table A.3 Growth rate in the Indian pharmaceutical sector

Year	Growth rate of bulk drug	Growth rate of formulation	Growth rate of the sector
1975–1978	0.14	0.18	0.18
1979–1982	0.13	0.12	0.13
1983–1986	0.08	0.08	0.08
1987–1990	0.17	0.20	0.19
1991–1994	0.19	0.18	0.18
1995–1998	0.20	0.15	0. 16
1999–1903	0.20	0.15	0.16

Table A.4 Proportion of diversified firms

Year	H-Index for the Sector	Highly specialized firms (1–.75)	Specialized firms (.74–.40)	Moderately diversified firms (.39–.25)	Highly diversified firms less than (.25)
1991	0.352	0.18	0.19	0.25	0.37
1992	0.329	0.19	0.22	0.31	0.28
1993	0.359	0.20	0.23	0.33	0.23
1994	0.423	0.24	0.27	0.32	0.17
1995	0.416	0.28	0.24	0.28	0.20
1996	0.453	0.28	0.26	0.32	0.15
1997	0.449	0.28	0.30	0.27	0.15
1998	0.475	0.24	0.26	0.19	0.10
1999	0.433	0.30	0.32	0.24	0.15
2000	0.481	0.28	0.33	0.26	0.13
2001	0.472	0.31	0.33	0.24	0.13
2002	0.403	0.27	0.29	0.23	0.21
2003	0.414	0.32	0.25	0.26	0.17
2004	0.432	0.27	0.29	0.32	0.12
2005	0.482	0.28	0.31	0.30	0.11

Source: Computed from the annual balance sheets of companies from the CMIE data base

Table A.5 New chemical entities invented

Companies	New chemical entities (NCE)
Dr Reddys lab	10
Ranbaxy	12
Cadila	4
Lupin	4
Glenmark	6
Wockhardt	4
Torrent	2
Kopran	2
Dabur	4
Orchid	2
Nicholas Primal	7
JB Chemical	2

Source: Calculated from the annual balance sheets of companies

Chapter 3
The Sources of Heterogeneity in the Efficiency of Indian Pharmaceutical Firms

3.1 Introduction

One of the objectives of the reform process initiated for the Indian pharmaceutical industry is to remove the hurdles of regulation and to allow firms to function freely in response to market forces. To fulfill this objective the Indian government pursued certain policies, like dismantling the complex network of industrial control and licensing policy, liberalizing and facilitating the flow of foreign direct investment and foreign trade, removing the restrictions on the import of bulk drugs, limiting the scope of price control etc. Such policies were implemented with the expectation that the liberalized market environment would allow pharmaceutical firms to function freely, enter into technological collaboration with foreign firms, introduce new products and processes and thereby achieve higher efficiency and productivity. However, such a competitive environment may not benefit all firms equally. In an industry where firms differ with respect to their access to technology and state-of-the-art knowledge, the process of liberalization may create gainers and losers. In other words, a performance differential may arise amongst firms. In this regard, analyzing the efficiency of firms is one of the most appropriate methods of examining performance differential. This chapter is primarily devoted to such an investigation.

In efficiency analysis, it is assumed that not all firms may be able to allocate their resources to carry out their objectives in the most optimal manner even when they operate in a similar environment. Therefore, given the estimated production frontier (which is arrived at by enveloping the input-output bundles of the best performing firms), there can be a gap in the output produced by the best performing firms and other firms considered in the sample. Such a gap or the distance of firms from the frontier indicates the level of inefficiency faced by them.

In efficiency related literature there are two ways of measuring the efficiency of the firm, namely, the output efficiency that captures how far an inefficient firm can scale up its output production to reach the frontier for the same level of inputs it employs and the input efficiency that identifies how far a firm can reduce its input usages for a given level of output it produces. The input and output oriented

M. Mazumdar, *Performance of Pharmaceutical Companies in India*,
Contributions to Economics, DOI 10.1007/978-3-7908-2876-4_3,

measures of efficiency may not be equal, particularly when the underlying production technology exhibits returns to scales property. Therefore, previous studies have either given priority to the output expansion of firms to compute their *output efficiency* or have computed the *input efficiency* by imposing an a-priori assumption that a firm minimizes its level of input usages.

However, a profit-maximizing firm strives to reduce its input usage and increase its output production at the same time. In this analysis, we have therefore attempted to measure the output and input efficiencies in a simultaneous fashion for Indian pharmaceutical firms. The model (Pastor Ruiz and Sirvent Model 1999) that we have applied to compute the efficiency of pharmaceutical firms allows them to expand each of the outputs[1] in its output bundle and at the same time it also in-corporates the possibility of reducing each of its input usages to arrive at the output and the input efficiencies of firms.

After calculating inefficiencies, we also wish to identify the reasons behind the efficient functioning of a firm by identifying its determinants. Such analysis will illuminate the effectiveness of, say for example, the R&D efforts of firms or new investment in plant and machinery to attain higher efficiencies. Policy suggestions can then be made to boost the R&D environment in the country or to make easy availability of loan if such moves on the part of firms are found to be effective for attaining higher efficiency. Thus, the analysis is also useful for policy purposes

Given this background, the rest of the chapter unfolds in the following way: the next section explains briefly the method used to measure the efficiency of firms and illustrates the non-parametric DEA methodology. Section 3.3 presents a review of some important studies related to efficiency measurement for manufacturing firms in general and the pharmaceutical sector in particular. Section 3.4 presents the data set used in this chapter. The main finding from the empirical analysis is discussed in Sect. 3.5. Section 3.6 identifies the determinants of the efficiency scores of firms through an appropriate model. This section is followed by a concluding section.

3.2 Measurement of Efficiency

The efficiency of a firm has two important components: one is purely the technical or physical component of the efficiency, which refers to the maximum output that can be produced by the best possible use of inputs allowing minimal wastage. Another is the allocative efficiency, which refers to the ability of a firm to combine inputs and outputs in optimal proportion in light of prevailing prices (Lovell 1993, p. 10). Here we are concerned with the technical efficiency of firms.[2]

[1] Since we have a single output case, the possibility of increasing each of the output in the output bundle at different proportions does not arise. While measuring the input specific efficiencies, we have, however, incorporated such possibilities.

[2] For a detailed discussion on Data Envelopment Analysis see Ray (2004) and Charnes, Cooper, Lewin and Seiford, eds *Data Envelopment Analysis: Theory, Methodology and Practice* (1994).

There are two different ways of estimating the frontier production function and the efficiency of firms, namely, (1) Parametric, and the (2) Non Parametric methods. The Parametric approach incorporates the randomness of the data generating process, however, it imposes an explicit functional form say a Cobb-Douglas or a Translog on the observed data point to estimate the frontier and the inefficiency of firms. In the current analysis, we use the non-parametric Data Envelopment Analysis (DEA) approach.

3.2.1 Non-parametric Measure of Technical Efficiency

DEA imposes certain minimum assumptions of a neo-classical production technology, uses linear programming approach to empirically construct the frontier, and arrive at the efficiency of firms.[3] While it does not impose any functional form on the observed data point, it also cannot take care of the randomness of the data generating process. We still prefer the non-parametric DEA approach because in the Indian pharmaceutical sector the structure of firms differs at different input levels. Thus while on the one hand, we have a large number of small firms with low market share, on the other hand, a few large firms capture about 75% of the market. Under such circumstances, the chances of mis-specification for the production function can always arise when we estimate the frontier parametrically. Further, in our analysis we have used firm level information from the audited balance sheet of the companies, which is less prone to randomness. Moreover, Banker (1993) has also shown that DEA based efficiency *estimates are weakly consistent* and converges faster than the efficiency estimates from other frontier methods (Grosskopf 1996; Kneip et al. 1998). In our book we have large sample of an unbalanced panel of 2,492 firms for 15 years; we therefore presume that DEA based efficiency estimates will satisfy weak consistency property.[4] This methodology also helps us to look at the efficiency of firms by both input and output usage in a combined fashion. Further, we have constructed the frontiers over the years sequentially. In sequential frontier, it is assumed that for any given year the input-output bundles or the technologies of the previous years is available but technology of future years is not available (see Sect. 3.4 for a detail description about sequential frontier). However, in the parametric approach a single functional form is fitted by considering the data points for all the years. In other words, it is

---

[3] See Ray (2004) for a detailed exposition on DEA.

[4] Simar and Wilson (1998a, 2000) have set the foundation for using bootstrap techniques to generate empirical distributions of DEA efficiency scores and correct various randomness in DEA based estimates. The technique has, however, not tickled down to common practice because of the lack of availability of statistical packages.

assumed that, in a given year, the technologies of future years is available. Thus, in our analysis, we have made a more realistic assumption about the availability of technology. Hence, efficiency estimates using DEA are more precise.

To construct the frontier, the input-output set (x, y) or synonymously the technology or production possibility set is defined as

$$T = \{(x, y); x \in R_+^N, y \in R_+^M : \text{ x can produce y}\} \tag{3.1}$$

Typically, it is assumed that (a) all input and output bundles are feasible $(X^*, Y^* \in T)$ and freely disposable, and (b) the technology set T is convex. Given the above assumptions the efficiency of firms is estimated with respect to the following technology set by using the technique of *mathematical programming*. There are two approaches for efficiency measurement in DEA, viz., the *radial* and the *non-radial* measure. The radial measure follows the Debreu (1951) and Farrell (1957) definition of efficiency and have either an input or an output orientation. For input efficiency, the input vector of a firm is scaled down by θ without any corresponding fall in output such that the adjusted input-output bundle is a feasible point of technology set T i.e.

$$TE^I(x, y) = \min \theta : (\theta x, y) \in T \tag{3.2}$$

Similarly, the corresponding output-oriented measure of technical efficiency is given by

$$TE^0(x, y) = \frac{1}{\varphi} \max \ \varphi : (x, \varphi y) \in T \tag{3.3}$$

Here the output bundle of the firm is scaled up by a constant fraction ϕ without any additional employment of inputs such that the adjusted input-output bundle is also a feasible element of the technology set T.

Unlike the radial approach, the non-radial measures follow the Koopmans (1951) definition of efficiency. According to Koopmans, a producer producing multiple outputs using multiple inputs is technically efficient if an increase in any output in the output bundle requires a reduction in at least one of the other outputs or an increase in at least one input (Lovell 1993, p. 10). If we take an *input conserving approach* the same concept may be defined for the production process where a reduction in any input requires an increase in one of the other inputs or a reduction in at least one output. The merit of the Koopman definition is that it incorporates the possibility whereby a firm can alter its input and output components in different proportions to arrive at its input and output inefficiencies.

Since the definition of Koopmans satisfies the Pareto optimality criteria, the measure is also known as Pareto-Koopman measure of efficiency.[5] In non-radial approach, the input and the output specific efficiencies are estimated with reference to the efficient subset of the input and the output set[6] of T. Once the input and output elements of an inefficient firm are projected on the efficient subset of the technology set T, no further expansion or contraction in the output or input elements is possible. Such is, however, not the case for the radial approach where the input or the output vector of the firm is projected on the boundary of the technology set. Hence it does not preclude the possibility of further reduction in input or an expansion in output in the input or output vector of the firm. Among the various non-radial measures proposed (for example, the Measure of Efficiency Proportion (MEP) developed by Banker and Cooper (1994), Range Adjusted Measure (RAM) of Cooper et al. (1999), two step Russell-extended Farrell measure by Zieschang (1984))[7] we use the *Pastor, Ruiz, and Sirvent* (*PRS* 1999) model to compute the input and output efficiency of firms.[8]

3.2.1.1 Output and Input Efficiencies: The PRS Model

In PRS model, it is assumed that the objective of firms is to minimize the ratio Γ

$$\Gamma = \min \frac{\frac{1}{n}\sum\limits_{i}\theta_i}{\frac{1}{m}\sum\limits_{r}\phi_r} \equiv \min \frac{\frac{1}{4}(\theta_L + \theta_K + \theta_E + \theta_{RW})}{\phi} \tag{3.4}$$

Here θ_i is the proportion by which the input i is scaled down, $\{i = L$ *(labor), K (capital), E (energy), RW (raw material)*$\}$. Thus, given the empirically constructed frontier, θ_L is the proportion by which labor is scaled down by an inefficient firm to reach the frontier. Minimizing the ratio Γ is like minimizing the value of θ_i and at the same time maximizing the value of ϕ_r, subject to

$$\sum_j \lambda_j y_j \geq \phi y_o \text{ (Output} - \text{constraint)} \tag{3.5}$$

[5] According to the Pareto criteria, an input-output bundle cannot qualify as an efficient point if there remains the possibility of any increase in output or reduction in inputs.

[6] For various properties of the input and output set and its relation with the technical efficiency of the firm one can refer to Varian (1984) and Ray (2004).

[7] See Färe and Lovell (1978) and Russell (1985) for the limitation of the above measures.

[8] The efficiency measure proposed by PRS is well defined, satisfies all the global properties of an efficiency measure compared to other non-radial measures. Additionally, it can also compute the input and output efficiencies of firms that other non-radial measures fail to capture. Further, Ray and Jeon (2007) has shown that the PRS measure of efficiency is a global generalized efficiency measure because all other radial and non-radial measures are a special case of PRS model.

$$\sum_{j} \lambda_j L_j \leq \theta_L L_0 \text{ (Labor – constraint)} \tag{3.6}$$

$$\sum_{j} \lambda_j K_j \leq \theta_K K_0 \text{ (Capital – constraint)} \tag{3.7}$$

$$\sum_{j} \lambda_j E_j \leq \theta_E E_0 \text{ (Energy – constraint)} \tag{3.8}$$

$$\sum_{j} \lambda_j RW_j \leq \theta_{RW} RW_0 \text{ (Raw – Material – constraint)} \tag{3.9}$$

$$\sum_{j=1}^{N} \lambda_j = 1 \text{ and } \sum_{j=1}^{N} \lambda_j \geq 0; j = 1(N) \tag{3.10}$$

Thus, while minimizing Γ we get the input and output efficiencies of the firm. The above constraints in the programming imply that potential outputs and inputs of a firm lie within the efficient subset of the technology set T. Inequality (3.5) ensures that the expanded output do not exceed the frontier constructed by the output sets of other firms in the sample. The other constraints are the input constraints which imply that minimized inputs do not fall below the average inputs employed by other firms in the sample. Finally, the constraints also ensure that while constructing the frontier the weights λ are selected in a way that they do not exceed the efficient input constraints for each of the inputs employed and the output produced by the firm. Finally, the constraint (3.10) ensures convexity of the technology set which implies Variable Returns to Scale (VRS) technology (see Ray 2004). To obtain the efficiency of the firms the programming has to be run separately for each firm in the sample. Note that the efficient input-output projection (x^*, y^*) satisfies the following property

$$x^* = \sum_{j} \lambda_j^* x^j \leq \hat{x} \text{ and } y^* = \sum_{j} \lambda_j^* y^j \geq \hat{y}$$

Thus, $(\hat{x}, \hat{y})$ is Pareto-Koopman efficient, iff $\phi_r^* = 1$ for each output r and $\theta_i^* = 1$ for each input i, implying that $\Gamma = 1$. The Pareto-Koopman efficiency measure is a global efficiency measure (GEM) and product of two factors γ_1 and γ_2. The first factor $\gamma_1 = \frac{1}{n}\sum_{i} \theta_i$ is the input oriented component (GEMIN) and the second factor $\gamma_2 = \frac{1}{m}\sum_{r} \phi_r$ is the output-oriented component (GEMOUT). Thus, $\Gamma = \gamma_1\gamma_2$. The objective function Γ in this mathematical programming problem is a non-linear problem. Applying the first order Taylor series for Γ at $\theta_i^* = 1 \forall$ i and $\phi_r^* = 1 \forall$ r, Ray and Jeon (2007) has shown that it is possible to lineralize the objective function as $\Gamma = 1 + \frac{1}{n}\sum_{i} \theta_i - \frac{1}{m}\sum_{r} \phi_r$

Thus solving the linear programming problem:

$$\Gamma = 1 + \frac{1}{n}\sum_i \theta_i - \frac{1}{m}\sum_r \phi_r \tag{3.11}$$

subject to the constraints (3.5), (3.6), (3.7), (3.8), (3.9), (3.10) and substituting the optimal (θ_i^*, ϕ_r^*) value in Γ i.e. $\Gamma^* = \frac{\frac{1}{n}\sum_i \theta_i^*}{\frac{1}{m}\sum_r \phi_r^*}$ the efficiency scores of a firm is arrived at.

3.2.2 *Determinants of Firm Efficiency*

In the non-parametric approach for efficiency analysis using DEA, it is a common practice to estimate a regression model in the second stage explaining the variation in the measured efficiency scores for a set of explanatory variables (Ray 1991; McCarty and Yaisawarng 1993; Duncombe et al. 1997; Chilingerian and Sherman 2004; Ray 2004; and Ruggiero 2004). The approach to link the mathematically computed DEA efficiency scores with its determinants was first introduced and further developed by Ray (1988, 1991). Since DEA efficiency scores are censored from below at unity, Ray (1991) justified the use of the Tobit model instead of the ordinary square regression. However, the approach lacks a serious data-generating process (DGP)[9] that would conceptually link the non-parametric deterministic DEA efficiency score with the statistical two-stage regression analysis. Responding to the need for developing a proper framework, Simar and Wilson (2007) defined a DGP that would make the second stage regression analysis sensible. Simar and Wilson's (2007) paper established that, due to the serial correlation in the efficiency estimates, the inferences drawn for the second stage regression are invalid. The authors suggested the use of maximum likelihood (ML) estimators of truncated regression and smooth bootstrapping for valid inferences in the second stage regression. Banker and Natarajan (2008) have advanced a DGP that has a much less restrictive form than the DGP advanced by Simar and Wilson (2007) and theoretically justifies the use of simple ordinary least square (OLS) or even Tobit

[9] Data generating process is a probability distribution that is supposed to characterize the population from which the data source has been drawn. It is the process by which the sample data is generated while the researcher estimates the statistical model of his interest. The set of data obtained depends crucially on the particular set of error terms drawn. A different set of error terms would create a different data set for the estimated statistical model (see Kennedy 1998; Härdle and Simar 1999 and so on for a detailed discussion on DGP).

estimation for the second stage parametric regression analysis.[10] *In the spirit of the Banker and Natarajan (2008) paper, we also employ an OLS model to evaluate the impact of contextual variables on the efficiency estimates of the firm.*

Since we have panel data for our analysis the OLS regression model is specified as

$$Ln(eff_{jt}) = x_{jt}\beta + \mu_{it} \tag{3.12}$$

where j represents the jth firm j = 1(1) N; subscript t denotes time in our model (that spans from 1991 to 2005). Utilizing a one-way error component model for the disturbance terms to account for the unobservable firm specific effect,[11] we can re-write $\mu_{it} = \mu_i + v_{it}$, where μ_i, s is the unobservable firm specific effect that is independent of x_{jt}. For estimating the above model, one can either treat μ_i, s as fixed parameters to be estimated with other parameters in the model. In panel data literature, this is known as fixed effect model. The random effect model, on the other hand assumed μ_i, s to be the random variable, satisfying the (following) property $\mu_i \sim N(0, \sigma_\mu^2)$. Since in our data the number of firms is more than the number of time periods, the random effects estimation technique is considered to be more appropriate to estimate the model (it will have more degrees of freedom) compared to the fixed effects model. However, if the assumption that the individual invariant effects (μ_i) are not correlated with the regressors i.e., if $E(\mu_i/X_{it}) = 0$ is not valid, the GLS estimator of the random effect model becomes biased and inconsistent (Baltagi 2003). In this regard, Hausman (1978) has developed a test, which suggests whether the fixed effect model or a random effect model is appropriate for estimation purposes. See Baltagi 2003; Wooldridge 2004 for a detailed illustration on the Hausman Specification test.

The independent variable in our model is x_{jt} which is a vector of k factors that explains the variations of the efficiency of the jth firms (=1–288) in the t-th time period (t = 1991–2005). In our study, the data for all 288 firms are not available for all the years and we therefore have an unbalanced panel of 2,437 firms for 15 years. The relevant variables for our study are obtained from the balance sheets of companies from the prowess database.

---

[10] The Monte-Carlo Stimulation carried out in the second stage indicates that the two stage method with DEA based efficiency in the first stage and OLS, maximum likelihood or even Tobit estimations, in the second stage performs far better than the parametric methods. The Banker and Nataranjan (2008) paper assumes a form of Data Generating Process (DGP) that is much more flexible and less restrictive than the one assumed by Simar and Wilson (2007) that has also examined the impact of contextual variables on the efficiency of firms in a two-stage process. While the Simar and Wilson (2007) paper argues that ML estimation of a truncated regression rather than the Tobit model is the preferred approach in the second stage, the Banker and Natarajan (2008) results are more robust and appropriate than the Simar and Wilson (2007) approach.

[11] The advantage of panel data is its ability to account for the unobservable firm specific individual effects like managerial skill, firm-specific capabilities and others. Not accounting for the firm specific individual effects can actually lead to a bias in the resulting estimates (see Baltagi 2003).

3.3 Review of Literature on the Efficiency of the Manufacturing Sector

Since measuring efficiency is a common way to evaluate the performance of any decision-making unit (DMU), the empirical application of this concept has been quite voluminous.[12] Given such wide application of the methodology, the review of applied empirical literature in this book has been limited specifically for a sample of studies pertaining to Indian manufacturing firms. In recent times, the issue of efficiency has evoked interest among Indian scholars because firm activities like entry, exit, and expansion were highly regulated by a number of public policies in the pre-liberalization era.

Using a time varying frontier production approach and the dataset from 1974 to 1988, Neogi and Ghosh (1994) estimated the inter-temporal movement of the technical efficiency of the manufacturing firms. The study shows that there has been a fall in the efficiency of firms in the pre-liberalization era. An inquiry into the sources of inter-industry efficiency variations shows that skill-upgradation, labor productivity and profit played significant positive roles, whereas capital intensity works against general beliefs. Other studies that have used the data from the pre-liberalization period have also examined a variety of issues like size of a firm and its efficiency (Bhavani 1991; Goldar 1985), the variation in efficiency levels across states and across different ownership patterns (Nikaido 2004 and Ramaswamy 1994).

A number of studies have also used the data of the post-liberalization era to specifically examine the impact of liberalization on the efficiency of firms. Some of the notable studies in this regard are by Mitra (1999), Kalirajan and Bhide (2005), Jayadevan (1996), Mitra et al. (2002a), Trivedi (2003), Srivastava (2001) and others. Using the methodology of Cornwell et al. (1990) to study the technical efficiency and productivity growth of Indian industries, Mitra (1999) indicated that for industries like food products, beverages and tobacco products, basic metals and metal products, there has been a sharp decline in efficiency in periods from 1985–1986 to 1992–1993 as compared to the period from 1976–1977 to 1984–1985, whereas few other industries have experienced a positive growth in efficiency during the study period. The study of technical efficiency by Parameshwaran (2002) for selective manufacturing industries like electrical, non-electrical, electronics, and transport indicates that although the industry has experienced positive technical change due to the liberalization policy of the government,

[12] As documented by Emrouznejad (2001), Tavares (2002) Gattoufi et al. (2004), and Cook et al. (2009) the total number of journal papers on efficiency analysis using only DEA exceeds 1,259. DEA methodology has also been widely applied mostly in the context of developing nations to evaluate the performance of public utilities like municipal corporations, education service providers, public sector and others and also for the traditional manufacturing sector. An internet search on a search engine like google.com on data envelopment analysis return about 1,000 hits, the vast majority of which appears to be working papers.

this has also led to a fall in efficiency for these industries. The study also indicates that the export activity, import of technology and raw materials of a firm contributes to its higher efficiency. The study by Kalirajan and Bhide (2005) is the first of its kind that has used the random coefficient model developed by Swamy (1971) and Swamy and Mehta (1977) to estimate frontier production function and the efficiency of the Indian manufacturing sector. The study indicates that due to liberalization, the productivity growth of the manufacturing sector has slowed down which is mainly due to a fall in the technical efficiency of the firms. Using the firm level data and employing the non-parametric technique of DEA to estimate the efficiency of the firms, a study by Ray (2002a) indicated that the average efficiency for the Indian manufacturing sector has declined over the period from 1991 to 1996. There was, however, some improvement in efficiency after 1996. The study also indicated that firms with foreign ownership contribute towards efficiency.

Since liberalization brings in FDI, Kathurai (2002) studied the impact of FDI flow and its spillover on the efficiency gain of the Indian manufacturing firms. The study indicated that after liberalization the efficiency of the Indian manufacturing industry has improved. However, the benefit of technical gains accrued mainly to foreign-owned firms. Categorizing the firms into various groups based on their innovative activities, the study also indicated that with increased globalization, FDI has a positive effect on the productivity and efficiency for scientific firms in the Indian manufacturing sectors whereas the productivity and efficiency have decreased for non-scientific firms.

Because of the federal structure of India, attempts have also been made in a number of studies to understand the differences in efficiency and productivity of the manufacturing firms across the states. In this regard, Mitra et al. (2002a, b) examined the effect of infrastructure for 17 major industries in 15 major states in India, using the stochastic frontier approach. The study indicates the significant role of infrastructure to explain the differences in the total productivity and efficiency of firms. Utilizing the concept of super-efficiency, Mukherjee and Ray (2004) show that there has been no change in the efficiency ranking of the states with respect to the manufacturing sector in the post reform period. In addition, no evidence of convergence of efficiency levels of the firms belonging to different states was noticed in the post-reform period. This may be because the technical efficiency of firms was affected by state-specific infrastructure and political climate.

The studies mentioned above were conducted mainly at the inter-industry level and hence they were done at industry level aggregation. One would expect that a firm level analysis within an industry would be more accurate because the chances of pooling heterogeneous units will be ruled out (Liu and Tybout 1996; Liu 1993; and Bartelsman and Doms 2000). Besides, it is possible to examine a number of issues when analysis is done at the firm level. Thus, a number of studies have also been conducted at the intra-industry level.

A number of research papers use the parametric stochastic frontier approach to evaluate efficiency of firms from specific industries like the sugar industry (Ferrantino and Ferrier 1995), engineering goods (Goldar et al. 2004), textile (Bhandari and Maiti 2007) and pharmaceuticals (Chaudhuri and Das 2006).

Goldar et al. (2004) in their study compared the efficiency of firms with different ownership patterns for the Indian engineering industry. The result clearly indicated that foreign firms in Indian engineering industry have a higher technical efficiency than the domestically owned ones. No significant difference in technical efficiency was, however, noticed between the public and the domestic private sector firms. The extent of inefficiency for the public sector units after liberalization was also studied by Agarwal (2001). Their findings suggest that the majority of firms have low levels of technical efficiency and that the efficiency has not improved significantly over time. However, an improvement in technical efficiency is observed in some firms in the engineering sector and firms in the petroleum-producing sector due to foreign collaboration.

Lall and Rodirgo (2001) first studied the role of infrastructure and location-specific factors for efficiency differences in industries like leather products, machine tools, motor-vehicles and electronic. The study indicated the importance of industrial cluster to achieve higher efficiency.

Using the firm level Annual Survey Industry (ASI) data the study by Bhandari and Maiti (2007) indicated that large sized firms are more efficient in the context of the Indian textile industry. Further, the study also indicated an inverse relationship between the age of the firm and technical efficiency. Constructing frontiers for selected years, the study indicated that there has been a modest improvement in the efficiency of firms from Indian textile industry in the post liberalization era.

Chaudhuri and Das (2006) estimated the stochastic frontier production function using firm level data for the years 1990–2001 to measure technical efficiency of the Indian pharmaceutical sector. The study has shown that the mean efficiency scores of the industry have improved over the sub-period 1999–2001 in contrast to the sub-period 1990–1998. Further, the study has also identified that large sized firms or firms exporting more of their products in the international market have reduced their inefficiency.

The second group of studies employs the non-parametric frontier technique to compute the efficiency of firms. In this regard, the study by Majumdar (1998) evaluates the slack in the resource utilization by state-owned enterprises due to soft budget constraints. The study indicates that in the face of crisis, private sector firms are not allowed to die but their ownership is transferred to the state sector. Also cheaper financial capital is also transferred to them. Such activities lead to the accumulation of slack in resource utilization, which cannot be corrected just by the policy of privatization and requires other institutional reform like eliminating budget constraints.

The non-parametric DEA approach has also been applied by Majumder (1994), Sarangi and Phani (2008) to study the efficiency of the Indian pharmaceutical sector. Majumder (1994) studied the capabilities and resource utilization of firms by employing the DEA methodology. The study covers only nine large firms and spans for the years 1987–1990. The inefficiency of public sector firms as compared to private players is the main finding of the study.

In conducting our literature review, we found that while there are a number of studies examining the efficiency for various industries in India, certain efficiency-related questions (see Chap. 1) have not been adequately addressed for the Indian pharmaceutical sector (see in this regard, Mazumder and Rajeev 2009a, 2010). Our study therefore aims to fill this gap. Moreover, studies that have examined the efficiency of Indian pharmaceutical firms either have limited sample coverage or have not examined the inter-firm efficiency differences adequately. The database that we have used in our analysis covers firms of different sizes and also for a longer period of time. Such a large sample is advantageous on various counts: first, its gives a precise estimate of the efficiency of firms and second, it is also possible to conduct a more in-depth micro-level study.

Moreover, the existing efficiency literature either has an output or an input orientation. However, there can be differences in the input and output efficiencies of a firm when the technology exhibits returns to scale property. In the Indian pharmaceutical industry, a large number of small enterprises co-exist with a handful of large firms. Compared to large firms, the small ones can be inputwise efficient because they operate at low scale and may have greater flexibility to employ the inputs of production. Nevertheless, in the presence of variable return to scale (VRS) or limited market reach, the small firms can be inefficient in terms of their output even if they are efficient in terms of their input. Therefore, to understand the differences in the ability of the firms to manage their input and output, it is necessary to study both output and input inefficiencies of firms. The conventional parametric approach, however, cannot measure the input inefficiency because it takes the corresponding input coefficients to be the same across all the firms and measures inefficiency through the random change in the intercept term.[13] Instead, the non-parametric model that we have applied incorporates the possibility of an increase in the output that the firm produces and also in the scope of a reduction in inputs that it employs to arrive at the output and input efficiencies of the firms. Use of this advanced technique is not common in the literature. Only a limited number of studies have used this approach (see Ray and Jeon 2007). In this respect, the findings from the current study are a new contribution to the literature. Also, we have already argued that with heterogeneity in the structure of the firm, the non-parametric method gives a more appropriate efficiency estimates even though it cannot filter out the random component from the inefficiency measures. Lastly, the second stage regression analysis done by researchers to identify the determinants of efficiencies consider mainly the size, age and ownership patterns of firms. However, our database allows us to consider a number of other important firm specific factors.

[13] Although Kalirajan and Shand (1997) and Kalirajan and Obwana (1994) have integrated the random coefficient model of Swamy (1971) (that can handle the heterogeneity in slopes and intercept of firms) for econometrically estimating the frontier models and the input inefficiency of firms, such technique is not widely used because of computational difficulties.

3.4 Data Sources and Modeling Frontiers Over Time

To examine the efficiency of pharmaceutical companies, firm level information is considered for the years 1991–2005.[14] The number of firms in the sample varies from 70 to 200 and 89 over the years and in total there is an unbalanced panel of 2,400 and 92 firms for 15 years. The firms considered in the study together account for about 85% of the total output and 87% of the input usage for the sector for almost all the years.[15] Thus, the sample of firms considered in the study can be viewed as representative of the sector. The relevant data necessary for the computation is collected from the financial balance sheets of companies provided by the prowess data source of the Centre for Monitoring of Indian Enterprises (CMIE). An ideal approach to compute the efficiency of firms will be to use the physical output and input of firms. However, in the absence of data on physical output and input we use information on values of production and input as done in the earlier literature (see Caves and Barton 1990; Tybout et al. 1991; Aw and Hwang 1995; Pavcnik 2002 and so on). Such an approach is useful particularly when firms produce differentiated products and/or face a differentiated input market. The efficiency measures computed in these research works, including the current one, closely correspond to indices of revenue per unit of input expenditure (see Katayama et al. 2009).

The study conceptualized a 1-output, 4-input production technology. Output in the model is the value of total output (y) defined as the total sales of a firm plus the change in the stock of output measured in terms of the opening stock minus the closing stock in output. The inputs in the model are (1) labor (l), measured in terms of wages and salaries for the workers; (2) material inputs (rw) ,measured in terms of the companies' expenditure for raw materials; (3) energy input (pf), measured is terms of the expenditure for power and fuel; and (4) capital (k), which is the book value for plant and machinery and building.

To bring the variables in real terms each variable is appropriately deflated. The value of output is deflated by the price index for the drug and the pharmaceutical sector collected from the Reserve Bank of India (RBI) monthly bulletins. Expenditure for worker is deflated by the Consumer Price Index (CPI) for the manual and the non-manual worker; expenditure for fuel and power is deflated with the price index for Fuel, Power Lights and Lubricants collected from the RBI bulletins to arrive at the real figure, the company expenditure for raw-material is deflated by the average price index for chemicals and chemical products from the ASI data base. The capital stock is available as book value for plant and machinery. Therefore, the

[14] The Prowess Data-Base provides firm level information from the year 1989 to the current year. However, data are consistently available only from the year 1991. Therefore, the study period from 1991 to 2005 has been considered in this paper. Also most of the policy changes for this sector were implemented between the year 1995 and 1998.

[15] The figures have been arrived at by taking the ratio of the output manufactured by the registered Indian pharmaceutical companies (provided by the CMIE prowess database) to the total value of output produced by the sector (provided by the Ministry for Chemicals and Petro-Chemicals).

Perpetual Inventory Method (PIM) (see Balakrishnan et al. 2000) is used to deflate the value of capital taking 2003 as the benchmark year.

To measure efficiency, one needs to account for the availability of technology and construct frontiers at different points in time. In DEA literature (see Tulkens and van den Eeckaut 1995) three forms of frontiers are distinguished, viz., (1) the *contemporaneous frontier;* (2) *the sequential frontier; and* (3) *the intertemporal frontier*. In this analysis, we use the sequential frontier. This is under the assumption that for any given year the input-output bundles or the technologies of the previous years is available but technology of the future years is not available. In the sequential frontier, interdependence is assumed between the production possibility sets. This allows an outward shift of the frontier and an enlarged production possibility set over the years. We choose to use sequential frontier under the assumption that, for the sample years, the sector might have experienced technological progress leading to a possible outward shift in the production frontier. This is possible due to greater involvement of the firms in R&D, import of capital goods and investments in modern plant and machinery.

3.5 Measuring the Efficiency of the Indian Pharmaceutical Sector

In our empirical analysis, the Pastor et al. (1999) model (see Eqs. 3.4, 3.5, 3.6, 3.7, 3.8, 3.9, 3.10, and 3.11) (that allows for the simultaneous increase in the output and decrease in the inputs) has been employed to get the output and input efficiency scores of a firm.

Since a single output four input technology has been conceived for pharmaceutical firms, efficiency scores are available for output and four inputs (1) Raw-material; (2) Power and Fuel; (3) Labor; and (4) Capital. Table 3.1 provides the average efficiency scores obtained for the firms in the sample for each year.

Let us first consider the case of output efficiency of a firm. The first column in Table 3.1 depicts the value of ϕ that represents the unrealized potential increase in the output of a firm that could be achieved without employing any additional inputs. More precisely, in the year 1991, the average efficiency attained by firms in the sample was 81%. This implies that on an average firms in the industry can further expand their output by about 19% without employing any additional inputs. The trend for the output efficiency reveals that there has been a fall in the average efficiency of the sector. Similar conclusions have been arrived at by the earlier studies as well (see Ray 2002; Mukherjee and Ray 2004; Ray 2004; Srivastava 2001; and Parameswarn 2002) for the Indian manufacturing sector. A consistent fall in the mean output efficiency for the sector also implies that, compared to the output produced by frontier firms, the production level of inefficient firms are falling over the years.

Table 3.1 Input and output specific efficiency of the Indian pharmaceutical sector (1991–2005)

(1) Year	(2) Output efficiency ϕ	(3) Material efficiency θ_{RM}	(4) Power and fuel efficiency θ_E	(5) Labor efficiency θ_L	(6) capital efficiency θ_K
1991	0.811	0.933	0.613	0.863	0.672
1992	0.662	0.681	0.418	0.854	0.547
1993	0.623	0.718	0.389	0.808	0.558
1994	0.603	0.724	0.442	0.923	0.638
1995	0.507	0.873	0.434	0.907	0.701
1996	0.462	0.869	0.399	0.926	0.713
1997	0.418	0.898	0.451	0.920	0.661
1998	0.531	0.984	0.387	0.886	0.362
1999	0.452	0.918	0.502	0.919	0.548
2000	0.415	0.891	0.347	0.895	0.708
2001	0.371	0.899	0.365	0.909	0.739
2002	0.318	0.911	0.323	0.885	0.700
2003	0.307	0.843	0.364	0.927	0.756
2004	0.402	0.928	0.322	0.928	0.614
2005	0.387	0.675	0.402	0.946	0.669

Three distinct possibilities might arise in this context. The first issue is methodological. Since we are using a sequential frontier, in the initial years, the degree of freedom is less and these have caused a number of observations to have an efficiency of one. That, in turn, has caused a higher average efficiency for the sector. Second, the form of production frontier constructed for the sector incorporates the possibilities of technological progress. In other words, an outward shift in the frontier is possible for the subsequent years. This implies that if there is technological progress for this sector leading to an outward shift in the production frontier, for the inefficient firms the distance from the frontier is increasing even though their performance may not decline in an absolute sense of the term. Finally, it may so happen that the efficiencies of firms that lie below the frontier worsen in absolute terms. We will be examining some of these possibilities in Chap. 5.

3.5.1 *Input-Specific Measures of the Efficiency of Firms*

Moving now to the input wise measure of efficiency, columns 3–6 in Table 3.1 summarizes the value of θ_i, s (see again Eqs. 3.4, 3.5, 3.6, 3.7, 3.8, 3.9, 3.10, and 3.11) the input efficiencies of firms. A value of 0.863 for the labor efficiency in 1991 implies that an average firm in this industry can cut down its labor cost by about 14%[16] without employing any additional inputs or hampering their output

[16] A value of 0.863 for labor efficiency implies that labor inefficiency is about 0.177. This is computed by deducting 0.863 from unity.

level. Similarly, a value of 0.933 for the raw-material efficiency implies that firms on an average can reduce its raw-material expenditure by about 7%. One can similarly interpret the efficiency scores for capital power and fuel. The average measures in terms of inputs in efficiency suggest certain interesting trends for the industry. It is noticed that even though the output efficiency reveals a declining trend, firms on an average have been able to make efficient use of labor, raw-material and capital. The average efficiency scores for labour, raw-material and capital are fluctuating around the mean value of 0.90, 0.85 and 0.63 respectively over the years. On the other hand, over the years, the mean efficiency for power and fuel is only 0.40. What could be the possible reasons for such efficient use of raw material and labor and inefficient use of power-fuel by Indian pharmaceutical firms?

Raw material is a factor of production which can be used in an appropriate quantity. India has a well-developed chemical industry (see Kaul 2007), which provides raw materials to the pharmaceutical industry. With good linkages with the raw material industry, it is expected that Indian firms will be able to use raw material efficiently and in appropriate quantities.

Labour is another factor of production showing high efficiency. In recent years, almost all firms can hire and fire labour with ease according to their needs. Thus, it can cut down the cost of labor if such a need arises. On the whole, therefore, we find that the efficiency of labour for this sector is high.

Another important factor of production is capital. The efficiency scores for capital reveal that it has a lower score compared to labor and raw material. On the whole, it can be argued that firms are moderately efficient in using capital. Generally, returns from capital flow over a period. Hence, it may not be possible for a firm to utilize fully the capital stock in the year it is installed. In India, most of the firms are investing heavily in plant and machinery to adhere to the new rules in the recently amended Drugs and Cosmetic Act. This may have led to a rise in the unused capital stock[17] for the sector. Underutilization of capital stock can arise in lean period when the demand for the product is low or when firms are slow in applying and adapting the new technology. Accumulation of underutilization of capital stock can be checked by plotting the growth rate of capital stock and the growth rate of output against time. Figure A.1 (Appendix A), reveals that for most of the years, the growth rate of the capital stock in this sector is higher than that of output, which implies the presence of underutilized capital stock. The Capacity Utilization Ratio has also reduced from about 0.80% to about 0.60% for the sector

[17] Discussion with companies reveals that a firm has to install high quality capital stock worth three crores to fulfill the requirement of the Schedule M of the newly amended Drugs and Cosmetic Act. Moreover, many firms have also upgraded their production system at par with the standard set by the regulatory body of the developed countries to export their product there. Since, return from capital stock generally takes time to realize, it may not be possible for a firm to realize fully the potential benefit of the capital stock at least in the short run.

for the study period. Thus, whatever inefficiency is noticed for the stock of capital is mainly due to its underutilization.

Power and fuel, such as electricity, coal, and natural gas and so on are utilized in the pharmaceutical sector to generate energy for the distillation process. The energy consumption notes of firms (available in the balance sheet of companies) reveal that firms (mainly the large ones) that have undertaken the initiative to conserve energy for the production process by replacing the old technology with modern ones, are the efficient ones. The rest of the firms still use technology that consumes more of energy per unit of the output generated and therefore cause energy wastage. It is noteworthy that the share of consumption of power and fuel has increased for the sector from about four and a half per cent to about eight per cent of the total cost of production from 1995 to 2005. However, for large sized firms the share of power and fuel consumption in the total expenditure has remained at around 2%. For tiny, small and medium sized firms, the share of power and fuel consumption has increased by around 4–5% leading to fuel usage inefficiency. It is important to note here that amongst the small and medium sized firms, a few firms that have replaced coal-based technology with diesel and gas to generate power, have lower share in power and fuel consumption. They are the efficient firms from the small and medium sized group.

On the whole, we can conclude that although the average efficiency of the sector in its use of the different factors of production is high, it has not reciprocated equivalently in its output efficiency. There can be two possible reasons for such an outcome. First, because of the non-availability of data for physical output, we have used the value of output in our efficiency analysis. Thus, price of the output may be a determinative factor for output efficiency of firms. The price of an output depends on the underlying market structure and the demand for the product. If a firm uses its input (comparatively) less inefficiently but fails to get a fair price for its product due to low level of demand, it will show a low level of output efficiency (also see Mazumdar and Rajeev 2009a, 2010). The second reason could be the economies of scale in production. In our analysis, we have assumed a Variable Returns to Scale (VRS) technology. For a VRS technology in the increasing returns to scale (IRS) zone, a unit employment in the factor of production leads to more than proportionate return for the output. Thus, compared to a firm that lies in the DRS zone and has same level of input inefficiency, the magnitude of output inefficiency will be much higher in the IRS zone (see Ray 2004).

Generally, for small scales of operation, a firm lies in the IRS zone and for large scales of operation, it lies in the DRS zone. If we look at the characteristic features of inefficient firms, we find an overwhelming presence of small inefficient firms in the IRS zone. Further, these small firms have low scale of operation and limited market reach. Thus, lower price realization coupled with the presence of economies of scale in production has resulted in a low level of inefficiency for the sector.

3.6 Determinants of Efficiency of Firms

An important component of this analysis is to identify the factors that may affect efficiency. This is achieved by doing the regression analysis for the logarithmic transformation of the output efficiency scores of firms.[18] The independent variables considered in our model can be broadly classified into three groups (A) Firm's Strategy Variables; (B) Firm's Structural Variables; and (C) Policy-related Variable.

3.6.1 Strategy Variables

The strategies that firms adopt reflect the changing behavior of firms in response to policy and other environmental and institutional changes. Two important strategy variables considered in our model are expenditure on research and development (R&D) and increased relation with the international market in terms of export and import.

R&D intensity measured in terms of the ratio of a firm's expenditure on R&D to its value of sales can be considered a suitable proxy for the R&D effort of firms. Firms successful in their R&D can invent superior processes technology. Consequently, a firm may produce better products for which they can earn higher level of revenue by employing the same or lower level of inputs (Aghion and Howitt 1992; Grossman and Helpman 1991). However, heavy allocation of resources for R&D activity can also reduce efficiency if firms fail to reap the benefit of R&D (Helpman 1992).

It can also be hypothesized that large sized firms have natural advantages to undertake more R&D related activities. This may arise if there is scale or scope or effect in R&D intensity of firms. Majumder and Rajeev (2007) in their study noted the presence of scale economies in the R&D activity of Indian pharmaceutical firms. Additionally, large firms have greater market reach and more reputation. Thus, it is easier for large firms to market their new products successfully. An interaction between the market share of firms and the R&D intensity is also considered to examine the joint effect of the size of the firm and its R&D efforts on its efficiency.

[18] We have also tried to estimate a regression model each for the input as well as the total input efficiency scores of the firms. Since the predictability powers of the models were low, we concentrate here primarily on output efficiency scores. Intuitively also it makes more sense to consider only output efficiency scores in our regression model because we notice that, on an average, firms are input wise efficient.

Exporting and importing behavior of firms may also have influence on efficiency. A number of studies have indicated that by exporting their products in the international market, firms can gain higher efficiency (see Aw and Hwang 1995; Robert and Tybout 1997; Clerides et al. 1998; World Bank Report 1997). There can be two sources of efficiency gain for firms selling their product in the international market. One is high prices for their product and hence higher return; the second source of efficiency gain could be through 'learning by exporting' (see Clerides et al. 1998; World Bank Report 1993, 1997). However, to export in the international market a firm also has to incur various forms of transaction costs like identifying the foreign market and the potential customers through market research, building off- shore marketing infrastructure, implementing necessary legal documents etc. (see Pradhan 2006a). The return from such investments may not be immediate and a firm may even incur loss if it fails to correctly identify the potential market.[19] Accordingly, the export earning of a firm per unit of its sales is included as an explanatory variable in our model to examine its impact on the efficiency of firms.

Here also we hypothesize that large sized firms have some advantage in selling their products in the international market. Consequently, we have also considered the interaction between the export intensity and the market share of the firm to examine the joint effect of the size of firm and its export earning on its efficiency.

Let us now consider the case of firm's exposure in the international factor market. This is captured through the imported raw-material intensity and imported technology.

Evidence suggests that the imported intermediary good is an important channel through which technological diffusion takes place (see Tybout 2000). This may affect the efficiency favorably. However, to import quality raw material, a firm has to pay more. More are the proportionate returns from its usages, more it improves the efficiency of firms. If, on the other hand, the cost for imported raw material exceeds the benefit in terms of value of output, the efficiency of a firm may fall.

Generally, Indian pharmaceutical firms re-engineer imported technology and learn about new designs, products and processes.[20] Such activities enable firms to build up its internal production capabilities and competence. All these may positively affect the efficiency of the firms. Imported technology is measured as the ratio of a firm's expenditure on imported capital good to its total value of sales. Since technology once imported, remains in the stock of the firm, the variable imported technology usages for the tth year is constructed by adding the figures for the imported technology from the base period to the tth period by taking 5% as the rate of depreciation.

We next move to other possible determinants.

---

[19] A number of studies have documented that because of various forms of entry barrier only the most productive firms self select for the global market.

[20] See World Bank Report (1993, 1997) about a firm's import of foreign technology and its positive impact on their efficiency.

3.6.2 Structural Variables

The structure of a firm is largely determined by its size, technological parameters and product mix (Caves and Barton 1990; Caves 1992). We take each of these factors into consideration.

From the theoretical viewpoint the relationship between the size of the firm and its efficiency is not clear (Audretsch 1999). On the one hand, it can be hypothesized that large sized firms will be more efficient because of the presence of threshold limits in production, scale economies and imperfection in capital markets (Kumar 2003). However, beyond a certain limit, higher market power may also plague a firm with X-inefficiency (Leibenstein 1966) which may lead to lower efficiency. The output share of a firm in the total industry (Kwoka 1978) is taken as a proxy for its size. To capture the possible non-lineralities between the output efficiency and the size of the firms, we have also included the size of a firm and its square in the regression analysis.

Capital-labour ratio[21] is a technological variable considered in our regression model. Measured in terms of the ratio of the company's expenses for plant-machinery, building, and other fixed assets to its expenditure for wages and salaries, it captures the degree of mechanization in the production process. It is hypothesized that higher the degree of automation in the production system, higher will be the efficiency of the firm because workers can perform more effectively with better capital goods.

With regard to product varieties, three categories of firms are distinguished on the basis of the product, viz., the formulation companies which produce only the final product, the bulk drug companies which produce the basic raw-material; and the bulk and formulation companies which produce both bulk and formulation products. Firms producing both the bulk and formulation variety are vertically integrated with raw-material industry and are expected to enjoy advantages of vertical integration (Coase 1937; Hess 1983; Williamson 1981) against the other two categories of firms. However, if the internal cost of organizing the activities exceeds the benefit of vertical integration and there is control loss (Coase 1937; Williamson 1967) firms may lose efficiency. Firms are differentiated on the basis of products with dummies treating the formulation companies as the benchmark for our analysis.

The age of firms, also determine its structure to an extent. The age of a firm is calculated from the year of its incorporation. From the point of economic theory, the relationship between a firm's age and its performance is again ambiguous. Some authors suggest that older firms give superior performance since they are more experienced and enjoy the benefits of learning (Sticchcombe 1965). Others have

[21] Capital–Labor Ratio = Expenditure on plant-Machinery, Building and other fixed Asset adjusted for historic prices by employing PIM/Expenses for salaries and wages.

however argued that older firms are prone to inertia and are less flexible to changed economic circumstances (Marshall 1920).

3.6.3 Policy Related Variable

A time dummy has also been introduced taking value 1 from 1995 onwards and 0 for the rest of the year to examine the impact of policy reform on the efficiency of the firms. The year 1995 is chosen because the first version of product patent was implemented. The Drug and Cosmetics Act, 1940 was also amended in 1995 to infuse competition for this sector. In other words, important policy changes pertaining to this sector has taken place for this year. The final equation used to estimate the determinants of efficiency scores is given by

$$\ln(eff)_{it} = \beta_0 + \beta_1(R\&D)_{it} + \beta_2(R\&D * MarketShare)_{it} + \beta_3(Export - \text{intensity})_{it} +$$
$$\beta_4(Export\text{intensity} * Marketshare)_{it} + \beta_5(\text{Imported technology})_{it} +$$
$$\beta_7(\text{imported raw-material})_{it} + \beta_8(Marketshare)_{it} + \beta_7(Marketshare * Marketshare)_{it}$$
$$+ \beta_9(Capital/labor)_{it} + \beta_{10}(Dummybulkdrug)_{it} + \beta_{11}(DummyFormulation)_{it} +$$
$$\beta_{12}(Age)_{it} + \beta_{13}(Age * Age) + \beta_{14}(TimeDummy)_{it} + \mu_i + v_{it}, \ldots\ldots\ldots\ldots\ldots$$
$$..(3.1) v_{it} \sim IID(0, \sigma_v^2)$$

Here 'μ_i' are unobserved firm specific effects (such as, entrepreneurial or managerial skills, firm specific intrinsic skill and resources). 'v_{it}' is the stochastic term which is assumed to be identically and independently distributed, IID(0, σ^2). It is assumed that the independent variables are independent of v_{it} for all i and t. The above econometric model is a panel data model and has been estimated following the appropriate method devised for panel estimation.

3.6.4 Findings

Table 3.3 summarizes the main findings from the regression analysis.[22] Based on the Hausman (1978) specification test (Table 3.2) statistic, we accept the null hypothesis that individual invariant effects (u_{it}) are not correlated with the regressors i.e., $E(u_{it}/X_{it}) = 0$. This suggests that the model should be estimated using the fixed effect estimation technique.

[22] For the robustness of our results, we have estimated the econometric model for various sub-samples of our data set and found that there are no significant differences in our result.

Table 3.2 Hausman specification test

Chi^2	Probability
130.93	0.000

Table 3.3 'F' test that all u_i = 0 to verify the presence of individual effect

F statistic	26.43
Probability	0.0000

An important component of panel data model (Fixed effect model) is the presence of firm specific effects. The estimated 'F' statistics (see Table 3.3) to verify the presence of fixed effects shows that fixed effects are really present in the data. They also indicate the presence of firm-specific effects. This implies the presence of unobservable firm-specific factors, such as managerial capability, to influence the efficiency of firms.

Let us consider the other explanatory variables in our study. Figures in the table suggest that the majority of individual coefficients are significant in our model. The model as a whole is also significant, as indicated by the 'F' test statistic, which is significant at a 1% level. The 'R' square of the model is about 0.24. This indicates that the efficiency of the firms is explained by around 24% by the variables included in the model. Thus, based on the 'R' square and also highly significant 'F' statistic, it can be concluded that the model fits well to the data.

3.6.4.1 Structural Variables

The size of a firm is positively significant for the efficiency of the firm. However, a negative coefficient with the square of the size of firm also implies that diseconomies of scale in production emerge beyond certain threshold limits and therefore the efficiency of the firm falls. This implies that small-sized firms can gain efficiency by merging.

Our analysis also revealed that by installing imported technology firms become efficient. We have argued that firms importing foreign technology also benefit from the training and knowledge transfer from the foreign seller, which is a common practice in the process of technology transfer (see Clerides et al. 1998; World Bank Report 1993, 1997).

Table 3.4 also indicates that firms producing both bulk and formulation products are efficient compared to firms that produce only bulk drug or formulation. This also reveals that in the context of the pharmaceutical industry, firms that are vertically integrated with the raw-material industry are more efficient. This implies that vertical mergers could be a strategic option for firms to grow and gain from efficiency in production.

The age of the firm is statistically significant with a negative coefficient. This indicates that young and more experienced firms are efficient in India. Generally, young firms tend to use advanced technology. This has resulted in better efficiency.

The coefficient for the capital-labor ratio is negative and statistically significant for efficiency. Most of the Indian pharmaceutical firms have installed new plant and

Table 3.4 Results from fixed effect model. Number of observations: 2,492, Number of groups: 289

Variables	Coefficients	*t*-values	Prob > $\lvert t \rvert$ > 0
R&D/sales	0.0494315	0.63	0.529
R&D/sales*firm size	40.2558**	2.1	0.036
Export/sales	−0.2397499*	−3.32	0.001
Export/sales*firm size	7.434762*	3.17	0.002
Imported raw-material	0.2289138*	4.15	0.000
Imported technology	0.319771**	2.42	0.016
Firm size	9.789846*	11.15	0.000
Square firm size	−49.77589*	−4.03	0.000
Capital-labor ratio	−0.0000527**	−2.45	0.014
Bulk drug	−0.287102	−1.24	0.215
Bulk and formulation	0.0729986**	2.55	0.011
Age	−0.0172499*	−8.58	0.000
Time dummy	−0.1165368*	−7.92	0.000
Constant	0.7006724*	19.5	0.000
R square (overall)	0.4205	F statistic	17.29*

*, **, ***–Significant at 1 %, 5 % and 10 % level

machinery recently. Such investment may have been made keeping future opportunities in mind and presently these capitals are not fully utilized. Figure A.2 in the Appendix A indicates this.

3.6.4.2 Strategy Variables

As expected, our analysis also reveals that the use of imported raw materials and foreign technology improves the efficiency of firms.

While the R&D variable is not statistically significant, the interaction between the R&D and the size of the firms is positively significant. This indicates that R&D is beneficial if it is done on a large scale. We have argued that this may happen either due to the economies of scale and scope in R&D activity or because of greater market reach and reputation of the large sized firms because of which it can successfully launch its new product and earn high.

Contrary to the general perception, we find that with the rise in export intensity, the efficiency of firms falls.[23] Export markets for generic products are of three types viz., the highly regulated generic market (such as the markets in the USA, the European Union, Australia and so on), the semi-regulated generic market (such as

[23] An interesting point to mention here is that a large number of pharmaceutical firms still sell their products in the domestic market. Though not reported we have differentiated the firms that sell their product in the domestic market from the firms that sell their product in the international one using a dummy variable. The result of our analysis confirms that firms targeting the international market are always better off.

in Russia, the Ukraine, Portugal and so on) and the unregulated generic market (such as Sri-Lanka, Arab Emirates and so on). Generally, most of the firms target either the regulated or the unregulated market. Exporting in the global regulated market for both the bulk drug and formulation is costly, given the stringent regulatory norm that a firm has to follow to sell its product (Chaudhuri 2005, pp. 188–95). If the returns from such markets is not enough to compensate the cost incurred to comply with regulatory barriers, it leads to a fall in the efficiency of firms. Although regulated markets account for about 38% of India's total export and 50% of the bulk drug export in 2005, only a handful of Indian firms have benefited from the regulated market because of a high cost of regulation.[24] In the unregulated market, there is no entry barrier, but the competition is intense and the returns are less. On the other hand, in the semi-regulated, the entry barrier is less compared to the regulated market and the benefit is more in comparison to the unregulated market. Few firms, however, target the semi-regulated market and almost all the small sized firms target the unregulated market. We, therefore, find that efficiency falls with rise in export intensity (this issue has been analyzed further in Chap. 4).

However, the interaction between the size of firms and their export intensity is significant with a positive coefficient. This implies that firms that are large and also export more in the international market are better off. Generally, large-sized firms have a better portfolio of products that they sell evenly across the regulated and semi-regulated markets. Thus, they can compensate for a loss of revenue in one market with gain in another. In addition, large sized firms have better marketing networks that also assist them to sell their product successfully.

3.6.4.3 Policy Related Variable

The coefficient of time dummy takes a negative value for the efficiency of firms. This may happen due to two reasons. First, on an average the efficiency of firms has deteriorated due to policy changes. Another option is that with liberalization and increased competition, it is possible that the frontier has shifted outward due to the entry of new efficient firms leading to a rise in the distance between frontier firms and the rest. Consequently, we find that there has been a fall in the average efficiency for the sector. This hypothesis needs to be tested rigorously. We do it in Chap. 5, where the analysis shows that the sector has indeed experienced technological progress for a considerable period, leading to an outward shift of the frontier and a fall in the efficiency of the firm.

---

[24] Even the largest company of India Ranbaxy incurred a significant loss in 2008 by exporting in the US market because it failed to fulfill the US Food and Drug Administration (FDA) regulatory requirement (see *Mint,* June 6, 2009). Similar was the plight for Dr. Reddys Lab and Cipla.

3.7 Conclusion and Direction for Further Research

The present analysis attempts to examine the firm heterogeneity in the Indian Pharmaceutical industry by measuring their input and output efficiency. Based on our analysis we can conclude that with policy changes the output efficiency of the Indian pharmaceutical sector has declined. It appears that a few large firms have been able to take the benefit of a liberalized regime, but rest of the large number of small firms in the industry lagged behind. Further, analysis of the input and output efficiency reveals that even though firms have been able to use their inputs efficiently there has been a persistent decline in the output efficiency of firms. We argue that such circumstance arises because of the 'economies of scale in production and the presence of large number of small firms that lie in the IRS zone of the empirically constructed production possibility set. Thus, one possible route to improve their efficiency will be to encourage merger to reap the benefit of economies of scale.

Our analysis also reveals the importance of firm specific characteristics to achieve higher efficiency. We find that increased investment in R&D will be a beneficial strategy for large sized firms. Thus, one possible way to encourage the firms to do more R&D will be to involve more private–public partnership in R&D. It is noticed that in the context of the developed nation public support played a very important role to boost the R&D climate of the country NICHM (2000). However, in India, public-private co-operation is currently not significant and it is necessary to improve such cooperation for the development of the industry (Chaudhuri 2005). Firms that are able to successfully market their product in the regulated market has to be technologically competent and this is seen through their efficiency scores as well. Small firms that cater mainly to the unregulated international or domestic market need to improve their efficiency to remain competitive in the long run and one way to do so is through merger. In this context our study indicates that vertical merger is better than horizontal merger. Therefore, firms producing only formulation or final product should merge with firms that produce the raw material or the bulk drug for the industry. Unless the inefficient firms internalized the changed market scenario and take up appropriate measures, it will be difficult to survive in a globally competitive market as they did in a protected market in the past.

3.7.1 Limitation and Direction for Further Research

A major limitation of the above study is that the DEA efficiency scores are mathematically computed and do not lend themselves easily to statistical testing. Thus, a potential fruitful extension of our research would be to do a bootstrapping of the DEA efficiency scores following the Simar and Wilson (2007) methodology to undertake various statistical tests for the DEA efficiency scores. One can follow the Bankers (1993) approach for statistical analysis of the efficiency estimates.

Given the heterogeneity in the structure of Indian pharmaceutical firms, one can also do a quantile regression analysis instead of the usual linear regression in order to trace the differential impact of the strategies of firms for firms from different efficiency groups. It is also possible to enrich the regression analysis by identifying other important determinants, such as the importance of the nature of R&D, the importance of geographical location and industrial clusters, ownership patterns, the nature of technological collaboration and so on, and their impact on the efficiency of the firms. As it is difficult to get such data for each firm, we have not been able to incorporate some of these variables. A detailed qualitative survey of some small, medium and large sized firms can also supplement the findings from the secondary sources of data and can provide additional insights into the efficient functioning of firms. Though we have carried out a field survey of a limited size to get certain insights (see Chaps. 1 and 7), a large survey is beyond the scope of the current work.

Appendix A

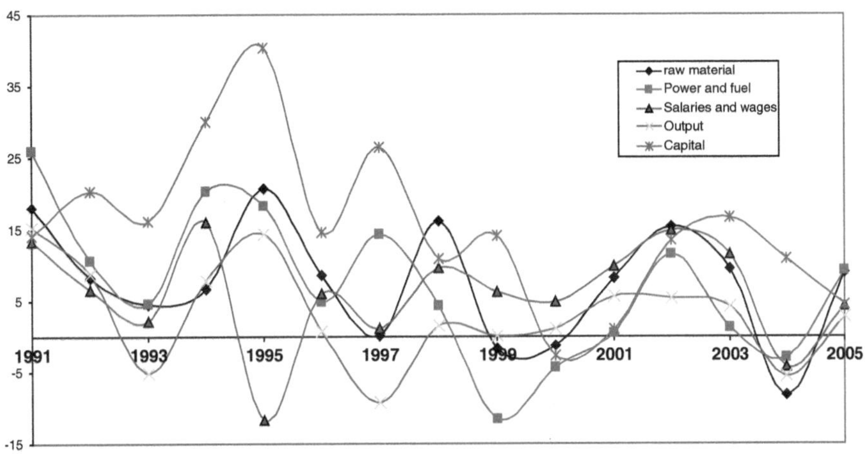

Fig. A.1 Growth of inputs and output

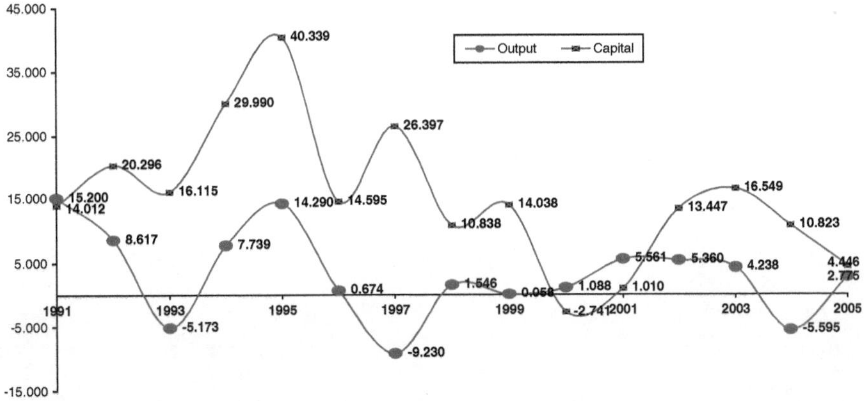

Fig. A.2 Growth of output and capital

Chapter 4
Comparing Efficiency Across Various Groups of Firms: A Meta-Frontier Approach

4.1 Background of the Study

In the previous chapter, we have analyzed the efficiency of Indian pharmaceutical firms and their determinants. However, little is known about the role of the frontier or the most efficient firms in the industry. To which strategic groups do they belong and how do they influence the efficiency of other firms within a group? In this chapter, we would like to take up these issues in detail.

To examine these issues we proceed in the following manner. We first classify the firms into common homogenous groups based on the strategies that they are adopting and construct two separate frontiers viz., the group specific local frontier that is constructed by including firms with similar characteristics and a global frontier that is constructed by taking into consideration all the firms in the sample. Computing the efficiency of a firm with respect to a group frontier will help us identify group specific frontier firms. It will also help us evaluate the efficiency level of firms with respect to their own group members. Such an analysis is useful to assess how best a firm performs when we compare them with firms having similar characteristics. Also, when the canvas of comparison is expanded to include all other firms in the sample, we can examine whether frontier firms from a group still remain efficient. Such an approach to efficiency analysis is also known in the literature as the Meta-Frontier approach to efficiency analysis and was pioneered by Battese and Rao (2002) and later taken up by Battese et al. (2004) and Rao et al. (2003).

The group specific local frontiers are computed with the assumption that firms from the same group face similar production opportunities whereas firms from diverse groups have diverse characteristics and opportunities. *The local frontiers are then the production possibilities that are available only for firms belonging to that group, whereas,* the global frontier is *characterized by the production possibilities that are available for all the firms in the sector*. When the local frontier coincides with the global frontier, group specific production possibilities also define

M. Mazumdar, *Performance of Pharmaceutical Companies in India*, Contributions to Economics, DOI 10.1007/978-3-7908-2876-4_4,

the global production possibilities. However, if the local frontier lies substantially below the global frontier, then firms from the group miss out the production possibilities that the sector is offering.

In the Indian pharmaceutical industry, differences in the production possibilities among firms arise due to certain factors. Among them we consider the R&D focus, focus on global market and the differences in product varieties produced by firms as some of the critical factors. Consider, for example, a set of firms that fail to fulfill the regulatory norms pertaining to the international market due to resource constraint. Certainly, these firms will be unable to export their products and miss out the opportunities in the global market. Under such circumstances, the average efficiency level for this set of firms computed against the global frontier may be considerably low, although firms may be quite efficient amongst themselves. The efficiency level estimated against the local frontier (constructed using the non-exporting firms) can be quite high. This implies that, compared to their group, member firms are on an average quite efficient. However, due to the inability of firms to capture global market opportunities, the efficiency of firms estimated against the global frontier (consisting of both exporting and non-exporting firms) may be *considerably low and consequently the local frontier lies way below the global frontier.*

In the literature on the subject, the ratio of the efficiency scores of firms from local and global frontiers is known as the *technological gap ratio (TGR). Alternatively, we can also define the gap between the local and global frontier that arises due to the differences in the efficiency scores of firms estimated against the local and global frontiers as the production possibility ratio (PPR).* Here the *PPR* captures the differences in the efficiency of firms with respect to local and global frontiers (and hence the distance between the two frontiers) due to differences in *production possibilities* for firms from varied groups. A cross comparison of the efficiency of firms at two different levels adds robustness to the analysis and gives a clear direction to correct efficiency at various levels. If firms from a group suffer from a low level of efficiency mainly because the local frontier lies *substantially below* the global frontier then policies should be directed to bridge the gap between local and global frontiers by removing constraints from which firms from a group suffer.. If, however, the low level of efficiency arises because, on an average, the distance of firms is high from both the groups specifically local as well as global frontiers, it implies that, on a whole, the efficiency of firms from a group are also low and hence there are only few efficient firms from that group. One can then identify the characteristics features of the group specific efficient firms and locate the sources of such differences. Such an analysis provides additional insights about the relative strength for various groups of firms and useful for micro-level policy intervention and public policy purposes.

Given this background, the present chapter is structured in the following manner. The next section discusses briefly the justification for constructing various groups in the context of the study. Section 4.3 will presents the empirical model that has been applied to calculate the efficiency of firms. The review of literature pertaining to the Meta-frontier technology has been illustrated in Sect. 4.4. Section 4.5 presents the data description. Empirical results are presented in the penultimate section and the final section presents the concluding observations.

4.2 Conceptualizing Different Groups

Two groups are constructed based on the R&D related strategy adopted by firms. Firms successful in their R&D or innovation effort can come out with new method or process of technology. Consequently, the production possibilities that firms from this group face will be different from those firms without any R&D related outlays. It is also expected that if firms are successful in their innovative effort, the group frontier constructed by considering only the firms undertaking innovative activity will lie close to the global frontier. Whereas the distance of the group frontier for firms without any R&D unit may actually increase from the global frontier, or in other words the PPR may be comparatively lower.[1] Alternatively, the high cost of R&D and the presence of the gestation period may pull down the frontier for firms with R&D in the short run. *Firms with R&D related outlays are therefore differentiated from firms without any R&D unit by classifying them into two alternative groups.*

The production possibilities that firms face might also differ due to exposure to the international market. With global exposure, firms may learn more about better product design or even better management techniques from foreign buyers (Tybout 2000). Further, firms exploring the international market produce their product keeping in mind the differences in the disease pattern, population structure, and regulatory norms in the global context. Additionally, increased exposure in the international market implies expanded market opportunities. Consequently, the production possibilities that firms from these groups possess are expected to be different from firms that target only the domestic market. In our analysis we have also classified the export-oriented firms into two different groups viz., the high export earning firms (i.e., firms earning more than 25% of their revenue in the international market) and the low-exporting firms (i.e., firms with an export earning of less than or equal to 25%).[2] The rest of the firms are defined as non-exporting firms.

Finally, firms are also classified according to the products they produce. Currently, the main activities of the Indian pharmaceutical industry are broadly restricted to the production of (1) bulk drugs and (2) formulations. The bulk drug business is essentially a business for the raw material for final product, whereas the formulation is a brand-oriented business for the final product. Given the differences in the market possibilities for producing these two types of product, firms in the industry are also classified into three product groups viz., (1) firms engaged in the production of bulk drug (2) firms engaged in formulation production and (3) firms engaged in the production of both varieties of product. Production of these varieties of drugs is also closely related to the organizational structure of firms. Thus, firms producing bulk drugs compete vertically in the intermediate good markets and firms

---

[1] A unit value of PPR implies that group and the global frontier coincide, whereas a fall in the value of PPR implies a rise in the distance between the local and the global frontiers.

[2] The classification is based on discussion with some pharmaceutical companies.

producing formulation compete in the final market horizontally. On the other hand, firms producing both bulk and formulation are vertically linked with the input market, and also compete in the final product market. Differentiating firms with respect to product variety also gives additional insights about the structure of a firm and its efficiency.

4.3 The Concept of Local and Global Frontiers: A Meta-Frontier Approach

The concept of Meta-production analysis was first propounded by Hayami and Ruttan (1970, 1971) and by Ruttan et al. (1978). It was subsequently integrated in the frontier approach for efficiency analysis by Battese and Rao (2002), Battese et al. (2004) and Rao et al. (2003) to study the efficiency of firms with potentially similar technology. In the Meta-Frontier approach for efficiency analysis, group-specific local frontiers are constructed for firms possessing similar production opportunities and a global or a Meta-frontier is also constructed by considering all the firms in the sample.

Following the definition of technology set, the Meta-frontier (henceforth we will use the word 'global frontier' in place of 'meta-frontier') is represented as

$$T^M = \{(X, Y); X \in R_+^N, Y \in R_+^M : \text{X can produce Y}\} \tag{4.1}$$

Here X is the input bundle selected from an arbitrarily chosen group that can produce the output bundle Y. It is assumed that the input–output set of T^M is (a) feasible (b) freely disposable, and (c) convex.

Similarly, the group specific local frontier for the kth group is represented by the following equation

$$T^K = \{(X^K, Y^K) X^K \in R_+^K, Y^K \in R_+^K : X^K \text{ produce } Y^K\} \tag{4.2}$$

To empirically construct the frontier[3] and the output distance of firms[4] we employ the Banker, Charnes and Cooper (BCC) model that calculates the radial

[3] In the previous chapter, we have noticed that, on an average, pharmaceutical firms are more efficient in utilizing their inputs. The differences in the efficiency of firms, however, arise mainly for the output case. Thus, it will be more appropriate to compare the efficiency of firms on the output front.

[4] In the previous chapter we have noticed that, on an average, pharmaceutical firms are more efficient is utilizing their inputs. The differences in the efficiency of the firms however arise mainly for the output case. Thus, it will be more appropriate to compare the efficiency of the firms on the output front.

distance of firms from the global and group frontiers for a VRS technology.[5] In order to construct group frontiers, the input and output set of firms are classified into H number of distinct and exhaustive groups. The production possibility set for the kth group is given by the following equation

$$S^k = \{(x, y)$$
$$: x \geq \sum_{t=1991}^{2005} \sum_{j \in k} \lambda_{kjt} x^{kjt}; y \leq \sum_{t=1991}^{2005} \sum_{j \in k} \lambda_{kjt} y^{kjt}; \sum_{t=1991}^{2005} \sum_{j \in k} \lambda_{jt} = 1; \lambda_{kjt} \geq 0;$$
$$(k = 1, 2, \ldots\ldots\ldots, H)\} \quad (4.3)$$

The set S^k is the free disposable hull of the observed input-output set of firms from the kth group. Let the input–output set of any arbitrarily chosen ith firm in the kth group be (x_k^i, y_k^i). A measure of the *within-group* (output-oriented) technical efficiency of the ith firm is given by

$$TE_k^i = \frac{1}{\phi_k^i} \quad (4.4)$$

To measure Φ_k^i one solves the following linear programming (LP) model Max Φ_k^i Subject to

$$\sum_{i \in k} \lambda_{ki} l_i \leq l_k^i \text{ (labor)} \quad (4.5)$$

$$\sum_{i \in k} \lambda_{ki} k_i \leq k_k^i \text{ (Capital)} \quad (4.6)$$

$$\sum_{i \in k} \lambda_{ki} pf_i \leq pf_k^i \text{ (Power - fuel)} \quad (4.7)$$

$$\sum_{i \in k} \lambda_{ki} rm_i \leq rm_k^i \text{ (Raw - material)} \quad (4.8)$$

$$\sum_{i \in k} \lambda_{ki} y_i \geq \phi y_k^i; \quad \text{(Output)} \quad (4.9)$$

[5] The non-radial approach, however, cannot be used here because it does not consider an equi-proportionate expansion in output or a contraction in input. Therefore, the projection of the efficient bundle of a firm can take place at different points on the local and the global frontiers. However, in a radial approach, the projected output bundle of a firm on a local -frontier is scaled up further along the same radial axis on the global frontier.

$$\sum_{i \in k} \lambda_{ki} = 1 \text{ and } \lambda_{ki} \geq 0 \text{ and } \phi^i \text{ unrestricted} \tag{4.10}$$

The LP is solved for each firm in the kth group. Here Φ is the factor by which the output bundle is scaled up along the ray to reach the boundary of the production possibility set S^k. While constructing the frontier constraints of the programming ensure that the projected output lies within the reference technology set S^k. In particular, the input-constraint (4.5), (4.6), and (4.8) ensures that while constructing the frontier, the weights λ are selected in a way, such that it does not exceed the inputs employed by firm i. The output constraint, on the other hand, ensures that the projected output does not exceed the reference frontier constructed by the output sets of other firms in the sample. Finally, constraint (4.10) ensures convexity of the technology set which implies Variable Returns to Scale or *(VRS)* technology.[6] To get the efficiency of the firms, the programming has to be run separately for each firm in the sample.

Consider next the technical efficiency of the ith *firm* in the kth group, relative to a *global* frontier. The *global-frontier* which is the outer envelope of all the *local frontiers* consists of the boundary points of the free disposal convex hull of the input-output vector of *all firms* in the sample and is given by the following equation

$$S^G = \{(x, y) : x \geq \sum_{k=1}^{H} \sum_{t=1991}^{2005} \sum_{j \in k} \lambda_{kjt} x^{kjt}; y \leq \sum_{k=1}^{H} \sum_{t=1991}^{2005} \sum_{j \in k} \lambda_{kjt} y^{kjt};$$
$$\sum_{k=1}^{H} \sum_{t=1991}^{2005} \sum_{j \in k} \lambda_{jt} = 1; \lambda_{kjt} \geq 0; (k = 1, 2, \ldots\ldots\ldots, H)\} \tag{4.11}$$

The technical efficiency of the firm with respect to the global frontier is given by

$$TE_G^i = \frac{1}{\Phi_G^i}.$$

where $\Phi_G^i = \max \Phi$

$$\text{s.t} \sum_{k=1}^{H} \sum_{i \in k} \lambda_{ki} x_i \leq x_k^i; (x = \text{labor, capital, power \& fuel, raw-material}) \tag{4.12}$$

$$\sum_{k=1}^{H} \sum_{i \in k} \lambda_{ki} y_i \geq \phi y_k^i; \sum_{k=1}^{H} \sum_{i \in k} \lambda_{ki} = 1 \ \lambda_{ki} \geq 0 (k = 1(1)H;$$
$$i = 1(1)n \text{ and } \phi^i \text{ unrestricted} \tag{4.13}$$

[6] If however, $\lambda_{ki} \geq 0$ we have the standard Charnes Cooper and Rhodes (CCR) model that assumes the underlying production technology to exhibit Constant Returns to Scale (CRS) technology.

The average output efficiency for kth group is given by $TE_k^i = \left(\prod_{k=1}^{n_k} \frac{1}{\Phi_k^i}\right)^{\frac{1}{n_k}}$ where $\Phi_k^i = \max \Phi : (x_k^i, \Phi y_k^i) \in S^k$ and n_k is the number of firms in group k. Similarly, when measured against the global frontier, the mean output efficiency for firms from group k will be given by

$TE_G^j = \left(\prod_{i=1}^{n_k} \frac{1}{\Phi_G^i}\right)^{\frac{1}{n_k}}$ where $\Phi_i^G = \max \Phi : (x_i^G, \Phi y_i^G) \in S^G$.

The distance of group k from the global frontier is then the geometric mean of β_k^i, $\left(\prod_{i \in k} \beta_k^i\right)^{\frac{1}{n_k}}$, where $\beta_k^i = \frac{\mathrm{TE}_G^i}{\mathrm{TE}_k^i}$. TGR *or* $PPR = \frac{\mathrm{TE}_G^i}{\mathrm{TE}_k^i} = \frac{\Phi_G^i}{\Phi_k^i}$. The ratio is defined in the existing literature as the technology gap ratio *(TGR)* and can be expressed as$\mathrm{TE}_G^i = TGR \times TE_k^i$. The efficiency of a firm with respect to the global frontier can then be decomposed into the product of the group specific efficiency and the gap between the group and the global-frontier (Battese et al. 2004) which we define in the context of our study as the *Production Possibility Ratio (PPR)* of firms.[7]

4.4 Meta-Frontier Technology and the Existing Empirical Studies

Although the concept of meta-production function was first pioneered by Hayami (1969) and by Hayami and Ruttan (1970, 1971) it was integrated in the frontier analysis quite recently. The application of meta-frontier technique to examine the efficiency of the firms is therefore limited. Concentrating first on the stochastic frontier approach, we observe that the earliest applications of the meta-production function of Hayami (1969), can be found in the work of Kawagoe and Hayami (1985), Lau and Yotopoulos (1989), Kudaligama and Yanagida (2000) and so on. Kawagoe and Hayami (1985) estimated a production function using inter-country agricultural cross-sectional data. Lau and Yotopoulos (1989) re-estimated the Kawagoe et al's model by using transcendental logarithmic form of the production function instead of the Cobb-Douglas specification.

A recent attempt to apply the frontier production approach of Farrell (1957) in estimating the meta-production function was made by Kudaligama and Yanagida (2000). This was further extended by Gunaratne and Leung (2001) and Sharma and Leung (2000) to examine the efficiency of aquaculture farms in several countries. However, Battese and Rao (2002) first pointed out that the global frontier constructed in earlier studies failed to envelope the group frontiers correctly. This is because the maximum likelihood estimate of the parameters of the stochastic

[7] The distance between the local and the global frontier is defined by Battese et al as the Technology Gap Ratio and by Bhandari and Ray (2007) as the Technological Closeness Ratio (TCR). It can also be synonymously called the production possibility ratio (PPR) that captures the differences in the production opportunities among firms.

global-frontier model may not necessarily result in an estimable function that correctly envelops the estimated parametric production function for the groups.

The problem was addressed latter by Battese et al. (2004) in a way such that the global production frontier for a specific functional form does not fall below the deterministic part for the stochastic frontier models of the groups involved. This was achieved in two stage viz., in the first stage the parameters for the groups are estimated using the stochastic frontier model of Coelli (1996). In the next stage the estimated coefficient are employed to estimate the global-frontier that best envelops the deterministic component of the estimated stochastic frontiers for the groups.

The framework thus developed was applied in a body of empirical research to compare the efficiency of the production units facing different production possibilities. Battese et al. (2004) first applied the framework to analyze the differences in the efficiency of garment firms in five different regions of Indonesia, by estimating region specific stochastic frontier production function. It was further applied by to study the technical inefficiencies and Technological gap ratio for the Australian dairy industry and by Chen Ku Hsieh (2007) to examine the impact of industrial dynamic externalities on the inefficiencies and the technological gap ratio for the Information and Communication Technology (ICT) firms in different region of Taiwan. In their empirical application Iyer et al. (2006) regressed the TGR of the technologically backward countries to explain their catch up with the world frontier. The analysis revealed that a host of factors like for example the FDI inflows, trade openness and human capital have been affective in bridging the technology gap of backward countries. The importance of region specific characteristics in agricultural efficiency was captured by applying the meta-frontier framework by Chen and Shunfeng (2008) for the Chinese agricultural efficiency, and by Biman et al. (2008) to study technical efficiency and the TGR for the cocoa production in West African countries. Empirical application of the technique can also be noticed in the work of Boshrabadi et al. (2007) to examine the technical efficiency and technological gap ratio for wheat production in the Kerman province of Iran and in the work of Assaf (2009) for examining the efficiency of airports in the UK due to size.

The concept of Meta-frontier was further advanced to construct cost and profit frontiers in a parametric fashion for European banking industry by Bos and Schmiedel (2007). Further advancement in the estimation procedure of the technique is also noticed in the work Sipilainen et al. (2008). In particular Sipilainen et al. (2008) have shown that instead of making the assumption of smooth concave envelopment of group specific frontiers (while estimating the global frontier) it is more realistic to assume a piece-wise concave envelopment of the data while estimating the global-frontier. This is achieved by applying the stochastic non-parametric estimation method by Kuosmanen (2006, 2008). The model was applied to estimate the technical efficiency and the technical gap ratio for milk production in the Nordic countries.

Compared to the parametric estimation, the non-parametric estimation of the meta-frontier by DEA is simple. In DEA, estimation the meta-frontier tightly envelopes the group specific local frontiers and therefore it does not suffer from the fall out of the parametric estimation (Rao et al. 2003). Given the simplicity in its application there has also been some empirical application of non-parametric meta-frontier technique. Das et al. (2007) used the concept to study the branch level labour-efficiency for the major public sector banks in India. The study constructed region specific frontier to examine how differences in the region specific work culture is reflected in the overall efficiency level achieved by the banks from that area. Bhandari and Ray (2007) also applied the non-parametric technique to compare the efficiency of textile firms in India for different ownership pattern, location and organizational structure by constructing group specific frontiers. Their analysis indicates that firms with less productive technology are gradually catching up with the global frontier. Further, the paper shows that firms organized as public limited companies performed better than firms of other organizational types.

From the above review, it is evident that the empirical application of the meta-frontier technique is limited. Further, the earlier applications are mainly cross-sectional in nature. In this empirical application, we have used panel data to construct the group and global frontiers for knowledge intensive sectors like pharmaceutical. Further, earlier studies have constructed group specific local frontiers either on the basis of ownership patterns or geographical locations. However, for the Indian pharmaceutical sector, firm-specific strategies like R&D export intensity and product varieties generate different production possibilities. We have therefore classified the firm based on these features and have examined their efficiency with respect to the local as well as the global frontier. This study therefore adds a new dimension to the applied empirical work relating to the Meta-Frontier technology by classifying firms into various strategic groups. Additionally, in contrast to the earlier applications that have constructed group and global-frontier at different points in time thus masking off any significant scope in the technological progress, the current study also constructs a sequential frontier that incorporates the scope of technical change or a shift in the frontier over a period.

4.5 Data Description and Variables Used

In this analysis, we consider a one output four input technology set (see Chap. 3 for a detailed illustration on variable selection and construction of the technology set). Similar to the previous exercise it is assumed that the technology is non–regressive in nature or in other words, we construct a sequential frontier for each year. Thus starting from 1991, we successively enlarge the reference sample by including the observations of one additional year. The LP is solved separately for each firm in the sample to calculate its efficiencies relative to the group specific local and global frontiers.

Table 4.1 Mean output efficiency scores for firms with and without R&D related outlays

Firms with R&D related outlays				Firms without any R&D units		
(1) Year	(2) (global)	(3) (local)	(4) PPR	(5) (global)	(6) (local)	(7) PPR
1991	0.887	1.000	0.887	0.789	0.796	0.992
1992	0.582	0.662	0.879	0.623	0.774	0.804
1993	0.301	0.646	0.845	0.521	0.542	0.750
1994	0.560	0.654	0.857	0.497	0.631	0.787
1995	0.550	0.616	0.893	0.461	0.501	0.790
1996	0.522	0.575	0.908	0.351	0.436	0.805
1997	0.508	0.556	0.914	0.285	0.359	0.795
1998	0.442	0.453	0.976	0.248	0.322	0.772
1999	0.502	0.559	0.898	0.289	0.366	0.791
2000	0.477	0.525	0.877	0.307	0.366	0.826
2001	0.466	0.488	0.954	0.275	0.328	0.829
2002	0.447	0.476	0.938	0.217	0.263	0.826
2003	0.415	0.455	0.912	0.219	0.250	0.875
2004	0.496	0.540	0.918	0.301	0.348	0.866
2005	0.474	0.519	0.912	0.307	0.359	0.856

4.6 Comparison of Technical Efficiency Scores Across Different Groups of Firms

In our empirical analysis, we have employed the standard BCC model (see Eqs. 4.3, 4.4, 4.5, 4.6, 4.7, 4.8, 4.9, 4.10, 4.11, 4.12, and 4.13) estimated the efficiency levels of the firms. We first take the case of firms with and without R&D related outlays.

4.6.1 Efficiency of Firm with and Without R&D Related Outlays

Table 4.1 summarizes the mean efficiency scores for firms with and without R&D related outlays.

Let us first consider the case of firms with R&D related outlays. Estimated against the global frontier the mean efficiency level of firms engaged in R&D activities is .887 in 1991. This implies that taking into consideration all the firms in the sample, on an average, firms engaged in R&D activity can further increase their level of production by 11% without employing any additional inputs. However, the efficiency figure takes a value of unity when it is estimated against the local frontier for the same year. This implies that compared to their own group members all firms are efficient and no further improvement in efficiency is possible. The differences in the efficiency scores estimated against the local and global frontier indicates a gap between the two frontiers that is captured by the PPR. Ideally, if firms are successful in their R&D effort the local frontier should lie close to the global frontier. However, the PPR takes a value of .887 in 1991 indicating that the gap between the local and global frontier for firms with R&D activity remains at 11%. Since most of the firms have invested in R&D activities only in the early nineties such gap might have arisen due to lagged effect in R&D.

The figures in the efficiency score also indicate a gradual fall in the value over the years. Estimated against the global frontier, the mean efficiency scores for firms with R&D related outlays over the years (i.e., from 1991 to 2005) turn out to be around 49%.[8] This increases to about 56% when efficiency is measured against the local frontier. A gradual fall in the efficiency of firms estimated against the local and the global frontier implies that even though a large proportion of firms[9] in the pharmaceutical sector engage in R&D related activities, their efficiency are falling over the years. However, the trend for the PPR indicates a gradual rise in its mean value from .88 (between 1991 and 1995) to about .92 (between 2001 and 2005).

Thus a gradual fall in the mean efficiency scores from firms from this group and a rise in the value of PPR over the years implies that few firms from this group have remained efficient (i.e., they have an efficiency score of one) even after undertaking R&D while the rest of the firms have fallen behind. One can then infer that the benefit for doing R&D accrues to only few firms while for the rest of the firms the benefit is either negligible or nil.[10]

We next consider the case of firms without any R&D related outlays. We notice that the efficiency score estimated against the global frontier turns out to be .789 in 1991. It improves marginally to .796 even when the canvas of comparison is restricted to own group member. The PPR also takes a value of .99 in 1991. This implies that in 1991 the local frontier for firms without any R&D related activity almost coincides with the global frontier. The trend in the efficiency scores estimated against both the local and the global frontier indicates there has been a gradual fall in the efficiency levels of firms from this group. We also notice that over the years i.e., from 1991 to 2005, the PPR for firms without any R&D units is about .85. As defined earlier, PPR is an index of proximity of the local frontier to the global frontier. Bounded between zero and one, a value of PPR close to unity does not necessarily imply that the firms from a group are on an average efficient. It only indicates that the maximum mean output that a group of firms could produce would be almost the same even if they had chosen to locate the corresponding alternative group. In the present context, the PPR captures the additional production benefit that firms without any R&D related outlays could get by investing in R&D. A cross comparison of the value of PPR for firms with R&D and without R&D related outlays suggests that if on an average firms without any R&D activities spend for R&D they could have gained an efficiency of around 8%.[11] Therefore by

[8] The figure has been arrived at by computing the geometric mean of the efficiency scores of the firms from 1991 to 2005.

[9] Almost 50% of the firms in this sector are engaged in R&D related activities, see Chap. 1.

[10] This issue has been investigated further in the next chapter where we have also computed the technical change of firms along with the efficiency change. Our analysis indeed brings out the fact that by undertaking R&D, few frontier firms have experienced technical change or an outward shift in the production frontier Such outward shift in the frontier has also reduced the efficiency of the rest of the firms in the sample.

[11] On an average, the PPR for firms with R&D related outlays is .84 and for firms with R&D is .91. The percentage differences is then about 8%.

spending on R&D firms have developed some capacity to enhance their *production capability* and catch up with the rest of the firms in the sample. This situation may even strengthen further in the future and R&D may play a significant role in enhancing the efficiency of firms.

4.6.1.1 Relation Between Efficiency Scores and Other Characteristics of a Firm

In the next step, we have also examined certain interesting features of the most efficient firms from both the groups (i.e., the firms that constitute the global frontier with an efficiency score of 1). We have first examined the relation between efficiency scores (levels) for firms undertaking R&D and their size measured in terms of sales volume. We find that a strong association exists in a statistical sense[12] with large firms that have engaged in R&D related activities and their efficiency scores whereas available statistics indicate that small or medium sized firms are the inefficient ones. In other words, a positive correlation of about 60% is noticed with the size of the firms and their efficiency scores. From the company reports[13] that are available from the CMIE database, we also observe that there is a noticeable difference in the thrust for R&D between large sized firms and smaller ones.[14] While the focus of R&D for the large sized firm lies in high value products and advanced process development, small or medium sized firms mainly do incremental variety of product innovation and simple process synthesis. We also notice that among the small firms that undertake R&D, firms that have more focused niche products lie on the frontier (i.e., they have an efficiency score of one).[15] The Herfindahl Index for diversification also stands at around .89 to about .75 for

---

[12] A Krusal –Wallis χ^2 test has been conducted to examine the mean differences in efficiency level across size firms with R&D related outlays. The size of the firms is measured in terms of sales volume. The differences in the mean efficiency scores are significant at 1% level across the size for firms with R&D related outlays (see Table A.1, Appendix A).

[13] CMIE database do not provide company reports consistently for all the years. It is available only from 2000 onwards. Though such information cannot be utilized for a rigorous econometric analysis it is useful to gather insights for certain features of the pharmaceutical firms and understand about their performance differences.

[14] This has been crosschecked and substantiated from the information provided by the companies in their respective websites. Almost all the registered companies maintain their websites and provide information about the agenda.

[15] From our field survey, we have also come to know that it is easier for small firms to enter into collaboration with MNCs if they have niche products under their command. Thus, for example, if a firm can build its expertise in novel drugs delivery system, MNCs might find it attractive to enter into collaboration with these firms. In turn, by undertaking process R&D for the global majors, these small firms also gain proficiency and expertise in production. The MNCs are also keen to outsource their process related activities because it is time consuming and laborious in nature. While such activities provide the much-needed benefit to the global majors, it is also a huge opportunity for smaller firms, making it a win-win strategy.

those firms (see Table A.2 in Appendix A). In other words, if R&D is targeted for a more focused product basket, the chances of success are high and consequently firms also reap the benefit by becoming efficient.

Examining the efficiency scores of small sized firms, we note that small firms that have undertaken R&D have lower efficiency levels compared to firms without any R&D related activities.[16] Since R&D is a risky venture that generally pays off with considerable time lag, possibly the small sized firms are investing in R&D activities with the expectation of higher returns in the long run (either to come out with some new processes or to enter into some technological collaboration with other firms). In the mean time, their capital expenditure has gone up, thus increasing their cost of production and pulling down the level of efficiency.

Let us now consider the case of firms without any R&D related outlays. From the company report, we noticed that efficient firms (i.e., firms with an efficiency score of one) have complied with the good manufacturing requirement or have installed imported plant and machinery. In other words, firms that have taken initiatives to upgrade their production base are also the efficient ones.[17]

4.6.2 *Efficiency of Exporting and Non-exporting Firms*

We next consider firms targeting the international market. Figures in Table 4.2, summarize the efficiency scores for the export-oriented firms in the Indian pharmaceutical industry. Let us first consider the case of firms with a high export earning.

The efficiency levels estimated against the global frontier for firms with high export earning indicates a gradual fall in value over the years. Thus, for example, the average efficiency scores estimated against the global frontier is 0.874 in 1991; this fell sharply to about 0.438 in 2005. We also notice similar trends when we estimate the efficiency of firms against the local frontier. However, as expected, the magnitudes of efficiency levels have remained at a higher level when it is estimated against the local frontier. Take, for example, the case of 2005; the efficiency figure with respect to the global frontier was .438, however, the efficiency levels of firms were as high as .646 with respect to the local frontier. A value of PPR of around 65% over the years also captures the above phenomenon. This also implies that the gap between the local and global frontier remains at around 35% level for firms

[16] Estimated against the local and the global frontier, we notice that, on an average, the efficiency scores of small firms with R&D related outlays are about .32 and .28 respectively. The corresponding figures for firms without R&D related outlays are about .42 and .34.

[17] Generally, firms from this group upgraded their production base to capture the outsourcing markets from MNCs in the form of contract manufacturing. MNCs are also keen to outsource their manufacturing activities to cut down their cost of production and allocate more resources in their R&D related activities (see Chaudhuri 2005). From our previous chapter we notice that firms can gain on the efficiency count by installing imported plant and machinery.

Table 4.2 Mean efficiency scores for the high export intensive, low export intensive and non-exporting group of firms

	[a]High exporting firms			[b]Low exporting firms			Non-exporting firms		
(1) Year	(2) (global)	(3) (local)	(4) PPR	(5) (global)	(6) (local)	(7) PPR	(8) (global)	(9) (local)	(10) PPR
1991	0.874	0.927	0.909	0.740	0.781	0.948	0.854	1.00	0.854
1992	0.694	0.900	0.771	0.585	0.642	0.911	0.566	0.916	0.618
1993	0.646	0.91	0.71	0.552	0.618	0.893	0.415	0.701	0.591
1994	0.561	0.944	0.594	0.535	0.631	0.848	0.528	0.645	0.751
1995	0.538	0.771	0.698	0.469	0.542	0.865	0.395	0.534	0.740
1996	0.513	0.686	0.749	0.401	0.466	0.862	0.394	0.538	0.731
1997	0.359	0.423	0.598	0.436	0.511	0.852	0.303	0.393	0.805
1998	0.332	0.555	0.48	0.385	0.422	0.913	0.223	0.316	0.706
1999	0.362	0.453	0.599	0.413	0.466	0.848	0.326	0.413	0.79
2000	0.388	0.638	0.608	0.423	0.476	0.889	0.28	0.371	0.753
2001	0.327	0.457	0.716	0.421	0.47	0.896	0.264	0.336	0.785
2002	0.34	0.503	0.675	0.378	0.426	0.887	0.198	0.25	0.790
2003	0.343	0.503	0.683	0.365	0.425	0.860	0.172	0.209	0.820
2004	0.435	0.600	0.725	0.452	0.500	0.905	0.261	0.337	0.776
2005	0.438	0.646	0.678	0.470	0.528	0.891	0.228	0.291	0.784

[a]Firms earning more than 25 % of their revenue in the international market
[b]Firms with an export earning of less than or equal to 25 %

from this group. The efficiency figures computed against the local frontier indicates that, on average, firms from this group are moderately efficient. However, with increased export the efficiency of firms falls.

Such decline in the efficiency of firms is possible when the revenue that they earn from the international market also falls. For firms from high export groups such circumstances arise because of two reasons. First, an overwhelming proportion of firms from the high export intensive group sell their products in unregulated markets of the less developed countries. The unregulated market resembles the perfectly competitive market. There is an almost cost free entry condition and even small firms can export their products without undertaking any substantial risk (Chaudhuri 2005, pp-186). To gain market share, the suppliers in those markets pursue the strategy of price cut. Consequently, this has resulted in poor price realization. Second, few firms from this group have also targeted the regulated and the semi-regulated market. The entry into such markets is difficult because firms have to comply with the legal and regulatory barriers that involve investment in plant and machinery. While the cost of investment is high, the returns are also higher. However, in recent years even the returns from such investment had turned out to be low particularly for firms from highly regulated market because the Indian firms have to compete with incumbent foreign firms that have already established a brand name for their product (see Chaudhuri 2005). Thus, we find that, even though firms on an average from this group are moderately efficient, a high cost of investment coupled with low returns have resulted in a fall in the efficiency of firms when it is estimated against the global frontier.

Moving now to the case of firms with low export earning (i.e., less than 25% of the total revenue) we also notice that there is no considerable difference in the magnitude of efficiency scores when it is estimated against the local and the global frontier. This is also reflected in the value of PPR that fluctuates within a range of around .95 to about .85. A gradual fall in the trend for the efficiency scores estimated both with respect to the local as well as with respect to the global frontier is also noticed over the years. We also notice a marginal decline in the trend of PPR from a value of around .91 to about .88 over the years. In other words, this implies that the local frontier has remained close to the global frontier and few efficient firms from this group have also remained efficient for most of the years. Generally, a moderate proportion of firms from the low export intensive group (almost 45%) sell their product in the semi-regulated market of the European Union (EU) and few firms (almost 10%) sell their product in the regulated market of the US. As a result, on an average, price realizations are found to be higher and hence, their efficiency scores are also high (it lies in between 1 and .75) The rest of the firms have targeted the unregulated market where the price realization is less and hence they are inefficient compared to firms that target the semi-regulated market.

Lastly, we consider firms that target only the domestic market. Consider, for example, the year 1992; the mean efficiency score estimated against the global frontier turned out to be .556; this increases to .916 when efficiency is estimated against the local frontier. This implies that local frontier for firms targeting the domestic market lies way below the global frontier in 1992. The PPR for firms selling their product in the domestic market captures the production possibilities that accrue to firms by exporting their product in the international market. A value of PPR at around .614 indicates that the low efficiency that we notice for firms from this group is not just because of its bad performance, but also due to the wrong choice of market, i.e., their exclusive focus for the domestic market. Trends in efficiency scores estimated against the local and global frontier clearly indicate a drastic fall in its value. Thus, for example in 1992, the mean efficiency scores estimated against the global frontier turned out to be .566 and it sharply reduced to about .22 in 2005. The situation improves to a moderate extent when we compare their efficiency with respect to the local frontier. This is also captured by the value of PPR, which fluctuates at around .74 over the years. If we compare the PPR of firms with a low export earning with the firms that target only the domestic market, we notice that, on an average, an additional efficiency improvement of a magnitude of around 18% is possible by just focusing on the global market.

A cross comparison of the efficiency scores (measured against the global frontier) for these three group of firms revealed certain interesting features.

First, by comparing the efficiency scores of firms that target the international market (column 1 and 5 of Table 4.2) with firms that target only the domestic market (column 8 of Table 4.2) we notice that, on an average, firms exporting their product in the international market have always fared better. For firms with export earning the mean efficiency is about .45 from 1991 to 2005. In contrast, firms that target only the domestic market have an efficiency score of .30.

Second, if we compare the efficiency figures estimated against local frontier for firms with a low export earning with firms that exclusively target the domestic market, we notice that, up to 1996, on an average even firms targeting domestic markets have performed equally. However, from 1997 onwards, on an average, efficiency of firms that target only the domestic market has deteriorated even when it is estimated against the local frontier. This implies that firms that are efficient (.i.e., firms with an efficiency score of unity) with respect to the local frontier from this group can bridge their efficiency gap from the global frontier by exporting their product in the international market; such a move may not be enough for inefficient firms to be efficient. However, a value of PPR of around .88 for firms with a low export earning and a value of .79 for firms that target only the domestic market from 1997 to 2005 implies that, on an average, even inefficient firms can gain efficiency of around 13% by selling their product in the international market.

Lastly, we also notice that among these groups of firms, the average efficiency scores estimated against the local frontier for firms with high export earning are also found to be the highest. The mean efficiency figure is about .62 for high exporting firms, .50 for low exporting firms and .41 for firms that target only the domestic market from 1991 to 2005. In other words, firms from this group are quite efficient among themselves. However, by selling more in the international market their efficiency has deteriorated. The PPR of firms that earn a large amount in the international market is around .66 over the years. For firms with a low export earning, the PPR is around .88. By comparing the PPR of high and low exporting firms, we find that, instead of focusing mostly on the international market (almost 75% of firms from this group earn about 60–90% of their revenue in the international market) if firms from the high export intensive group maintain a balance between the global and domestic market, they can, on an average, gain an efficiency of around 33%. This is particularly true for firms that target the unregulated global market. Alternatively, they can also sell their product in the global semi-regulated market, which a large proportion of firms from the low exporting group do and gain on the efficiency count.

4.6.2.1 Characteristic Features of Efficient Firms

Examining the characteristic features of efficient firms from these three groups revealed certain interesting facts. First, among the high export intensive group, frontier firms (i.e., firms with an efficiency score of one) have evenly distributed their market in the regulated and semi-regulated country. In other words instead of venturing into only the regulated market, firms have also targeted the semi regulated market. In 2002, out of the total revenue earned from abroad, on an average efficient firms from the high export intensive group generated about 45% of their revenue from the regulated market and the rest 55% from the semi-regulated market. Overseas investment with marketing or technological collaboration seems to be an attractive strategy for frontier firms from this group. Generally, Indian firms either merge or take over firms from abroad. Such a strategy is highly

Table 4.3 Mean efficiency scores of firms from different product groups

	Bulk drug			Bulk and formulation			Formulation		
(1) Year	(2) (global)	(3) (local)	(4) PPR	(5) (global)	(6) (local)	(7) PPR	(8) (global)	(9) (local)	(10) PPR
1991	0.853	0.906	0.942	0.734	0.778	0.944	0.630	0.917	0.758
1992	0.629	0.847	0.742	0.605	0.627	0.966	0.421	0.913	0.675
1993	0.588	0.725	0.811	0.632	0.667	0.948	0.375	0.856	0.591
1994	0.535	0.638	0.839	0.587	0.665	0.882	0.375	0.855	0.596
1995	0.458	0.458	1.000	0.539	0.559	0.965	0.332	0.614	0.701
1996	0.403	0.459	0.879	0.526	0.632	0.832	0.301	0.534	0.709
1997	0.352	0.412	0.855	0.518	0.668	0.775	0.241	0.470	0.658
1998	0.304	0.385	0.790	0.509	0.622	0.818	0.216	0.401	0.715
1999	0.316	0.391	0.808	0.489	0.573	0.852	0.227	0.415	0.688
2000	0.328	0.371	0.882	0.379	0.536	0.708	0.279	0.504	0.836
2001	0.273	0.319	0.856	0.457	0.507	0.900	0.223	0.444	0.708
2002	0.285	0.279	0.858	0.444	0.471	0.942	0.180	0.441	0.603
2003	0.270	0.347	0.777	0.392	0.415	0.946	0.158	0.347	0.777
2004	0.379	0.502	0.754	0.464	0.483	0.962	0.229	0.529	0.630
2005	0.337	0.537	0.627	0.441	0.464	0.950	0.233	0.581	0.587

effective because it becomes easier for Indian firms to sell their product with the already established brand name of foreign firms. Additionally, with merger and take over, the possibility of input and knowledge sharing arises which in turn enables firms to gain competency in production.

Among the low export-intensive group, firms that lie at the frontier also have technological collaboration with foreign partners, spend more on marketing related outlays and have greater automation in the production process. All frontier firms from this group target either the semi-regulated or the regulated market. Efficient firms that target only the domestic market are the relatively new entrants, capital intensive in nature and spend more on imported technology. Further, firms from this group also have some form of association with foreign or domestic multi-national firms mainly in the form of contract manufacturing and produce niche products (see Table A.3 in Appendix A).

4.6.3 *Efficiency for Firms from Different Product Groups*

Lastly, we consider how the efficiency of firms varies in the production of different varieties of products. Figures in Table 4.3 summarize the mean efficiency scores for firms from different product groups. We first consider the case of firms that produces both bulk drug and formulation.

A cross comparison of efficiency levels estimated against the local and global frontier for firms producing both bulk drug and formulation indicates that until 1995 there are no noticeable differences in the efficiency levels of firms. Thus, for example in 1992, we notice that the efficiency score estimated with respect to the global frontier is 0.605. Similarly, with respect to the local frontier, we find that the efficiency score is .630. Thus, there has been a marginal improvement in the efficiency of firms when we compare firms amongst themselves. The PPR here captures the benefit that accrues to firms for producing a different product mix. We find that, until 1995 the group frontier has remained close to the global frontier for firms producing both bulk drugs and formulation. The firms were also moderately efficient with an average efficiency score of around .61. The trend in the PPR signifies that the distance magnified after 1995. However, from 2001 onwards the local frontier has moved closer to the global frontier. This implies that marginal differences exist in the efficiency scores of firms computed against the local and the global frontier (see the efficiency figures in columns 4 and 5 of Table 4.3). The trend in the efficiency levels of firms estimated against the local and global frontier also indicates a gradual fall in the value. On a whole, we however, find that firms from this group have an efficiency score of around .47 in recent years (i.e., from 2001 to 2005). A mean value of PPR of around .95 in recent years also implies that the local frontier has remained closer to the global frontier. This implies that frontier firms from this group have remained efficient throughout the period of our study, while the efficiency of firms that lie below the frontier has actually declined. A mean value of PPR close to unity also implies that inefficient firms from this group would not be able to overcome their inefficiency just by producing a different product variety (i.e., by producing either bulk drugs or formulations).

Let us now consider the case of firms producing only bulk drugs. A cross comparison of efficiency scores measured against local and global frontiers for firms producing bulk drugs again reveals a gradual fall in value. However, a discrepancy is noticed in the efficiency score estimated against the local and the global frontier. Thus, for example, in 1992 the efficiency score estimated against the global frontier turned out to be around .62. It increases to about .85 when we estimate the efficiency with respect to the local frontier. In other words, firms are quite efficient when they are compared amongst themselves. However, the low level of efficiency that is noticed when we estimate it against the global frontier arises mainly because of the choice of product mix. A value of .74 for the PPR in 1992 also indicates that firms can gain additional efficiency of around 30% by producing both bulk drugs and formulations. For the rest of the years we again notice a gradual fall in efficiency scores of firms estimated against the local as well as the global frontier. On an average, differences in the efficiency scores estimated against the local and global frontier lie within 8–20%. For certain years like 2004 and 2005, differences in efficiency scores estimated against the local and global is quite striking. Thus, we find that, in 2005, the efficiency score estimated against the local frontier is about .54. This reduces to a value of about .34 when it is estimated against the global frontier. This is also captured by a low value of PPR at around .63. A cross comparison of the PPR with firms that produces both bulk drug and formulation in the recent years i.e., from 2000 to 2005 indicates that, if firms producing bulk drugs would have produced both bulk drugs and formulations, an additional efficiency gain of around 22% would have been possible.

For firms producing formulations we notice that, compared to other groups, on an average the efficiency levels of the firms is low with respect to the global frontier. However, on an average, firms producing formulations are quite efficient when they are compared amongst themselves. Thus, we find that until 1994 the efficiency levels of firms are quite high with an average value of around .82 when it is estimated against the local frontier. In contrast, firms producing bulk drugs or bulk and formulations have an efficiency score of around .69 and .65 estimated against the local frontier for those years. For the rest of the years firms producing formulations are moderately efficient with respect to the local frontier. Another important observation is that differences in the efficiency score between the local and the global frontier for firms form this group is quite high. Thus, for example, in 1992 the efficiency score of firms estimated against the local frontier turned out to be around .92 whereas, when computed against the global frontier, the efficiency score is only .42. Differences in efficiency scores between the local and the global frontier is striking in the years 2002 and 2003. This is also captured by the low value of PPR that stands at around .68 over the years. Comparing the PPR with firms producing both bulk drugs and formulations, we notice that firms producing only formulations can gain an efficiency of around 38% by producing both bulk drugs and formulations.

A cross comparison of the efficiency scores estimated against the global frontier for firms from these three groups (i.e., the efficiency figures in column 2, 5 and 8) indicate that firms producing both bulk drugs and formulations are the most efficient ones followed by firms producing only bulk drugs and firms producing formulations. We find that, on an average, the efficiency level of firms producing both the products are about .51 over the years. For firms producing bulk drugs, it is about .40 and for firms producing formulations it is .28.

Among the firms producing only formulations or bulk drugs, we find that firms producing formulations are the most efficient ones when we estimate their efficiency against the local frontier. It is almost close to the efficiency score computed against the local frontier for firms producing both bulk drugs and formulations. This indicates that firms producing formulations are quite efficient amongst themselves and they can further increase their efficiency by producing both bulk drugs and formulations.

Together this indicates that, in the context of the Indian Pharmaceutical industry, firms producing both bulk drugs and formulations are the most efficient ones. This also implies that integrating vertically with the downstream intermediary industry reduces the cost of transaction and, hence, a higher efficiency gain is possible. The value of PPR for firms producing bulk drugs and formulations also indicates that, if firms, producing only formulations or bulk drugs, re-orient their production strategies in order to produce both categories of products, a significant gain in the efficiency level can be achieved with respect to the global frontier. This can be as high as 30% for firms producing formulations and 10–20% for firms producing bulk drugs for certain years.

4.6.3.1 Characteristic Features of Frontier Firms

Frontier firms (i.e., firms with an efficiency score of one or unity) from all these three product groups also revealed certain interesting features. First, frontier firms producing both bulk drugs and formulations are comparatively large (together the efficient firms from this group capture about 25–30% of the total revenue of the industry in 2000–2005) and spend more on R&D (about 8–10% of its revenue). They also have overseas operations and earn both from regulated and semi-regulated markets.

Firms producing bulk drugs or formulation are generally medium sized or small sized firms. About 15% of small firms producing bulk drugs are also efficient (i.e., they have an efficiency score of one). Generally, the efficient small firms producing bulk drugs or formulations have complied with the new regulatory requirements and do contract manufacturing for Indian as well as foreign MNCs. We also find that frontier firms producing only bulk drugs or formulations possess either niche process or products or produce licensed products of foreign MNCs. On an average the Herfindahl Index for diversification for efficient firms producing bulk drugs or formulations is around .88 to .90, i.e., it is close to unity (see Table A.4 in Appendix A).

4.7 Conclusion and Direction for Further Research

In this chapter, we have examined the efficiency of firms at two levels viz., first, at the group level and also at the global level. The groups have been have formed based on R&D, export intensity and product varieties. The two-way analysis helps us to bring out certain interesting features about firms in this industry. We notice that, on an average, by spending on R&D, firms have not benefited substantially.

Based on export intensities and the efficiency of firms, we notice that firms can gain higher efficiency by selling their products in the international market. We however, notice that higher efficiency gain is possible by exporting the product in the global regulated or the semi-regulated market. However, firms have to invest in new plant and machinery to fulfill stringent global norms pertaining to quality control and good manufacturing practices. Not all firms have the financial capacity and resources to upgrade their production system at par with international standards. Even after investing in plants and machinery, a firm may not be able to get an appropriate return for its product because returns from global markets are shrouded with certain degrees of uncertainty. Thus, like firms with low export earnings, it is more economical for firms to maintain a balance between the domestic and global market . In the long run firms can target the regulated market when it has already established a reputation and brand name for its product.

With respect to different product groups, our study also indicates that firms producing formulations are efficient and hence can gain considerably by producing both bulk drugs and formulations. This also implies that vertical mergers are an effective strategy mostly for firms that produce only formulations to achieve higher efficiency.

A look at the characteristics of the frontier firms also reveal certain interesting features, which inefficient firms can adopt. It is noticed that almost all efficient firms have complied with good manufacturing requirements and entered into technological collaboration with foreign MNCs. From our previous analysis, we also notice that installing imported technology is an important route for upgrading the technology base. Easy availability of finance may be a possible way to assist firms in upgrading their technological base in the face of resource constraints.

4.7.1 Direction for Further Research

A possible extension of the above analysis is a boot strapped meta-frontier model by Assaf and Matawie (2008) to undertake various forms of statistical testing for the DEA efficiency scores. One can also classify firms according to geographical location or the size of firms and identify the importance of regional clustering of firms on their efficiency gain. This would be useful to find out how best firms in the Western region of the country (where it is historically located) perform compared to firms in the emerging areas of Bangalore and Chennai in the Southern region and the adjoining region of Noida in Northern India because of the bio-tech revolution. PROWESS however, does not provide precise location wise database of firms. It goes by the place of registration of a firm. Thus, such analysis is beyond the scope of the current research.

Appendix A

Table A.1 Mean efficiency differences across large and small firms with R&D related outlays

Hypothesis		
$H_0 : \phi_{\text{large}} = \phi_{\text{small}}$	χ^2 value	***P* value**
$H_1 : \phi_{\text{large}} \neq \phi_{\text{small}}$	**9.455**	**0.008**

Table A.2 Herfindahl Index of diversification for small efficient firms and inefficient firms with R&D related outlays

Year	Efficient small firms	Inefficient small firms
1991–1995	0.77	0.57
1996–2000	0.85	0.54
2001–2005	0.93	0.57

Table A.3 Herfindahl Index of diversification and imported capital for efficient and inefficient firms targeting domestic market

	Efficient firms		Inefficient firms	
Year	H-index	Imported capital/sales	H-index	Imported capital/sales
1991–1995	0.65	.39	0.57	.01
1996–2000	0.74	.42	0.54	.02
2001–2005	0.83	.56	0.57	.05

Table A.4 Herfindahl Index of diversification for small efficient firms and Inefficient firms with R&D related outlays

	Efficient firms		Inefficient small firms	
Year	Bulk drug	Formulation	Bulk drug	Formulation
1991–1995	0.78	0.91	0.57	0.65
1996–2000	0.80	0.92	0.54	0.67
2001–2005	0.92	0.94	0.57	0.71

Chapter 5
Examining the Efficiency, Technical, and Productivity Changes of Indian Pharmaceutical Firms: A Malmquist -Meta Frontier Approach

5.1 Background of the Study

In previous chapters, we have noticed that efficiency of firms in this industry has declined over the years. Such a fall in the efficiency of firms is possible, if firms become inefficient in the true sense of the term, or, if frontier firms become technologically more advanced, leading to a shift in the production possibility frontier. In other words, if technical change has generated more production possibilities that are enjoyed by few firms and has also eliminated some of the production options that were previously available for a large section of firms, efficiency of the sector will fall, thereby magnifying the distance of firms that lie below the frontier.

We have argued in our previous chapters, that most pharmaceutical firms in this industry have evolved around the soft patent regime of 1970. Thus, they were never engaged in R&D related activities. Further, a number of protectionist policies of the government encouraged a 'large number of infant firms to continue to remain infant' (Pradhan and Sahu 2009) and practice imitation. Given the assured market due to government policy, most of these firms continue to produce age old products and have undertaken little initiative to upgrade their production base. Making themselves up to date with the changed scenario might be difficult for these firms. On the other hand, the imposition of product patents, increased liberalization, global exposure and the bio-technological revolution in drug discovery and manufacturing process have led to rapid technical change and opened up new production opportunities that these firms might have failed to appropriate.

In continuation with our earlier analysis, in this chapter, we examine the extent to which technical changes in this industry affect efficiency changes of firms. In particular, we want to analyze the firms that drive technical change in this industry and to which group of firms they belong. This will help us find out if there are any relations between the recent moves of the firms, like for example investment in R&D, export of products and their technical change. We also want to supplement our analysis by examining the determinants of technical change. Towards this end, we proceed in the following manner. We first compute the productivity changes of firms.

M. Mazumdar, *Performance of Pharmaceutical Companies in India*,
Contributions to Economics, DOI 10.1007/978-3-7908-2876-4_5,

The productivity of a firm is defined as the ratio of output to the level of input it employs. The concept of productivity is therefore closely related to the concept of efficiency. It follows that a firm with higher efficiency also achieves a higher level of productivity. However, once a firm reaches the frontier of the production function, the sources of efficiency gain are exhausted. Consequently, it has to look for some other avenues to maintain a positive productivity growth and sustain competitiveness. One possible way to achieve higher productivity for an efficient firm will be to move along the production frontier and produce more output by employing additional inputs. However, if we assume diminishing returns to factors of production, then further improvement in productivity is not possible just by employing more input. It is, therefore, necessary for firms to innovate and gain technical change. In other words, an outward shift in the production frontier is necessary to experience a technical and productivity gain. We therefore find that there are two main sources of productivity growth of a firm viz., one is its efficiency in the level of production and the other is technical change. While the former is understood as the change in the distance of a firm from the production frontier, the latter is understood as the shift in the production frontier over time (Grosskopf 1993).

In our analysis, we apply the frontier approach for productivity measurements because it takes into account the efficiency of a firm. Particularly, we apply the Färe et al. (1989)[1] version of the *Malmquist productivity index* (1953) introduced by Caves et al. (1982) to estimate the productivity changes of firms. Further, group specific local frontiers along with the global frontier are constructed to estimate productivity changes of firms at two levels viz., one at the group level and the other at the global level. Such an approach will help us to capture the shift in the production frontier that we have constructed for the group of firms. In other words, we can find out the extent of technical change for various groups of firms and to what extent it is different from the technical change of the sector. However, to capture this phenomenon we have further decomposed the Färe et al. (1989) version of the Malmquist productivity index using a local and a global frontier. The standard decomposition is therefore further modified (see Sect. 5.3) to bring in changes in the productivity measurement when one uses both local and global frontier that the previous literature has not considered .In this respect the study, throws new light on the issue of productivity gain in the context of Indian pharmaceutical firms and also add to the growing body of applied empirical literature on the Malmquist productivity index. Finally, using an appropriate econometric model we have also identified the determinants of technical change components of the firms.

Given this brief background, the rest of the chapter unfolds in the following manner. The next section follows up with a brief empirical review on productivity related studies in the context of India. Section 3 introduces the basic concept of the Malmquist productivity index and illustrates the framework for examining the Malmquist productivity index for local and global frontiers. The framework is

[1] See also Grosskopf (2003).

applied to study the productivity changes for the Indian pharmaceutical firms in Sect. 4. In Sect. 5, we identify the determinants of technical change of firms. A concluding section follows thereafter.

5.2 Review of Literature on Productivity-Related Issues

The literature on frontier approach to productivity analysis is quite voluminous both on theoretical and empirical fronts. One can refer to the papers of Färe et al. (1989, 1994), Balk (2001), Grosskopf (2003) and Lovell (2003) that summarize the theoretical development of such an approach. On the empirical front, the application of such productivity related studies are also vast. Given the enormity of such an application, in this book, we review in brief mainly the studies pertaining to the Indian case.

Empirical application of the productivity index in the context of India mainly examines the impact of liberalization policy of the government on the productivity of the firms. Some of the notable studies that have examined the productivity of the Indian manufacturing sector by estimating the production function using the industry level aggregate data are by Goldar (1986), Ahluwalia (1991), Srivastava (1996), Krishna and Mitra (1998) and Balakrishnan and Pushpangadan (1994). On the whole, studies indicate that the productivity of Indian manufacturing firms has improved in the post-liberalization era. The second group of studies have used the disaggregated firm level data to examine the productivity of firms (Balakrishnan et al. 2000; Srivastava 2001). Studies reported that there has been no significant improvement in the productivity (growth) of Indian manufacturing firms in the post-reform period. The studies concluded that, due to liberalization, the technologically advanced firms have benefited from the productivity gain whereas the rest of the firms have been left behind in the competition. This has resulted in a fall in the overall productivity of the sector.

A number of studies have also applied the frontier production function (that incorporates the inefficiency of a firm) to examine a variety of issues like for example the impact of FDI (Vinesh 2002) and that of the presence of MNEs (Siddharthan and Lal 2004) on the productivity of firms (see Chap. 3 for a detailed review).

The use of non-parametric Malmquist productivity index to examine the productivity of manufacturing firms is also noticed in the existing literature. Malmquist productivity index was used because it is computationally easy, and does not impose any restriction like for example Hicks neutral or Harrod neutral technical change (Lovell 1993) that the parametric form does while calculating the technical change of firms. The earliest attempt to employ the Malmquist productivity index and examine the regional variations of productivity of manufacturing firms was made by Ray (1997). The study by Ray (1997) employed the Ray and Desli (1997) decomposition of the Malmquist productivity index (that assumes the underlying technology to be of VRS form) and indicated that there was evidence of productivity decline in most of the states principally caused by technical regress. A second stage regression analysis revealed that greater urbanization and higher capital-labor ratio tend to promote productivity growth. On the other hand, preponderance of non-production workers and higher incidence of industrial disputes hinder productivity increase. Using a more recent database and the same version of the Malmquist productivity index, Ray (2002b), however, noticed that, on an average, productivity growth has been higher in the post reform period.

Since an overwhelming proportion of firms in the manufacturing sector undertake various forms of informal activities, Raj and Duraisamy (2008) also studied the productivity of the informal manufacturing sector. Evidence suggests that the productivity of the informal sector registered a growth during the post reform period. The study also indicates that improvement in technical efficiency rather than technical progress had contributed to the observed acceleration in the productivity growth rate. Econometric analysis of the determinants of total factor productivity growth demonstrates that ownership pattern, literacy, and infrastructure availability significantly influence total factor productivity growth in the sector.

The Malmquist productivity index has also been applied to compute the productivity change at a disaggregated level for certain emerging sub-sectors of the Indian economy like the IT and ICT Industry (Mathur 2007), selected capital and labor intensive industry (Manjappa and Mahesha 2008) and sugar industry (Singh and Agarwal 2006). The studies indicated that the total productivity growth in the IT and ITC sectors and the sugar industry were mainly propelled by technical change.

It became evident in the course of the literature review that there is a lack of studies examining the productivity of the Indian pharmaceutical industry. In fact, even globally, we found only one study that is the work of González and Gascón (2004) that has examined the Spanish pharmaceutical industry using the Malmquist productivity index. Their analysis revealed that efficiency change explains most of the productivity growth of the Spanish pharmaceutical industry. On the other hand, the contribution of technical change was negligible, indicating a poor association with the R&D undertaken by firms and their productivity growth for the Spanish pharmaceutical industry.

Given the lack of studies, our research aims to fill the gap in productivity related studies of the Indian pharmaceutical industry. We have argued that in recent times Indian pharmaceutical firms are investing in plants and machinery to undertake various forms of innovative activities. Consequently, it is expected that these firms might have experienced technical change. To understand these issues in a rigorous manner it is necessary to examine productivity and its various components in the Indian pharmaceutical sector.

Further, earlier studies have decomposed the productivity of firms by constructing a single frontier at different time points. However, keeping in mind differences in the production opportunities across various groups of firms (see Chap. 4), we have also constructed specific production frontiers and decomposed the productivity of firms at the group level and also at the global level. Under such circumstances, it is essential to employ the meta-frontier technique pioneered by Battese and Rao (2002) to measure the productivity of the firms. Although the meta-frontier technique is widely employed to compute the efficiency of the firms, there is lack of studies that has used this approach to measure the productivity of firms. In this chapter, we have, therefore, made an attempt to apply the concept of meta-frontier to measure productivity changes and its various components, that is, efficiency and technical change, for the various groups of firms.

5.3 The Methodology Employed and the Malmquist Productivity Index

5.3.1 Malmquist Productivity Index

The Malmquist productivity index was first introduced by Caves et al. (1982) in terms of distance functions[2] to measure the productivity of firms. Subsequently, Färe et al. (1989) extended the Malmquist productivty index to incorporate the efficiency and technical change of a firm. They calculated an adjacent period productivity index that consists of the geometric means of two Malmquist productivity indices[3] viz., the base period and the final period Malmquist Productivity Index. In our book we also use the Färe et al. (1989) adjacent period version of the Malmquist productivity index which is defined in terms of distance function for period t and $t + 1$ as

$$MI = \left[\frac{D^t(X^{t+1}, Y^{t+1})}{D^t(X^t, Y^t)} \times \frac{D^{t+1}(X^{t+1}, Y^{t+1})}{D^{t+1}(X^t, Y^t)}\right]^{\frac{1}{2}} \quad (5.1)$$

where $D^t(x^t, y^t) = \min\{\Phi_j : (x_j, \Phi^{-1}y_j) \in S^t\}$. The distance function indicates the maximum proportion by which the output bundle of the firm in period t is expanded

[2] They named it the Malmquist firm specific productivity index after Malmquist (1953) who had proposed that in a consumer setting, an input quantity index that requires the notion of proportional scaling for year 2 observed quantities for a consumer generating the same utility as observed in year 1. The proportional scaling factor was the quantity index that unlike the other quantity index does not require any price information but that the utility function has to be known (Førsund 1999). Under the assumption of Constant Return to Scale (CRS) and certian other conditions Caves et al. (1982) established that Malmquist productivity index is equivalent to Törnqvist index and also established the intuitive link with the traditional productivity growth defined in terms of the growth in output per unit of input employed for two adjacent periods.

[3] Later Berg et al. (1992) also introduced a base period Malmquist productivity index. The base period Malmquist productivity index satisfies the circular test of index number which the adjacent period index does not satisfy. However, the base period index suffers from some drawbacks. As noted by Althin (2001), in the base period Malmquist productivity index, an alteration of the base period directly affects the subsequent measurement of the productivity changes of a firm. Also, when there is rapid technological change, the measurement of the productivity index can become incorrect when the final period is too distant from the base period. In the Indian pharmaceutical industry, we expect rapid technological change because of innovative activites of firms. Hence, it is more appropiate to use adjacent period productivity index.

holding the input vector constant, relative to the frontier in period t i.e., S^t. Similarly, $D^{t+1}(x^t, y^t)$ captures the proportional expansion of the same output bundle of the firm relative to the technology set in period $t + 1$. $MI > 1$ indicate productivity growth and $MI < 1$ productivity decline. To measure the productivity changes of a firm for two adjacent periods, two separate frontiers are constructed viz., one for the initial period and the other for the target period. The ratio of the distance function $\frac{D^t(X^{t+1}, Y^{t+1})}{D^t(X^t, Y^t)}$ measures the changes in the productivity of a firm taking the frontier for the base period as the benchmark for comparison. Alternatively, if one targets the frontier for the final period as the benchmark for comparison, the productivity changes are captured by the ratio of the following distance function $\frac{D^{t+1}(X^{t+1}, Y^{t+1})}{D^{t+1}(X^t, Y^t)}$. *Since there is no particular reason to prefer the base period to the target period frontier (or* vice versa*), the index number is calculated as the geometric means of these two distance function ratios.* The main rationale for considering the Malmquist index is that it explicitly accounts for the efficiency of a firm and hence its distance from the frontier. Stated otherwise, the *MI* can be decomposed into two mutually exclusive and exhaustive components: technical change (*TC*) and efficiency change (*EC*) components Färe et al. (1989).[4]

$$MI = TC \times EC \tag{5.2}$$

$$where\ \ EC = \left[\frac{D^{t+1}(X^{t+1}, Y^{t+1})}{D^t(X^t, Y^t)}\right] \ \ and\ \ TC = \left[\frac{D^t(X^{t+1}, Y^{t+1})}{D^{t+1}(X^{t+1}, Y^{t+1})} \times \frac{D^t(X^t, Y^t)}{D^{t+1}(X^t, Y^t)}\right] \tag{5.3}$$

Values greater than 1 for *TC* indicate technological progress whereas values less than 1 indicate technological regress. The *EC* component can be interpreted as a relative shift of an inefficient firm towards (or from) the production possibility frontiers at two different time periods and measures the catching up effect of the firms. In the empirical context, the *TC* component represents the change of the best practice technology, while the *EC* component represents the adoption of best practice technology.

The decomposition of the Malmquist productivity index into efficiency and technical change component can also be best illustrated with the help of a diagram. Consider Fig. 5.1 below, which depicts the case of one output (*Y*) and one input (*X*) *Malmquist* productivity index.

Let $f(y^t)$ be the frontier at the base period and $f(y^{t+1})$ be the frontier at the subsequent period. Let F be the position of the firm relative to the base period

---

[4] The Färe et al. (1989) decomposition measures the technical change with respect to CRS reference technology. The CRS technology is interpreted as a "global" benchmark for productivity improving technical progress. Ray and Desli (1997) proposed an alternative decomposition, which measures technical change by means of a variable returns to scale (VRS) benchmark technology (see also Grosskopf 2003, and Lovell 2003 for a critical discussion on various issues of Malmquist Productivity Index).

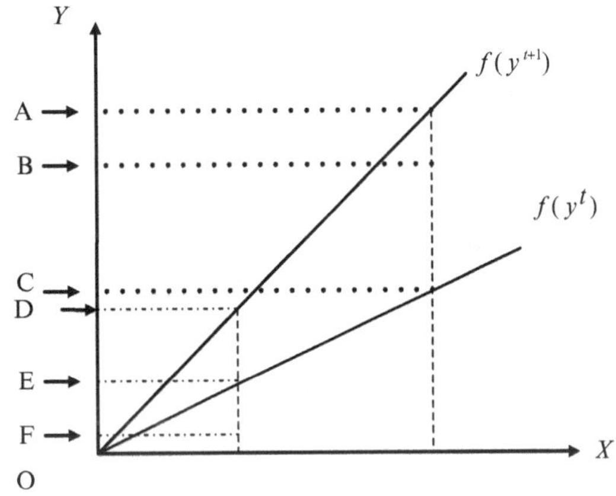

Fig. 5.1 Malmquist productivity index and its decomposition

frontier and B be the position of the firm relative to the final period frontier. The efficiency change of the firm is captured by the ratio

$$EC = \left[\frac{D^{t+1}(X^{t+1}, Y^{t+1})}{D^t(X^t, Y^t)}\right] = \frac{OB}{OA}\Big/\frac{OF}{OE}.$$

The technical change component captures the shift of the frontier. Since Malmquist productivity index allows the frontier to shift in a non-uniform manner, the technical change component can differ at different input levels. Here the technical change component is captured, relative to the base period and final period input level/employment. The first component of the technical change that is $\frac{D^t(X^{t+1},Y^{t+1})}{D^{t+1}(X^{t+1},Y^{t+1})}$ is measured relative to the base period input level of the firm and captured by the ratio $\frac{OB}{OC}/\frac{OB}{OA}$. Whereas $\frac{OF}{OE}/\frac{OF}{OD}$ represents the second component i.e., $\frac{D^t(X^t,Y^t)}{D^{t+1}(X^t,Y^t)}$ of the technical change measured relative to the final period input level. The TC component of the firm according to Malmquist productivity index is therefore given by $TC = \left[\frac{OF}{OE}/\frac{OF}{OD} \times \frac{OB}{OC}/\frac{OB}{OA}\right]^{1/2}$.

We next apply the Malmquist productivity index to measure productivity changes and their components, namely the efficiency and technical change, for Indian pharmaceutical firms.

5.3.2 Empirical Application of the Malmquist Productivity Index

Malmquist Productivity Index has been applied to estimate and analyze the efficiency change, technical change and the PPR for a panel of 2,500 Indian pharmaceutical firms for 15 years (1991–2005). To estimate Malmquist Productivity Index, it is necessary to obtain the cross- period and the same period distance functions. If one uses the frontier in period t to evaluate the distance function of a firm at its input-output combination observed in period t it is known as the *same period distance function*. If, on the other hand, the distance function of a firm is based on the technology from one period evaluated at the input–output bundle from another period, it is defined as *cross-period distance function*. The same and cross period distance functions for the global-frontier is arrived at by taking into consideration all the input–output sets of all the firms for each of the years. Equivalently, the same and cross period distance function for the groups are arrived at by considering only the sample points for firms belonging to the same group (see Ray 2004 for details).

5.3.2.1 Description of the Data and the Findings from Empirical Analysis

Here also, we perceive a one output four input technology (see Chap. 3 for a detailed illustration on technology) Since we have an unbalanced panel set of data, we have constructed a year-wise balanced panel to compute the productivity changes of the firm. In other words, for each of the two consecutive years, we have the same firms. More precisely, when we compare productivity of firms between 1991 and 1992 for instance, we consider the common set of firms. However, when we shift our years of comparison to 1992 and 1993, the common set of firms differs. Thus, for the year 1992, two different sets of firms are considered, depending on the year with which we are comparing. This approach is generally used in the literature.

5.3.2.2 Empirical Findings

The Malmquist productivity index (MPI) and its components viz., the efficiency and technical changes in the Indian pharmaceutical sector is arrived at by solving equation 5.14 to 5.19 and reported in Table 5.1.

A more than unit value for MPI implies a percentage increment in the total factor productivity for firms in this industry. Thus, a value of 1.219 in 1994 implies that, compared to 1993, there was a 21% increment in the total productivity for firms; whereas a value of 0.968 in 1992 implies that total factor productivity regressed by 4%. The available figures indicate that out of the 14 years under consideration, the sector on an average has experienced an increment in its productivity change for 7 years. The productivity performance registered a positive two-digit increment of around 22% in 1994, 12% in 1997, 24% in 1999 and a high rate of around 67% in 2004 and 36% in 2005. On the other hand, productivity regressed marginally in 1992, 1995, 2001 and 2002. We notice that the average productivity performance is at a rate of around −5.5% for these years. The productivity performance was abysmally low and registered a fall in its value by about 13.5% in 1996, 21.1% in 1998 and 16% in 2003. To understand what drives the productivity gain for firms, we first consider one of its important components, namely the technical change of firms.

A value of greater than one for the technical change component implies technological progress whereas a value of less than one implies technological regress.

Table 5.1 Malmquist productivity index and its components for Indian pharmaceutical sector

Year (1)	Total factor productivity change(TFP) (2)	Technical change(TC) (3)	Efficiency change(EC) (4)
1991	–	–	–
1992	0.968	1.511	0.641
1993	1.095	1.134	0.966
1994	1.219	1.051	1.160
1995	0.930	0.896	1.037
1996	0.864	0.591	1.461
1997	1.122	1.657	0.678
1998	0.789	0.420	1.879
1999	1.243	1.764	0.705
2000	1.090	1.361	0.801
2001	0.944	0.942	1.002
2002	0.985	1.713	0.575
2003	1.017	1.039	0.980
2004	1.309	1.531	0.856
2005	1.018	1.326	0.768

More precisely, a value of 1.511 for technical change in 1992 implies that relative to 1991 the production frontier for the Indian pharmaceutical sector has shifted out by about 51%. The technical change component of the Malmquist Productivity Index indicates that, on an average, the industry experiences technological progress for 10 years. It regresses by 10% in 1995 (the year of accession of India to the WTO) and by 40% in 1996 and 58% in 1998. However, for the rest of the years the sector has registered technological progress. This implies that, due to technological progress, the sector is experiencing new production possibilities. Such outward shift in the production frontier is possible either because of the entry of new efficient firms in the market with superior technology or because frontier firms are also experiencing technological change due to new investment.

However, it is interesting to note that the technological progress has not reciprocated equivalently for efficiency gain for most of the firms in this industry. In other words, the shift in the frontier has also magnified the output distance of firms that lie below the frontier. This has regressed the efficiency of the firms in this industry. This is also evident from the efficiency change component for firms summarized in column 4. The efficiency change component captures the relative change in the efficiency of firms at two different periods. More precisely, a value of 0.641 for the efficiency change component in 1992 implies that compared to 1991 the average efficiency of firms has regressed by 36%, whereas a value of 1.46 in 1996 implies that, on an average, the efficiency of firms has improved by 46% in 1996 in comparison to their efficiency in 1995.

A cross comparison of the values of efficiency and technical change component implies (see column 3 and 4 in Table 5.1) that, on an average, the efficiency for firms in this sector has regressed whenever there has been technological progress. This indicates that most of the firms in the industry are unable to appropriate the benefits of the technological progress that the sector has offered. While the industry has experienced an increment in its efficiency change in 1995, 1996, 1998 and 2001, technology has also regressed for those years. In other words, an outward shift in the production frontier has always deteriorated the efficiency of this sector. Thus, there exists a strong negative correlation (of about 82%) with the efficiency and the technical change components for firms in this sector. Such circumstance arises mainly because a large chunk of firms in this industry came into business because of the lack of strong patent protection. In the absence of patent protection these firms were never engaged in R&D related activities and also lack their own genuine products with good margin. On the other hand, the opening up of the economy, new regulation, imposition of product patent and biotechnology revolution has brought forth certain changes in technology. This has also opened up new production opportunities for this sector. Thus, they are unable to appropriate the benefit of technological changes and lose the new opportunities that the sector is experiencing in recent years.

5.4 Malmquist Productivity Index for the Meta (Global) and the Local Frontiers

We next classify firms in various groups and estimate and decompose the Malmquist productivity index at the group level. Just like the meta-frontier approach to efficiency measurement, we construct group specific local frontiers. This will give us a precise estimate of the shift in the production frontier constructed for various groups of firms at different points of time.[5] Thus, for example, by estimating the Malmquist productivity index at the group level, we can assess whether compared to firms without any R&D spending, firms that spend for R&D have experienced technical change more number of times or not. Additionally, by comparing the magnitude and direction of technical change of the global frontier with the local frontier, we can also assess the role of a group of firms to drive the technical change of the global frontier. *However, the Färe* et al. *(*1989*) version of the Malmquist productivity index is generally estimated with respect to a single global frontier. Therefore, further decomposition of the index is needed to incorporate global and local frontiers. Such decomposition has been attempted in this chapter. More precisely, we decompose the productivity index of firms with respect to local and the global frontiers.*

Two types of Malmquist productivity indices are generated when we measure the productivity of firms with respect to the local and the global frontiers viz., (1) the Group Specific Local Malmquist Productivity Index (LMPI) and (2) the

[5] In other words, when we construct a single grand frontier for the pharmaceutical sector, we can only capture the technical change for the sector. However, by classifying the firms into various groups, we can estimate the technical change for these groups of firms.

Global Malmquist Productivity Index (GMPI). For the kth group with observed input-output combinations (X^t, Y^t) and (X^{t+1}, Y^{t+1}) in period t and $t+1$ respectively the LMPI is captured by the following equation:

$$LMPI = \left[\frac{D_k^{t+1}(X^{t+1}, Y^{t+1})}{D_k^t(X^t, Y^t)}\right]\left[\frac{D_k^t(X^{t+1}, Y^{t+1})}{D_k^{t+1}(X^{t+1}, Y^{t+1})} \times \frac{D_k^t(X^t, Y^t)}{D_k^{t+1}(X^t, Y^t)}\right]^{1/2}$$
$$= EC^k \times TC^k \tag{5.4}$$

Similarly, the GMPI is also captured by the following equation

$$GMPI = \left[\frac{D_M^{t+1}(X^{t+1},\ Y^{t+1})}{D_M^t(X^t, Y^t)}\right]\left[\frac{D_M^t(X^{t+1}, Y^{t+1})}{D_M^{t+1}(X^{t+1}, Y^{t+1})} \times \frac{D_M^t(X^t, Y^t)}{D_M^{t+1}(X^t, Y^t)}\right]^{1/2}$$
$$= EC^M \times TC^M \tag{5.5}$$

In the presence of local and global frontiers, our next task is to decompose the productivity change of a firm estimated against the global frontier into three important components viz., *the within group* ***efficiency change*** *of a firm relative to the local frontier. The within group* ***technical change*** *which captures the shift of the local frontier* at two different periods and the ***technological growth effect*** *which captures the changes in the distance of the local frontier and the global frontier at two different points of time*. We explain each of the components in turn. Let us first take up the case of the efficiency change component of a firm.

5.4.1 *Efficiency Change with Respect to Global and Local Frontiers*

Consider Fig. 5.2, which depicts the efficiency change of a firm for a single output y and single input x case.

Let $f(y_k^t)$ and $f(y_k^{t+1})$ be the frontiers for a group of firms at period t and period t + 1. Also, let $f(y_M^t)$ and $f(y_M^{t+1})$ be the global-frontiers at period t and period $t+1$. The efficiency of a firm with respect to the global frontier in the base period is given by the ratio $\frac{OA}{OB}$, and the ratio $\frac{OD}{OE}$ is its efficiency relative to the global frontier in period $t+1$. *The change in the efficiency of a firm with respect to the Global-Frontier is given by the following ratio*

$$EC^M = \frac{\frac{OD/OE}{OA/OB} \Rightarrow \frac{OD/OF}{OE/OF}}{\frac{OA/OC}{OB/OC} \Rightarrow \frac{OD/OF \times OF/OE}{OA/OC \times OC/OB}} = \text{change in the efficiency of firms with respect to group}$$

specific local frontier change in PPR at the input-output levels of period t and $t+1$.

Generalizing the above finding for a group of firms, we can then argue that the efficiency change for a group of firms with respect to the global-frontier can be decomposed into two important components. First, efficiency change with respect to the local frontier which captures changes in the distance of firms from the local

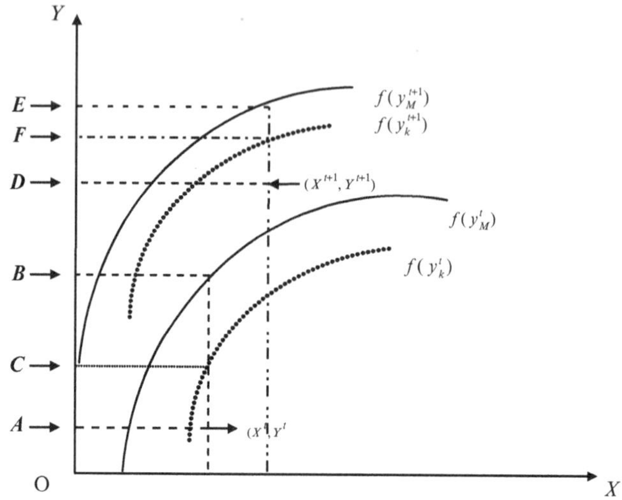

Fig. 5.2 Decomposition of the efficiency change with respect to local and global frontiers

frontiers for two adjacent time periods, and finally, the change in the PPR which captures changes in the relative distance of the local frontier from the global frontier over two adjacent time periods. Two distinct possibilities can arise in this context.

First, the output distances of firms may reduce with respect to the global frontier but may increase with respect to the local frontier. This implies that even though inefficient firms from the group are as a whole moving close to the global production possibility frontier, frontier firms or the most efficient firms from the group have also moved even closer to the global frontier. This brings the local frontier closer to the global frontier. In other words, by comparing the efficiency change estimated against the local and global frontiers, we capture the relative shift of two different frontiers i.e., the local and the global frontiers at two different times. The change in the value of PPR is more than 1 under such circumstances. Such a case may also arise when there is efficiency improvement with respect to both the local as well as the global frontiers. However, the magnitude of efficiency change is higher with respect to the global frontier but lower with respect to the local frontier. Clearly, such a measure captures the 'catch-up' of frontier firms without any ingredients of technical inefficiency and we connote it is as the *Catch up of the Frontier Firms* or *(CFF)*.

Second, the output distance of inefficient firms may increase from the global frontier but may reduce from the local frontier. This implies that the distance between the local and global frontiers has increased and the group as a whole has failed to appropriate the global production opportunities. The value of *CFF* will be less than 1 under such scenario.

Algebraically, $EC^M = \left[\frac{D_M^{t+1}(X^{t+1},Y^{t+1})}{D_M^t(X^t,Y^t)}\right]$ denotes the distance of the firm from the global frontier and $EC^k = \left[\frac{D_k^{t+1}(X^{t+1},Y^{t+1})}{D_k^t(X^t,Y^t)}\right]$ is the distance of the firm from the local frontier.

$$\frac{EC^M}{EC_k} = \frac{\left[\frac{D_M^{t+1}(X_{t+1},Y_{t+1})}{D_M^t(X_t,Y_t)}\right]}{\left[\frac{D_k^{t+1}(X_{t+1},Y_{t+1})}{D_k^t(X_t,Y_t)}\right]}$$

$$= \frac{D_M^{t+1}(X_{t+1},Y_{t+1})}{D_M^t(X_t,Y_t)} \times \frac{D_k^t(X_t,Y_t)}{D_k^{t+1}(X_{t+1},Y_{t+1})}$$

$$= \frac{PPR}{PPR_t^{t+1}}$$

$$EC_M = EC_k \times \frac{PPR}{PPR_t^{t+1}} = CFF_K \tag{5.6}$$

5.4.1.1 Technical Change with Respect to the Global and the Local -Frontier

Let us now consider the case of the technical change component of the Malmquist Productivity Index. Algebraically

$$TC^M = \left[\frac{D_M^t(X^{t+1},Y^{t+1})}{D_M^{t+1}(X^{t+1},Y^{t+1})} \times \frac{D_M^t(X^t,Y^t)}{D_M^{t+1}(X^t,Y^t)}\right]^{1/2}$$

$$and\ TC^g = \left[\frac{D_k^t(X^{t+1},Y^{t+1})}{D_k^{t+1}(X^{t+1},Y^{t+1})} \times \frac{D_k^t(X^t,Y^t)}{D_k^{t+1}(X^t,Y^t)}\right]^{1/2}$$

$$\frac{TC^M}{TC^g} = \left[\frac{D_M^t(X^{t+1},Y^{t+1})}{D_M^{t+1}(X^{t+1},Y^{t+1})} \times \frac{D_M^t(X^t,Y^t)}{D_M^{t+1}(X^t,Y^t)}\right]^{1/2} \Big/ \left[\frac{D_k^t(X^{t+1},Y^{t+1})}{D_k^{t+1}(X^{t+1},Y^{t+1})} \times \frac{D_k^t(X^t,Y^t)}{D_k^{t+1}(X^t,Y^t)}\right]^{1/2} \tag{5.7}$$

$$= \left[\frac{PPR_t\ (X_t,Y_t)}{PPR_{t+1}(X_t,Y_t)} \times \frac{PPR_t(X_{t+1},Y_{t+1})}{PPR_{t+1}(X_{t+1},Y_{t+1})}\right]^{1/2} \tag{5.8}$$

$$= \left[\frac{PPR_t\ (X_t,Y_t)}{PPR_{t+1}(X_t,Y_t)} \times \frac{PPR_t(X_{t+1},Y_{t+1})}{PPR_{t+1}(X_{t+1},Y_{t+1})}\right]^{1/2} = FTC^k \tag{5.9}$$

The above term captures the full shift of the local frontier towards the global frontier at two different times. It captures the strength of the local frontier to catch up with the shift in the global frontier. Intuitively, this implies that, if the magnitude of the technical change with respect to the local frontier is higher than global frontiers, the gap between the local and the global frontiers reduces and hence the value of the above term will be greater than 1. The above term can then be dubbed as the *Technological Growth Effect* or TGF^k.

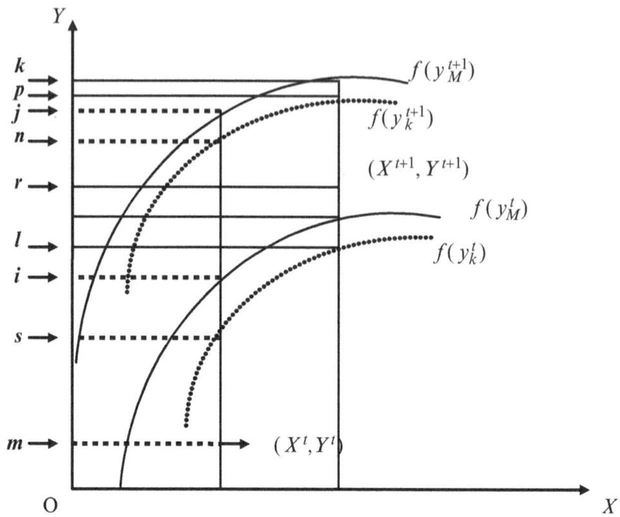

Fig. 5.3 Decomposition of the technical change with respect to local and global frontiers

One can also illustrate the above decomposition diagrammatically. Consider Fig. 5.3.

The ratio $\frac{oj}{oi}$ is the technical change of a firm relative to the global-frontier with respect to the input-output combination in period t and $\frac{ok}{ol}$ is the technical change relative to the global-frontier with respect to the input–output combination in period $t + 1$. According to the Malmquist Productivity Index $\left(\frac{oj}{oi} \times \frac{ok}{ol}\right)^{1/2}$ is the value of the technical change taking the benchmarks of period t and period $t + 1$.

$$\left(\frac{oj}{oi} \times \frac{ok}{ol}\right)^{1/2} = \left[\frac{\frac{oj}{on} / \frac{om}{on}}{\frac{oi}{os} / \frac{om}{os}} \times \frac{\frac{ok}{op} / \frac{or}{op}}{\frac{ol}{oq} / \frac{or}{oq}}\right]^{1/2} \Rightarrow \left[\frac{\frac{oj}{on}}{\frac{oi}{os}} \times \frac{\frac{om}{os}}{\frac{om}{on}}\right]^{1/2} \times \left[\frac{\frac{ok}{op}}{\frac{ol}{oq}} \times \frac{\frac{or}{oq}}{\frac{or}{op}}\right]^{1/2} \tag{5.10}$$

$$\Rightarrow \left[\frac{\frac{os}{oi}}{\frac{on}{oj}} \times \frac{on}{os}\right]^{1/2} \times \left[\frac{\frac{oq}{ol}}{\frac{op}{ok}} \times \frac{op}{oq}\right]^{1/2} \Rightarrow \left[\frac{\frac{os}{oi}}{\frac{on}{oj}} \times \frac{\frac{oq}{ol}}{\frac{op}{ok}}\right]^{1/2} \times \left[\frac{on}{os} \times \frac{op}{oq}\right]^{1/2} \tag{5.11}$$

$$\frac{1}{TGF^k} \times TC^k \tag{5.12}$$

The above decompositions validate that the technical change with respect to the global frontier can be decomposed into two important components viz., the inverse of the growth rate of the PPR for period t and $t + 1$ and technical change with respect to the local frontier.

Combining the above results, the global Malmquist productivity index can then be written as

$$GMPI = EC^k \times TC^k \times CFF^k \times TGF^k \tag{5.13}$$

5.4.1.2 Comparing the Productivity and Its Components Across Different Groups of Firms

In the next step, we have estimated the productivity changes and its components across various groups of firms. Just like the previous chapter (i.e., Chap. 4), here also we have conceived two groups. The first one is based on R&D and the second one on export earning (see Chap. 4 for a detailed illustration of the groups).

We estimate the productivity changes of a firm at two different levels viz., first, with respect to the group specific local frontier and also with respect to the global frontier. We first start with firms undertaking R&D.

5.4.1.3 Firms with and Without R&D Related Outlays

Tables 5.2 and 5.3 summarize the productivity change and its various components (i.e., the efficiency and technical change) for firms with and without R&D related outlays estimated against local and global frontiers. We first start with the efficiency change component for firms with R&D related outlays.

Columns 2 and 5 of Table 5.2 summarize the efficiency change component estimated against global and the local frontiers for firms with R&D related outlays.

Efficiency Change

We notice that, for firms with R&D related outlays, the magnitude of efficiency change is more than unity for 8 out of the 14 study years when estimated against the global frontier. If we estimate the efficiency change with respect to the local frontier, we find that, on an average, a more than unit value is also observed for almost the same years. However, in the year 2001, the efficiency change for firms with R&D related outlays is more than unity with respect to the global frontier but it is less than unity when we estimate it relative to the local frontier. We also notice that, out of the 14 study years, *CFF* also take a value of more than unity for 8 years. For the rest of the years, it is less than unity (in 2000, 02 and 05) or close to one (in 1995, 96, 97). Overall, we cannot conclude that firms with R&D related outlays have achieved higher efficiency over the years. However, it is interesting to note that with efficiency gain, the magnitude of efficiency change is higher with respect to the global frontier than the local frontier (except the year 2001).

This can happen when firms that constitute the local frontier for the R&D group (i.e., firms with an efficiency score of 1) experiences an increment in their efficiency change component, the magnitude of which is even higher than the change in the efficiency of inefficient firms. . More precisely, the *frontier firms from the R&D group are becoming more efficient with respect to the global frontier and* this pulls the local frontier closer to the global frontier. Thus, we notice that the inter-firm differences in efficiency increases within the R&D group when there is efficiency improvement.

Table 5.2 MPI for global and local frontiers for firms with R&D related outlays

	Global frontier			Local frontier				
(1) Year	(2) EC	(3) TC	(4) TFP	(5) EC	(6) TC	(7) TFP	(8) *CFF*	(9) *TGF*
1992	0.605	1.545	0.936	0.528	1.700	0.897	1.147	1.100
1993	1.077	1.001	1.078	1.011	1.065	1.077	1.065	1.064
1994	1.161	1.040	1.207	1.032	1.342	1.384	1.125	1.290
1995	1.040	0.901	0.937	1.059	0.875	0.926	0.983	0.971
1996	1.462	0.586	0.857	1.632	0.506	0.826	0.896	0.863
1997	0.656	1.772	1.162	0.713	1.661	1.185	0.919	0.937
1998	1.902	0.415	0.790	1.886	0.404	0.763	1.008	0.974
1999	0.709	1.752	1.242	0.709	1.775	1.258	1.001	1.013
2000	0.822	1.380	1.134	1.176	0.650	0.764	0.699	0.471
2001	1.008	0.963	0.971	0.938	0.981	0.920	1.074	1.018
2002	0.639	1.553	0.992	0.933	1.044	0.974	0.685	0.672
2003	1.463	0.561	0.820	1.389	0.584	0.811	1.053	1.042
2004	1.113	1.594	1.775	1.021	1.629	1.663	1.090	1.021
2005	0.473	2.983	1.413	0.697	2.063	1.438	0.679	0.692

Table 5.3 MPI for the global and group frontiers for firms without R&D related outlays

	Global frontier			Local frontier				
(1) Year	(2) EC	(3) TC	(4) TFP	(5) EC	(6) TC	(7) TFP	(8) *CFF*	(9) *TGF*
1992	0.654	1.499	0.979	1.037	0.927	0.961	0.630	0.619
1993	0.914	1.224	1.118	0.844	1.335	1.127	1.082	1.091
1994	1.159	1.068	1.238	1.187	0.864	1.025	0.977	0.809
1995	1.033	0.890	0.920	0.964	0.923	0.890	1.072	1.036
1996	1.459	0.596	0.870	1.037	0.842	0.874	1.407	1.412
1997	0.701	1.542	1.082	.6412	1.616	1.037	1.093	1.047
1998	1.861	0.424	0.789	1.631	0.495	0.807	1.141	1.167
1999	0.585	2.135	1.250	0.740	1.111	0.822	0.791	0.520
2000	0.785	1.346	1.057	0.661	1.792	1.184	1.188	1.332
2001	0.997	0.925	0.922	0.982	0.950	0.933	1.016	1.028
2002	0.520	1.882	0.978	0.538	1.815	0.975	0.967	0.964
2003	1.333	0.641	0.854	1.018	0.812	0.826	1.310	1.267
2004	1.045	1.578	1.648	1.079	1.542	1.663	0.969	0.977
2005	0.469	2.780	1.303	0.428	2.950	1.263	1.096	1.062

The local frontier can also move closer to the global frontier due to technological regress. This may arise if the downward shift in the local frontier is less than the global frontier. Under such circumstances, the value of the *CFF* will also be more than one.

Technical Change

To understand what pulls the local frontier closer to the global frontier, we next examine the technical change component for firms with R&D related outlays. Consider for example the case of 1992. A value of 1.542 for the technical change component in 1992 implies that, compared to 1991, the global frontier has shifted outwards by about 54% for firms with R&D related outlays. However, a value of 1.700 for the technical change component estimated against the local frontier in 1992 implies that technical change has been more than 70% when it is estimated against the local frontier. The technical change component is estimated against the local frontier corresponding to the actual shift in the local frontier for firms from this group. Thus, in 1992, firms undertaking R&D have experienced technical change, the magnitude of which is even higher compared to the shift in the global frontier. This also brings the local frontier for firms with R&D related outlays closer to the global frontier. This is also captured by the value of TGF that is around 1.10. This implies that there has been a technological growth of about 10% in the year 1992. In other words, the distance between the local and global frontier has reduced by about 10% due to technological progress. A cross comparison of technical change component estimated against local and global frontiers clearly indicates that the distance between the two frontiers has reduced for most of the years, *particularly when there is technological progress.*

However, the distance between local and the global frontiers has also magnified in 1997, 2000, 2002 and 2005 even when there is technological progress. Such circumstances arise when firms that constitute the global frontier experiences technological progress, but do not belong to the R&D group. The production frontier also regressed marginally in the year 1995 and 2001 and registered a significant fall in 1996, 1998 2000 and 2003. For firms undertaking R&D the production frontier can regress only when there is a heavy allocation of resources in R&D related activity without any noticeable returns. *Thus during the period under consideration, firms undertaking R&D may not have experienced significant technological progress.*

Firms Without Any R&D Related Outlays

Let us now consider the case of firms without any R&D related outlays. Table 5.3 summarizes the productivity changes for such firms.

Efficiency Change

A cross comparison of the efficiency change component for firms without any R&D related outlays (estimated against the local and global frontiers) reveals that firms from this group have also registered a more than unit value in its efficiency change component (6 out of the 14 years under consideration). Estimated against the global frontier, the efficiency change component registered an increment in its value in 1994, 1995, 1996, 1998, 2003 and 2004. On an average, similar trend are also observed when comparison is done against the local frontier except in 1992 and 1995. For the rest of the years the efficiency change components have, however, regressed. It is noticed from column 8 in Table 5.3 that *CFF* takes a value of more than unity for a considerable number of years (9 out of 14 years under consideration). This implies that even for firms without any R&D related outlays the local frontier has moved closer to the global frontier for a considerable number of years. Again, to understand what brings the local frontier for firms without any R&D related outlays closer to its global frontier we examine the technical change component.

Technical Change

We notice that efficiency of firms from this group has improved whenever technology has regressed. Take, for example, the case of the year 1992. The efficiency change component is 1.037 in 1992. It implies that, compared to 1991, in 1992 the efficiency of firms has improved by about 3.7%. However, technology has also regressed by 7% in the same year. We also notice similar trends in 1994, 1996, 1998, and 2003. We estimated a negative correlation of about 80% between the efficiency and technical change component for firms of this group. In other words, the efficiency progress that is noticed for this group mainly arises because of downward shift in the production frontier itself.

Nevertheless, firms from this group have also experienced technological progress for a considerable number of years. Thus, out of the 14 years, the frontier firms from this group have experienced technical progress for 7 years. The magnitude of technological progress is also high when it is computed against the local frontier. On an average, it is close to 50% for 1993, 1997, 1999, 2000, and 2004 and more than 100% for 2005.

Cross-Comparison of Technical Change for Firms with and Without R&D Related Outlays

A cross comparison of the technical change component for firms with and without R&D related outlays (column 6 of Tables 5.2 and 5.3) does not, however, indicate that firms with R&D related outlays have experienced a growth in their technical change for a greater number of years. On the other hand, we notice that production frontiers for both these groups of firms have shifted up or there is technological progress for almost equal number of times. More precisely, we notice that there has been technical progress in the years 1992, 1993, 1994, 1997, 1999, 2002 and 2005 for firms with R&D related outlays and in 1993, 1997, 1999, 2000, 2002, 2004 and 2005 for firms without any R&D related outlays. We notice that the magnitude of technical change for firms without any R&D related outlays are also as high as 31% in 1993, 61% in 1997, 79% in 2000, 81% in 2002, 54% in 2004 and more than 100% in the year 2005. We, therefore, cannot *establish any association between R&D initiatives of firms and technical progress.*

Another interesting trend that is observed for firms from both these groups is that the efficiency of firms has regressed whenever there is a technological progress.

In other words, the frontier has shifted up only because of few firms from both these groups.

Features of Frontier Firms

Consistent with our previous analysis (see Chap. 4), we find that firms that are large have come out with some success in their R&D effort and have experienced positive technical change.[6] It is also noticed from company reports that frontier firms from R&D groups have some technological collaboration with foreign multi-national companies that have age long experience in R&D related activities. Furthermore, most of the firms also have some technological collaboration with public research institutes.[7]

For firms without any R&D related outlays, we notice that firms that have invested newly in plant and machinery and have undertaken initiatives to upgrade their technological base by importing foreign technology are ones that have experienced growth in their technical change component. The average spending for imported technology is about 36% per unit of revenue generated for most of the years. For inefficient firms, it is either nil or less than 5%. We also find from company reports that firms that have experienced an increment in technical change from this group produce licensed products of foreign and domestic multi-national companies.

5.4.1.4 Firms Selling Their Product in the International Market and Firms Targeting Only the Domestic Market

By exporting their product in the international market, firms can also benefit from technological change when firms undertake overseas direct investment and enter into collaboration with host country firms while they export their products. In this analysis, we also estimate productivity changes for firms selling their products in the international market. Like in the previous chapter we have classified firms in three groups viz., firms with high export earnings (for earning more than or equal to 25% of their revenue in the international market), firms with low export earnings (for earning less than 25% of their revenue in the international market) and firms that target only the domestic market.

[6] Here also we have conducted a Krusal –Wallis χ^2 test to examine the mean differences in technical change across size of firms with R&D related outlays. The size of firms is measured in terms of sales volume. The differences in the mean technical change are significant at 5% level across the size of firms with R&D related outlays (see Table A.1, Appendix A).

[7] Most frontier firms with R&D related outlays like Dr Reddys Lab, Ranbaxy, Cipla, Glenmark and others have technological collaboration with foreign companies and with public research institutes like Central Drug Research Institute, Indian Institute for Science etc.

Table 5.4 MPI for global and local frontiers for firms with high export earning

(1)	Global frontier			Local frontier			Changes in production possibility ratio	
Year	(2) EC	(3) TC	(4) TFP	(5) EC	(6) TC	(7) TFP	(8) *CFF*	(9) *TGF*
1992	0.693	1.740	1.206	1.158	0.901	1.044	0.598	0.518
1993	0.941	1.142	1.074	0.965	1.101	1.062	0.975	0.964
1994	1.160	1.172	1.360	1.019	1.054	1.074	1.139	0.899
1995	0.994	0.920	0.915	0.894	0.978	0.874	1.112	1.063
1996	1.394	0.667	0.930	1.109	0.862	0.956	1.257	1.292
1997	0.682	1.661	1.132	0.890	1.051	0.935	0.766	0.633
1998	1.801	0.476	0.858	1.061	0.845	0.897	1.698	1.776
1999	0.680	1.524	1.037	0.861	1.243	1.069	0.790	0.816
2000	0.809	1.328	1.074	1.303	0.939	1.223	0.620	0.707
2001	0.971	0.915	0.888	0.800	1.021	0.817	1.213	1.116
2002	0.512	1.816	0.930	1.102	0.836	0.921	0.464	0.460
2003	1.288	0.694	0.895	1.110	0.815	0.905	1.161	1.174
2004	1.062	1.532	1.627	0.977	1.746	1.705	1.087	1.139
2005	0.515	2.949	1.519	0.898	1.461	1.312	0.574	0.495

High Export Earning

Let us first consider firms with high export earnings. Table 5.4 summarizes the MPI and its various components for firms with high export earning.

Efficiency Change

Estimated against the global frontier, the efficiency change component registered an increment in its value in 1994, 1996, 1998, 2003 and 2004 (see column 2 of Table 5.4). We also notice that the efficiency change takes a value that is more than unity in 1992, 1994, 1996, 1998, 2000, 2002 and 2003 even when it is estimated against the local frontier (see column 5 of Table 5.4). The change in *CFF* that captures the change in the distance of the local frontier from the global frontier indicates that the distance between the local and global frontier has magnified in 1992 and 2002. Thus, for example, in 1992, the value of *CFF* turns out to be 0.813. This implies that, compared to 1991, the distance between the local and global market has magnified by about 20%. In 2002, the distance magnified by about 44%.

The *CFF* corresponding to the efficiency change component also takes a value which is more than unity in 1994, 95, 96 2001, 03 and 04. This again indicates that the local frontier has moved closer to the global frontier for those years.

We next consider the technical change component for firms from this group.

Technical Change

The values in the technical change estimated over the years suggest that (see column 6 of Table 5.4) firms from this group have experienced an increment in their technical change for 7 out of the 14 years under consideration. For certain years like 1999, 2004 and 2005, firms registered a technical change that is as high as 74%. Discrepancy is also noticed in the direction and the magnitude of technical change estimated against the local as well as the global frontier. Thus in 1992, 2000 and 2002, we notice that technical change is more than unity when it is estimated against the global frontier. However, the value is less than one when it is estimated against the local frontier. This is also captured in the value of TGF for those years.

We also notice an increment in productivity changes of the firms (see column 7 of Table 5.4) for 7 out of 14 years driven mainly by the efficiency or the technical change of the firms. Thus in 1993, 1999, 2004 and 05 there is an increment in the productivity changes of firms driven mainly by technological change, whereas in 1994 and 2000 the productivity increment is mainly propelled by the efficiency change. It is interesting to note that in 2002 and 2003 even though the efficiency change is more than unity the technical change has also regressed drastically. Together these have also regressed the productivity changes of firms.

Low Export Earning

Let us now consider the case of firms with low export earning. Table 5.5 summarizes the MPI and its various components estimated against local as well as global frontiers.

Efficiency Change

We find that firms from this group have also experienced an increment in their efficiency change component for a considerable number of years (almost 8 out of the 14 years under consideration). Further, there are no significant differences in the direction or in the level of efficiency change when we compare the figure estimated against local as well as global frontiers except in 2000 (compare columns 2 and 5 in Table 5.5). Thus, from the efficiency change component we cannot conclude that firms with low export earning have really benefited.

Technical Change

However, out of the 14 years under consideration, firms from this group have experienced an outward shift in the production frontier for 10 years (see column 6 in Table 5.5). We also find that the magnitude of technical shift is high for most years. Thus, for example in 1997, 1999 and 2005, the outward shift in the

Table 5.5 MPI for the global and local frontiers for firms with low export earning

(1)	Global frontier			Local frontier			Changes in production possibility ratio (PPR)	
Year	(2) EC	(3) TC	(4) TFP	(5) EC	(6) TC	(7) TFP	(8) *CFF*	(9) *TGF*
1992	0.609	1.577	0.960	0.612	1.585	0.970	0.995	1.005
1993	1.011	1.137	1.150	1.042	1.012	1.054	0.970	0.890
1994	1.146	1.034	1.186	1.026	1.280	1.313	1.117	1.238
1995	1.068	0.898	0.959	1.077	0.887	0.955	0.992	0.987
1996	1.573	0.530	0.834	1.540	0.516	0.796	1.021	0.975
1997	0.698	1.618	1.129	0.601	2.170	1.305	1.161	1.340
1998	2.038	0.375	0.765	2.080	0.387	0.806	0.980	1.033
1999	0.700	1.892	1.326	0.637	2.142	1.365	1.099	1.131
2000	0.826	1.358	1.121	1.082	1.036	1.121	0.763	0.763
2001	0.996	0.961	0.957	0.908	1.010	0.917	1.097	1.052
2002	0.658	1.579	1.038	0.901	1.130	1.018	0.730	0.716
2003	1.420	0.560	0.795	1.500	0.529	0.793	0.947	0.944
2004	1.003	1.685	1.690	1.033	1.580	1.633	0.970	0.937
2005	0.462	2.797	1.295	0.668	2.386	1.594	0.692	0.853

technological frontier is more than 100%. For the rest of the years i.e., in 1992, 1993, 1994, 2000, 2001, 2002 and 2004, on an average, firms experienced a shift in their local frontier by about 25%. In addition, not much difference is noticed in the direction of technological shift when it is estimated against the global frontier, although there are some differences in the magnitude of technical change. We also notice that barring the years 1997, 1999 and 2005 when the outward shift in the frontier for this sector was exorbitantly high (i.e., more than 100%), the corresponding figures for the efficiency change also shows sign of improvement. In other words, there has been technical progress and also the inefficient firms from these groups have also caught up with the frontier firms (compare for example the efficiency and technical change components in 1993, 1994, 2000, 04). For the rest of the years, i.e., in 2001 and 2002 the efficiency change component has remained constant or close to unity. Another interesting finding is that among these three groups, firms with low export earnings have experienced an outward shift in their production frontier for the maximum number of years.

Firms Selling Their Product in the Domestic Market

Lastly, we consider the case of firms targeting the domestic market. Table 5.6 summarized the finding for firms targeting only the domestic market

Efficiency Change

We first consider the efficiency change component. We notice that in 1994, 1995, 1996, 1998, 2001, 2003 and 2004 even firms targeting only the domestic market

Table 5.6 MPI for the global and local frontiers for firms targeting only the domestic market

(1)	Global frontier			Local frontier			Changes in technological gap ratio	
Year	(2) EC	(3) TC	(4) TFP	(5) EC	(6) TC	(7) TFP	(8) *CFF*	(9) *TGF*
1992	0.809	1.046	0.847	0.995	0.815	0.811	0.813	1.233
1993	0.867	1.112	0.964	0.908	1.374	1.247	0.955	0.802
1994	1.213	0.976	1.185	1.201	0.860	1.033	1.010	0.968
1995	1.002	0.869	0.871	0.901	0.945	0.852	1.112	1.174
1996	1.288	0.673	0.866	1.484	0.562	0.833	0.868	1.200
1997	0.637	1.728	1.101	0.887	1.215	1.078	0.718	0.928
1998	1.648	0.430	0.709	1.402	0.506	0.710	1.175	1.408
1999	0.930	1.110	1.033	1.009	1.028	1.037	0.922	0.959
2000	0.759	1.389	1.054	1.841	0.617	1.136	0.412	0.880
2001	1.047	0.934	0.978	1.185	0.911	1.079	0.884	0.927
2002	0.505	1.870	0.944	0.515	1.830	0.942	0.981	1.062
2003	1.501	0.564	0.846	1.096	0.729	0.799	1.370	1.252
2004	1.150	1.482	1.704	0.946	1.718	1.625	1.216	0.615
2005	0.423	2.969	1.253	0.487	2.565	1.250	0.869	0.800

have experienced an increment in their efficiency change component, when it is estimated against the global frontier. With respect to the local frontier, the efficiency change component shows a sign of increment in 1994, 1995, 1998, 2003, and 2004. The *CFF,* is more than unity in 1994, 1995, 1998 and in 2003, and 2004. In other words, the local frontier has moved closer to the global frontier for those years. To examine whether the local frontier has moved closer to the global frontier due to technological progress, we next examine the technical change component.

Technical Change

A look into the technical change component for firms from this group indicates (see column 6 of Table 5.6) that for most of the years, either the technical change component has remained close to unity or it has regressed. We however, notice that in 1992, 1997, 1999, 2002, and 2004 there has been an increment in the technical change component even for firms targeting the domestic market.

Here also, we notice that the efficiency of firms regresses whenever there is an outward shift in the technological frontier. It is also interesting to note that the efficiency of the firm shows signs of improvement only when technology has regressed. Thus, for example in 2000, the frontier has regressed by about 40%. On the contrary, the efficiency of firms has improved by about 84%. Similarly in 2002 the technical change was as high as 83%, the corresponding figure for efficiency change is, however, 0.515. This implies that with an outward expansion in the technological frontier, the efficiency of firms from this group has regressed by about 49%. In other words, we find that few firms from this group have experienced an increment in their technical change component (though for a lesser number of times compared to firms with export earning). However, such shift in the frontier has also magnified the output distance of firms that lie below the frontier. In other words, it has also regressed the efficiency for the firms in this industry. This implies that few efficient firms from this group have also experienced a spurt in their production possibilities. However, the rest of the firms have failed to appropriate the benefit of the new technology and inefficiency figures have correspondingly magnified.

Overall, we can then conclude that firms with low export intensity have performed best when evaluated in terms of technical and productivity changes. We have argued that most of the firms with low export earning, mainly caters to the semi-regulated global market. To comply with requirements for good manufacturing practice firms have upgraded their plant and machinery. This might have favorably affected the technological and the productivity changes of firms. However, we notice that efficiency has regressed whenever there is an outward shift in the production frontier for firms from these three groups mainly driven by the increment of technical change.

In the next step, we have therefore examined the characteristics of frontier firms from these groups.

Features of Frontier Firms

In consonance with our previous analysis (see Chap. 4), we notice that frontier firms with high export earning, have evenly distributed their market in the regulated and semi-regulated country. From company reports, we notice that large firms from this group (see Chap. 2 for the definition of large sized firms) have adopted the strategy of overseas investments in production with marketing or technological collaboration with foreign MNCs. A large proportion of small sized firms from high exporting groups are found to have experienced technological change mainly by using imported technology and capital-intensive techniques in the production process. On an average, the capital intensity for small frontier firms from this group turned to be around 0.65 over the years and for small inefficient firms, it is less than 0.25. The spending on imported technology is around 45% per unit of the revenue generated. For efficient firms it is less than 5%.

Among the low export-intensive group firms, we have observed from studying their annual reports that those, which lie at the realm of technological frontier, also have technological collaboration with foreign partners, spend more on marketing related outlays and have greater automation in the production process. Compared to the less efficient firms that have capital intensity of less than 13% over the years, the capital intensity for frontier firms from this group are close to 66%.

Frontier Firms that target only the domestic market have complied with the GMP norms of the government and have some form of association with foreign or domestic multi-national firms (mainly in the form of contract manufacturing) producing niche products.

5.5 Determinants of Technical Change

The above analysis demonstrates a close association with R&D activities, international exposure and technical change of firms. By examining the characteristics features of frontier firms, we also notice that firms have benefited from technical growth by importing and installing new capital good and machinery. However, to explore further we do a multiple regression analysis that incorporates possible determinants that can have possible impact on the technical change of the firms.

In the next step, we conduct a regression analysis for the technological change arrived at by using the global frontier to find out its determinants. Since in the earlier chapters we have already identified the determinants of the efficiency of firms, here we conduct the regression analysis for the technical change of firms. Applying the Banker and Natarajan framework (2008, see Chap. 3) we estimates the following panel regression equation.

$$\begin{aligned} TC_{it} = {} & \alpha_{it} + \beta_1\, Time\ Dummy + \beta_2 Market\ Share_{it} + \beta_3\ Marketin\ Intensity_{it} \\ & + \beta_4\ Export\ Intensity_{it} + \beta_5\ R\&D\ Intensity_{it} + \beta_6\ Capital - Labor\ Ratio_{it} \\ & + \beta_7\ \text{Imported Capital} + \beta_8\ \text{Market Share} * \text{R \& D}_{it} \\ & + \beta_9\ \text{Imported Ra - Material}_{it} + \mu_i + v_{it} \end{aligned} \quad (5.14)$$

Drawing insights from a number of theoretical and empirical literatures and from our understanding about the pharmaceutical industry, we hypothesize that the following relationship holds with the explanatory variables[8] considered in our model and the technical changes of firms.

We first consider the technological parameters of our model. The technological parameters of the model are captured by capital-labor ratio and imported plant and machinery. The capital-labor ratio is measured in terms of the ratio of company's expenses for plant-machinery, building, and other fixed assets to its expenditure for wages and salaries. It captures the degree of mechanization in the production process of a firm. By installing capital-intensive technique, firms employ large volume production systems like flow manufacturing system, efficient assembly lines production. This enables firms to do repetitive works in a better way and hence we expect it to have a positive impact on the technical change of firms.

Similarly, the use of imported plant and machinery indicates the use of globally acceptable equipments and tools of production in the production process by Indian pharmaceutical firms. Installing imported technology also enables firms to experience more technological change provided firms adapt imported technology to local conditions (see Chap. 3 to know about the measurement of the variable). Hence, its

[8] The explanatory variables are measured in changes using the standard approach of the literature (Ray 2004).

effect on technical change can be ambiguous depending on how best the firms are using the imported technology.

A number of studies (see Kumar and Siddhartan 1994; Siddharthan 2004; Lall 2000; Tybout 2003) have also indicated that firms from developing countries benefit from knowledge exchange in the process of international transaction for imported technology and intermediate goods. Thus, we also consider the imported raw material intensity measured as expenses for imported-raw material deflated by the total revenue of firms as an additional channel through which international trade in raw material diffuses new knowledge and skill. We expect that the variable will have a positive impact on the technical change of firms.

It has been argued in Chap. 3 that firms undertake R&D with the possibility of coming out with new processes or new products, which can lead to technological change of this sector. Therefore, in the analysis to follow R&D intensity is considered as one of the determinants for technical change. Keeping in mind that large-sized firms may have an edge in R&D activities (see Chap. 3 for a detailed illustration on this term) an interaction between the size of firms and its R&D intensity is also considered.

It is also argued that exposure in the international market can benefit firms in terms of positive technical change if there is technology transfer and collaboration. Such activity arises when firms undertake overseas direct investment and enter into collaboration with host country firms while exporting its product in the international market. Thus, export intensity is also included as an additional variable in our regression model.

Marketing intensity is also considered as an additional variable in our analysis. Marketing intensity is considered keeping in mind the possible relation between product development, its promotion and resultant technological gains of firms. In a differentiation product market, the marketing intensity of a firm also serves as a measure of product differentiation (Greer 1971). Firms successful in their marketing effort can influence the demand for their product favorably. This in turns can increase their market size and can enable them to benefit from technological progress.

Lastly, in our model we also control the size of firms and the time dummy. The size of firms has been measured by taking the output share of firms in the total industrial output. The time dummy takes a value of one from 1995 onward when the first version of product patent and other regulatory changes were implemented for the sector.

5.5.1 Findings from Regression Analysis

The model (5.14) is estimated using the standard panel-data estimation method.[9] As mentioned in Chap. 3, one of the important decisions in a panel data analysis is whether the model should be estimated as a fixed effect or a random effect model. In this regard, the Hausman (1978) specification test is conducted. In the present

[9] The use of panel data model is justified in Chap. 3.

Table 5.7 Hausman specification test results

Chi^2	Probability
2.89	0.9412

Table 5.8 Breusch and pagan lagrangian multiplier test for random effects

Chi^2	Probability
34.04	0.0000

case, the Hausman (1978) specification test (Table 5.7) statistic fails to reject the null hypothesis that individual invariant effects (u_{it}) are not correlated with regressors i.e., $E(u_{it}/X_{it}) = 0$. This suggests that the model should be estimated using the random effect estimation technique.

After deciding that the model should be estimated as a random effect model, it is essential to check whether random effects are indeed present in the data. If random effects are not present in the data, then, it reduces to the Classical Linear Regression (CLR) model, which can be estimated using the Ordinary Least Square (OLS) technique. In this regard, the Breusch and Pagan (1980) test is used to check the presence of random effects (see Baltagi 2003 for a detailed illustration on the test).

By rejecting the null hypothesis, which states that random effects are not present in the data, the results of Breusch Pagan test (Table 5.8), validates the use of the random effect model instead of the OLS model. The model is estimated using the Generalised Least Square (GLS) method. When the model is estimated using GLS, its overall significance is tested using the Wald test statistic, which is essentially a Chi Square test. In the present case, the Wald test statistic is significant at a 1% level, which shows that the model as a whole is significant (Table 5.9). The value of 'R' square is 0.30 which is reasonably high. A common problem encountered in the regression model is the violation of constant variance and the normality assumption. The standard error computed in the model is a robust standard error, which is immune to heteroscedasticity and non-normality problems.

We next explain the relationship between explanatory variables and technical change considered in regression analysis.

The results in Table 5.9 suggest that firms installing capital-intensive technique experience technological progress. Generally, pharmaceutical firms install capital-intensive technique to comply with the new requirement in the Drugs and Cosmetic Act. Such technological up-gradation has also opened up new opportunities among firms by getting contract manufacturing from domestic or foreign MNCs. Even small firms that have complied with this requirement have started producing licensed products of MNCs.[10] All these have led firms to technologically advance.

Figures in the above table also suggest firms adapting to advanced imported plant and machinery also benefit from technological growth. A cross comparison of the coefficient of imported technology and capital intensity also reveals that, by importing globally acceptable equipments and tools of production, firms have

[10] Insights into emerging opportunities for Indian Pharmaceutical firms were gathered in the survey conducted with a few firms.

Table 5.9 Determinants of technical change

Variables	Coefficient	Robust standard error	Z	$P > \|z\|$
Capital –labor ratio	0.0000772[a]	0.0000352	2.19	0.028
Imported technology	1.694115[b]	0.8837128	1.92	0.055
Imported raw-material	−0.4051781[c]	0.1397189	2.9	0.004
R&D/sales	0.0539315	0.2242608	0.24	0.81
R&D/Sales[c]firm size	98.33048[b]	51.23027	1.92	0.055
Export/sales	−0.1012165	0.1402452	−0.72	0.470
Firm size(Market Share)	1.257646	2.191637	0.57	0.566
Marketing/Sales	0.4658311[c]	0.0067216	69.3	0.000
Time dummy	0.2655703[c]	0.0300697	8.83	0.000
Constant	1.131965	0.0193604	58.47	0.000
Wald chi2(9)	6269.89[c]	R Square 0.30		

[a]Significant at a 10 % level
[b]Significant at a 5 % level
[c]Significant at 1 %

benefited more from technological progress. Generally, Indian pharmaceutical firms additionally benefit by importing foreign technology by de-engineering imported goods. These in turn enable them to learn about new products and process design and even new management techniques when there is knowledge sharing with foreign firms that import their products to Indian firms. Thus by importing foreign technology, pharmaceutical firms also learn about expertise and operating skills from foreign sellers.

We however, find that, contrary to the conventional wisdom of importing raw materials and intermediaries, technology of firms regress. In recent years, many pharmaceutical firms started importing cheap bulk drugs from China. While firms have been able to cut down their cost of production by importing low cost raw material, they have also escalated their cost of process synthesis. Further, many pharmaceutical firms have failed to fulfill the regulatory requirements of the international standard by importing raw materials. Together this has regressed the technology for this sector.

Although spending more on R&D does not benefit firms in terms of technological change, it is noticed that large, more R&D oriented firms also benefit most from such activity. There can be two possible reasons for such a relationship, the first of which could be the presence of economies of scale and scope in R&D related activity. Majumder and Rajeev, (2007) in their study noted the presence of scale economies in the R&D activity of Indian pharmaceutical firms. Second, there is also a qualitative difference in the thrust for R&D among large and small sized firms. Generally, large sized firms undertake R&D for high-end process, product and custom synthesis. Such activities have also enabled Indian pharmaceutical firms to establish their reputation in processes engineering. A large number of foreign MNCs have also entered into technological collaboration with Indian pharmaceutical firms to learn about process design. In turn, large firms also learn about product R&D from foreign MNCs and benefit from technological progress. If we compare our finding from group wise analysis, we find that large sized firms from the R&D group contributed significantly for the technological progress for this sector. The evidence here also suggests that R&D makes an important contribution for their superior performance.

Marketing intensity turns out to be a significant variable in our model. This implies that in the context of our study, firms that differentiate their product also benefit more in terms of technological change and growth.

However, our analysis reveals that neither the *size of firms nor increased export or export earning* has any relation with technical change of firms.

Finally, evidence also suggests that changes in regulation have positively affected the technology change for this sector. Thus, with policy change the frontier has shifted. We also notice from our efficiency analysis that, with the change in regulation, the efficiency of firms has deteriorated. This confirms our argument that the gradual fall in the efficiency that we notice for this sector arises mainly due to technological change.

5.6 Conclusions and Directions for Further Research

The productivity analysis of Indian pharmaceutical firms revealed that the sector has experienced technological change a significant number of times. This has opened up new production possibilities for the sector. However, only few firms have access to new technology. On the other hand, the emergence of new technology has also eliminated some of the productive options that were previously available for a large section of firms. It is therefore noticed that inefficiency of the sector has magnified whenever there is technological progress.

A group wise classification of firms based on important criteria like R&D and export intensity help us identify frontier firms. On a whole, we find that frontier firms generally spend on R&D on a large scale. They also use capital-intensive technique for their production process and have also upgraded their technology by installing imported plant and machinery. It is also noticed that almost all frontier firms have some technological collaboration with foreign or domestic multi-national companies either in the form of contract R&D or in contract manufacturing.

Regression analysis also strengthens the findings from productivity analysis. Thus, one notices that firms can experience technological progress by either installing imported technology or capital-intensive technique. However, small firms may not have the capacity to purchase and install imported foreign technology. Thus, easy availability of finance is a possible route to assist firms in adapting capital-intensive techniques. Another possible option for small sized firms would be to install capital-intensive techniques at par with good manufacturing requirements set by the Government of India that continue to get the assured market from public hospitals and health care units. Such strategy will help small firms to get a fair return from their product by which they can recoup the cost of investment in new plant and machinery. The analysis also indicates that R&D is beneficial if it is done on a large scale. However, our study also indicates that by importing raw-material, a firm's technology regresses. We have argued that the root cause for such technological regress lies in the importation of low quality bulk drug from China. We here reiterated that India already has an excellent raw material bulk drug industry. Firms should therefore continue to purchase their raw material from the domestic market. Increased demand in the domestic market will further propel growth in the domestic bulk drug industry and enable firms to strengthen their presence in the global market.

5.6.1 Directions for Further Research

A possible extension of the above analysis would be to estimate the productivity of firms with respect to variable returns to scale technology (VRS) and account for productivity changes due to input use. In the available literature the decomposition of the Malmquist index, with respect to the VRS technology is not straightforward. There are various versions of it (see Grosskopf 2003). One can apply the VRS version of the Malmquist productivity index for the meta-frontier approach to productivity analysis. As usual, one could also bootstrap productivity, technology and the efficiency scores of firms to undertake various statistical testing. Further, the group wise comparison of productivity of firms can also be done based on geographical location or ownership pattern or size of the firms. As argued in chapter four, the PROWESSES database however does not provide precise location wise data for firms. It goes by the place of registration of a firm. Thus, such analysis is beyond the scope of the current research.

Appendix A

Table A.1 Mean differences in technical change (TC) across large and small firms with R&D related outlays

Hypothesis		
$H_0 : TC_{\text{large}} = TC_{\text{small}}$	χ^2 value	P value
$H_1 : TC_{\text{large}} \neq TC_{\text{small}}$	8.45	0.038

Chapter 6
Profitability of Indian Pharmaceutical Firms

6.1 Introduction

Apart from achieving higher efficiency and productivity, one of the important objectives of firms is to earn high profit. While attaining higher efficiency and productivity, it is necessary for firms to earn high profit. However, the former might not be sufficient. To gain high profit a firm must also obtain an appropriate price for its products. In the Indian pharmaceutical market where a large number of firms compete for multiple products, a firm should be able to convince consumers about the utility of its product and generate a higher demand for their product than its rivals. Further, a firm's profitability depends not only on the level of production and realized prices but also on the costs of production.[1] Thus, one has to take into consideration the supply side, demand side and market conditions while doing a profitability analysis of firms. Consequently, factors that favorably influence efficiency and productivity of firms may not have the same degree of influence on their profitability. This motivated us to move beyond the efficiency framework and consider the important questions of profitability of a firm.[2] While illustrating the

[1] In our book, we have, however, measured the efficiency and productivity of firms in value terms. In a sense, the productivity and efficiency measures of firms are revenue earned per unit of input expenditure incurred by firms. Consequently, the efficiency and productivity of firms are also influenced by the prices for the product or the demand side factors. However, there was no consideration for the cost of production in our efficiency or productivity related analysis.

[2] In the spirit of efficiency analysis one could also compute the profit efficiency of the firms. However, in the context of our study, there are two major difficulties in estimating the profit efficiency of firms. The first is the non-availability of data on input and output prices at the firm level. The second is conceptual; in particular, the framework for profit efficiency is developed in a competitive scenario where firm faces competitive input and output prices. Apart from incorporating technical efficiency, one has to take into consideration the allocative efficiency while estimating the profit efficiency of a firm. The question of allocative efficiency arises because firms try to produce their output and employ factors of production in light of the prevailing market prices and in accordance with the marginalist principle while they maximize their profit. Thus, a

M. Mazumdar, *Performance of Pharmaceutical Companies in India*, Contributions to Economics, DOI 10.1007/978-3-7908-2876-4_6,

determinants of the profitability of firms, we would like to see how the change in the structure of the industry from 1991 to 2005 and firm specific factors, like managerial capacity, the strategies adopted and related factors, contribute to the understanding of the profitability of Indian pharmaceutical firms. We would also like to see whether the factors that favorably influence the efficiency and technological growth of firms have similar influence on the profitability of firms.

Given this background, the rest of the chapter is structured in the following manner. Section 6.2 lays down the conceptual framework for the study. The next section reviews empirical studies related to the issue. Section 6.4 deals with the analytical part. The empirical results from the analysis are discussed in Sect. 6.5 and that is followed by a concluding section.

6.2 Conceptual Framework

An empirical analysis of the determinants of profitability empirically had invoked the interest of economists as early as the 1940s (see Mason 1939; Bain 1951). Two strands of literature are noticed in the existing field. The first one is by Bain (1951, 1956). Popularly known as the Structure-Conduct-Performance (SCP) paradigm, the scholars from this strand of literature argue that a firm's profit depends primarily on the structure of the industry under which it operates. Industrial structure is determined in terms of *concentration level, extent of barriers to entry* and *degree of product differentiation* (Scherer and Ross 1990). The concentration level captures the degree of collusion among firms, whereas scale economies determine the level of entry barrier. If an industry requires heavy investment in plant and machinery and there exist substantial scale economies, it can sustain only a small number of firms. In such a scenario, it is likely that the degree of collusion will be high and firms will earn above normal profit. However, the SCP theorist also argued that, even in the absence of scale economies and market concentration, a firm can still earn above normal profit if it can differentiate its product from its competitors. The degree of product differentiation in an industry determines the level of imperfection or substitution among various outputs. It also refers to the extent to which the buyers differentiate, have specific preferences among competing outputs of various sellers established in an industry (Bain 1956). The concentration ratio in conjunction with scale economies and the degree of product differentiation,

---

firm is profit efficient when it is technically as well as allocatively efficient. However, in a monopolistic market it is optimal for a firm to remain allocatively inefficient in the product market. If a firm is monopsonist, it also remains allocatively inefficient even in the input market. Though competitive, the Indian pharmaceutical industry resembles a differentiated monopolistic market condition and firms have some degrees of market power for various product groups. Consequently, for a profit-maximizing firm it is optimal to remain allocatively inefficient. It, therefore, makes little sense to compute the profit efficiency of firms.

therefore, determine the structure of the industry that in turn also determines the profitability in an industry.

The second strand of literature emphasized the importance of firm-specific factors as opposed to the industrial structure on its profitability. The scholars of the Chicago School of Economist first identified the importance of firm-specific factors, namely the "efficiency" of the firm. They argued that rather than concentration and imperfect competition leading to higher prices and profit, it is the higher *efficiency* of firms with a larger market share that leads to higher profit earning and hence concentration (see Demsetz 1973a, b and c). After the seminal paper by Demsetz (1973), further studies identified the technological, historical and organizational consideration of firm as the leading factors in determining firm performance (Röller and Sinclair-Desgagn´e 1996).

Based on the above arguments, a number of studies have also been conducted to empirically test the relative importance of the industry and firm specific factors for the profitability of firms. Some notable studies in this regard are by Scott and Pascoe (1986), Cubbin and Geroski (1987), Kessides (1986, 1987), Amel and Froeb (1991), Rumelt et al. (1991) and McGahan (1999). An unequivocal finding from all these studies is that at the industry level, firm level and even the line-of-business seem to together determine the profitability of a firm in an industry.

Apart from the above arguments put forward by scholars from the above strands of literature, in the context of our study, we think that emerging moves of Indian pharmaceutical firms, namely the investment in R&D, spending on marketing related outlays and export of products are important factors that also determine their profit. We call them strategic variables of firms. These variables also correspond to 'firm centric strategies' that management theorist Porter (1980, 1985) has delineated in his widely acclaimed theory of competitive advantage of firms. According to Porter (1980), the strategies of firms are fundamentally aimed either at achieving a low-cost position or to differentiate its products from the rival. Low cost position can be achieved either by managerial efforts like control on overhead cost or through process innovation. Differentiation, on the other hand, can be achieved in two forms: one based on marketing and promotion aimed at creating a superior brand image of the product, and the other founded on innovation aimed at creating new product varieties.[3]

The following diagram gives a synthetic view of the conceptual framework that we have used to analyze the profitability of firms.

[3] Porter has also suggested that the simultaneous pursuit of both strategies is not possible on the ground that each of these involves a different set of resources and organization arrangements. Firms should therefore emphasize any one of the generic strategies instead of getting *"stuck-in-the-middle"*, which is characterized as a lack of distinctive emphasis on any particular strategy.

6.3 Empirical Studies Related to Profitability

The empirical literature examining the profitability of firms is voluminous. Given the gamut of issues involved in analyzing the determinants of the profitability of a firm, we have reviewed only the most illustrative and pioneering studies in this area.

The earliest attempt to test the predictions of SCP framework[4] was made by Bain (1951, 1956) himself. His study confirmed the co-existence of a high rate of return, high concentration and entry barrier. Bain's (1956) pioneering work inspired further research in this area. Two classic studies that are widely quoted are by Comanor and Wilson (1967) and by Collins and Preston (1969). The major contribution of Comanor and Wilson (1967) lies in the use of advertisement-sales ratio as an index for overall differentiation in an industry and in approximating the Minimum Efficient Scale (MES) as the ratio of the average size of the largest plants accounting for half of the industry output and the size of the smallest of these plants. The contribution by Collins and Preston (1968, 1969) lies in disaggregating the data for industry from three digits to four-digit level, using the price-cost margin or the return to sales as an index for profitability, and in identifying a number of alternative specifications to test the SCP hypothesis.

Measuring MES as an entry barrier is a debatable issue. Comanor and Wilson (1967) adopted the definition of MES on the assumption that the size distribution of observed plants relative to MES do not vary much from industry to industry. However, studies by Weiss (1976), Baldwin and Gorecki (1985) did not provide any evidence for stable size distributions of firms. Caves et al. (1975) defined the *Cost disadvantage ratio* (CDR) variable along with MES to approximate the measure of scale economies. They argued that a large MES will be relevant only if there are substantial cost disadvantages at a lower level of output. A number of studies have also measured MES using survivorship technique. In the survival technique, one observes the size distribution of firms and tries to locate a 'size group' at which firms are moving over time. The size group in which all firms are clustered contains the MES (Saving 1970; Stigler 1968; Weiss 1976).

A large number of studies have also been advanced to measure the degree of product differentiation in an industry. Inspired by the theoretical work of Nerlove and Arrow (1962) that suggests that advertisement adds to the 'stock of good will', for a company, Weiss (1969) first estimated the 'stock of good will' using a depreciation rate in the range of 50–80%. Subsequently, Grabowski and Mueller (1978) and Nakao (1979) estimated the relationship between profitability and the 'stock of good will' for the pharmaceutical industry and for Japanese manufacturing companies. Both the studies established a significant and positive relationship between advertisement and profitability of the companies. The degree of

[4] For good surveys the empirical findings in SCP see Schmalensee (1989), Scherer and Ross (1990), Hay and Morris (1991), and Martin (2002).

product differentiation in a spatial sense (Eaton and Lipsey 1978) was also empirically verified by Collins and Preston (1969).

Opinions among researchers also differ regarding the correct measurement of the degree of collusion in an industry (see for example, Kwoka 1981; Hay and Morris 1991,). While most of the studies have used concentration of top four firms or C4 as the measure of concentration, studies by Cowling (1976), Cowling and Waterson (1976) and others have also used the Herfindahl H-index for concentration, based on the argument that it is theoretically more appealing and sound (Stigler 1964).

The role of buyer concentration to serve as an active restraint on profitability of an industry was empirically first verified by Lustgarten (1975). Besides the role of R&D as an entry, Mansfield (1983) first acknowledged barriers in an industry. Studies have also included other variables like diversification (Carter 1977; Jacquemin et al. 1980) and growth of firms (Bardburd and Caves 1982) as additional determinants of firms' profitability. A number of studies have also examined the role of foreign trade on the domestic profitability of an industry.[5] To mention a few, we have studied Jacquemin et al., for Belgium (1980), Chou's (1986) study for Taiwan, and Neumann et al.'s (1979, 1985) study for Germany,. These studies indicated a negative relationship between the import ratio and the profitability of firms.

Opinion also differed among scholars about the presence of simultaneity and the problem of endogenity among the structural variables considered in the study. To overcome the problems of simultaneity bias and to establish the multiplicity of causal links among structural variables, a simultaneous equation framework was developed. The first study of this kind was done by Strickland and Weiss (1976). The main thrust of the paper was to analyze the role of advertisement on profitability and concentration and the extent to which profitability and concentration also determine advertisement. Other pioneering papers examine that simultaneity problems were by Martin (1979a, b) and Gupta (1983).

Most of the empirical works that have followed the SCP tradition have industry as the fundamental unit of analysis. In recent years, there has been a shift in the emphasis from industry to the firm level. In general, the econometric specification for firm-level analysis is similar to industry-level specification, except that now those additional variables are considered to capture the impact of firm characteristics. Such variables include market share (as distinct from concentration ratio) and firm size (measured in terms of asset size). Shepherd's (1974) study was the first to use such firm specification to look at its profitability.

Moving now to the case of India, we find that a modest number of studies have also been conducted to examine the profitability of Indian manufacturing firms. One of the earliest applications of the SCP framework can be noticed in the work by Sawhney and Sawhney (1973). The authors examined the impact of capacity utilization ratio in their industrial profitability model because under utilization of capacity was a chronic problem in many industries in India. The study found that

[5] See Hay and Morris (1991), pp. 236–239 for an excellent review on this issue.

concentration had a non-linear relationship with the profitability of the industry and that the capacity utilization ratio had a positive and significant relationship with the profitability of industries. The study was extended by Apte and Vaidynathan (1982) to incorporate economies of scale and certain other features (like price ceiling and licensing) that are peculiar to Indian industries. The study indicated that economies of scale, capital-ratios, price and licensing controls have little effect on the profitability of an industry, whereas controls over distribution and product-mix have a significant adverse impact on the profitability of firms. An important dimension of Indian industry is the presence of multinational firms. Kumar (1990 and 1991) analyzed 43 Indian manufacturing industries in 1980–1983 to understand the superior performance of multinational enterprises (MNE). It was observed that MNE as groups are more protected by entry barriers compared to their local counterparts. Additionally, it was also noticed that in knowledge intensive sectors, MNEs were found to enjoy advantages over local enterprises both with respect to technological and human skills precisely because MNEs have greater access to the resources of global enterprises. Chhibber and Majumdar (1999) also studied the differences in the performance of manufacturing firms due to differences in ownership pattern. The result shows that only when property rights devolve to foreign owners at 51% i.e., when foreign owners have full control over their companies, firms display relatively superior performance. Majumdar (1998) also studied differences in the profitability of firms due to their size and age. The study indicated that, in India, old firms are less profitable whereas large sized firms are more profitable. The study explained that the market-restricting industrial policies that have been followed in India have put old firms at a disadvantageous position over the past three decades. In addition, case specific studies for specific industries have also been conducted, for example, by the motor vehicle industry Narayana and Joseph (1993) and the tyre-industry (Sen 1992)

Regarding the pharmaceutical industry, which is our main concern, we find that, in the context of the global pharmaceutical industry, the question of the above mentioned normal profit of firms has generated debate in the academic circle (Commanor 1986). Such debates arise because of the co-existence of high profit and low concentration in this industry (see for example the studies by Santerre and Stephen 2004: 467; Viscusi et al. 2000: 820; Schweitzer 1997: 25). These studies explain the role of marketing and R&D efforts of firms for such high profit earning of firms in spite of low concentration.

In conducting the review of literature, we found that the question of profitability in the Indian pharmaceutical sector has not been studied in detail. However, such an analysis is necessary to examine how effective the strategies of firms are to gain high profit. As efforts on the part of firms are new, how successful these strategies are in terms of higher profitability is an important question that needs to be probed at this juncture. If firms' profit fall due to certain production or marketing decisions, the question of feasibility of such effort arises. Given the changes in policy structure that governs this industry, a rigorous analysis will no doubt enhance our understanding of this life-line industry.

6.4 Analysis of Profitability

The analysis employs data collected from the annual balance sheet of pharmaceutical companies provided by the CMIE prowess database. The total number of firms in the sample varies from 70 to almost 289 over the years and in all, there is an unbalanced panel of over 2,372 firms for 15 years. The relevant explanatory variables, the profit earned by companies are computed from the financial balance sheet of companies. To calculate the cost of capital, the rate of interest and the price of capital is collected from the RBI monthly bulletin

The profitability of pharmaceutical firms is measured in terms of the *Return on Sales (ROS)* which also closely corresponds to the price cost margin (PCM) employed in the empirical literature. The use of ROS as compared to Rate on Asset (ROA) or Rate on Equity (ROE) has been preferred because of various reasons: First, it approximates a rate of return on sales measure and therefore constitutes the concept of profit. Second, the return from asset flows over a period of time, thus firms that have invested heavily for plant and machinery will show a lower value of profit earned if ROA is used for approximating the profit. In the Indian pharmaceutical sector, due to the heavy investment that is taking place in recent years, any measure of ROA will underestimate the true profits earned by firms.

Here $\Pi_{it} = \frac{y_{it}-c_{it}}{y_{it}}$, where Π_{it}= profit earned by the *i*th firm in the *t*th year and y_{it} = revenue earned by the *i*th firm in the *t*th year and c_{it} = is the variable cost of production. The variable cost of production includes the cost of labor measured in terms of wages and salaries, cost of raw material of companies and cost of power and fuel. To measure the economic rate of return, we have to account for the cost of capital. Measuring the cost of capital is a difficult task. Generally, the opportunity costs of capital services, that is, the total amount a firm could earn by renting the capital to other firms is considered as the cost of capital. The following procedure is applied to impute the rental rate of firms (see Chakroborty 1995). Suppose that a firm can earn an interest rate r by investing in risk-free asset. If δ denotes the depreciation of the plant and machinery during the period under consideration, then the rental cost of capital is $(r + \delta)$. Finally, if the price of the capital goes up at a rate of τ over the years, then the firm will enjoy a capital gain on the fraction $(1 - \delta)\tau$ of its capital stock remaining at the end of the period. This gain in the value of the capital stock should be deducted from the rental cost of the capital to get the price of the capital. The cost of the capital services that could be purchased for one unit of money is then given by $[r + \delta - (1 - \delta)\tau]$. The total capital cost then turned out to be $kp[r + \delta - (1 - \delta)\tau]$ where p is the purchase price of the capital; k is the stock of capital and the value of capital and kp is the value of capital. To compute the rental rate of the capital, it is required to get information for (δ, r, τ). The data for r and p is obtained from the monthly bulletin of RBI. The change in p over the years is employed to calculate the value of τ.[6] The figures for the depreciation of the capital δ are obtained from the balance sheet of companies.

[6] The price for plant and machinery is taken as a proxy for capital goods

6.4.1 *Determinants of Profitability*

6.4.1.1 Industry Specific Variables

The industry-specific variables considered here are as follows: (1) extent of concentration, (2) economies of scale, and (3) degree of product differentiation.

- The extent of concentration in the industry is measured in terms of the Herfindahl-Hirschman index (HI) of concentration. The Herfindahl index (H) is measured as the sum of square of each firm's share in output in the total industry output
  Thus, $H = \sum s_i^2$ where $s_i = \frac{i^{th}\text{firm output}}{\text{Total industry output}}$
- Industry wide measure of economies of scale and initial capital investment for different years (1991–2005) is arrived at by computing the Minimum Efficient Scale of production (MES). MES is measured as the average size of the largest plants accounting for 75% of the total industry output (Comanor and Wilson 1967; Caves et al. 1975). The variable has been considered because companies capturing 75% of the market in the industry are the most efficient firms in this industry.[7] The average capital stock for these firms then gives a proxy of the initial capital required to build an efficient plant in the Indian pharmaceutical industry.
- The 'overall measure of the product differentiation' in the industry is measured as the ratio of the total industry advertisement expenditure by the volume of total volume of sales in the industry (AMI) for each of the years i.e., from 1991 to 2005 (Comanor and Wilson 1967).

6.4.1.2 Strategic Variables

Advertisement Variable

We consider advertisement expenditure of firms as an important determinant of the profitability of firms. Three indicators are used here to capture the advertisement expenditure of firms. The first one is the industry-specific advertisement. As defined earlier, it captures the overall measure of product differentiation in the industry (see Table 6.1).

The second variable is called the marketing intensity of firms. It is measured as the ratio of marketing expenses of a firm by its sales. It captures the efforts of firms to market its product through sales representative and in turn increase the market

---

[7] While computing the output efficiency of firms, we noticed that firms capturing 75% of the market share are the most efficient firms in the industry with an average efficiency of around 75 to about 80%. Further, the total number of firms from this group is consistent over the years and varies from 25 to 30.

Table 6.1 Summary of the variables considered

Variables	Measurement of the variable	Notation used
Extent of concentration	Sum of square of each firms share in output in the total industry output	HI
Economies of scale	Average size of the largest plants accounting for 75 % of the total industry output	MES
Product differentiation	Ratio of the total industry advertisement expenditure by the volume of total volume of sales in the industry	AMI
Marketing intensity	Ratio of marketing expenses of a firm by its sales	MK
Marketing over time	Measured by adding up the past marketing expenses of the firms taking 25 % as the rate of depreciation	MT
R&D intensity	Ratio of R&D by sales	R&D_1
Export intensity	Ratio of export by sales	EXP
Marketing R&D interaction	Product of R&D intensity and marketing intensity	R&D_1*MK
R&D export interaction	Product of R&D intensity and export intensity	R&D_1*EXP
Market share	output share of a firm in the total industry output	MS
Herfindahl index of diversification	Measured as the sum of square of the share for the ith commodity in the total revenue earned by a firm. Thus, $H = \sum_{i=1}^{n} s_i^2$ where $s_i =$ share of the ith commodity in the total revenue earned by a firm	DI
Efficiency of the firms	Arrived at by solving a LP Model see Chap. 3	EFF
Imported technology	The variable stock of imported technology for the *t*th year is constructed by adding the figures for the imported technology from the base period to the *t*th period by taking 5 % as the rate of depreciation	IT
Imported raw-material	Expenses for imported-raw material deflated by the total revenue of the firms	IRW
Time dummy	Takes value one from 1995 onward zero for the rest of the years	TD

demand for their product (see Table 6.1). We, therefore, expect that the variable will have a positive impact on the profitability of firms. However, if rivals also spend on an equal scale and firms are unable to increase the market demand, the effect of marketing on the profitability of firms can be ambiguous (see Hurwitz and Caves 1988 for a theoretical discussion on this issue).

The third variable considered is also called 'marketing over time'. A firm may have a low marketing expenditure in the current year but may have already built a brand name for its product with long-term investment by investing more on marketing in the past. To capture this phenomenon the variable 'marketing over time' is considered in our profitability equation (for theoretical justification, see Nerlove and Arrow 1962). The variable is measured by adding up the past marketing expenses of firms taking 25% as the rate of depreciation ($\rho = .25$). Thus for the t th year the accumulated effect of marketing activities over time (S_{it}) is given by the following formula

$$S_{it} = \sum \rho^t S_{i,t-1} \tag{6.1}$$

We expect that this variable will have positive impact on the profitability of firms because of the following reasons. First, physicians develop 'prescribing patterns' whereby they become more familiar with the mode of action and side effects of a particular drug and tend to prescribe it more often (Hurwitz and Caves 1988). Thus, promotional activities undertaken by a firm in one period induces physicians to gain experience with a particular drug and are likely to have a lasting effect. Second, for chronic diseases, once a patient starts taking a particular product, he is unlikely to switch products unless a significant innovation is made.

R&D Variable: The second important variable considered is R&D. It is measured as the ratio of R&D by sales. Since the benefit of R&D can be appropriate only after a certain time period, we have also considered a lag of 1 year in R&D[8] (Geroski et al. 1997).

Export intensity (EI): The third important strategic variable considered is the export intensity of firms. It measures the shift in the business focus of firms from the narrow domain of the domestic market to the ever-merging opportunities in the global market. The competitive advantage of Indian pharmaceutical companies to sell its product in the international market broadly emerges from two causes viz., (1) advantage due to low cost of factors of production (endowment factor) and (2) long run experience in reverse engineering (technological factor). To expect that this variable will have a positive effect on the profitability of firms due to the above mentioned factors.

The study also recognizes the joint effect of (1) marketing and R&D and (2) R&D and export earning of a firm.

R&D-Marketing Interaction

Let us first explain the R&D marketing interaction. In the pharmaceutical industry, the R&D and marketing expenses of firms are closely interlinked. If a firm comes out with a new product, it has to market the product and generate demand for the newly invented product. Firms also get additional information about the new diseases pattern and about the effectiveness of its product to cure diseases while it markets its product through sales representative. This in turn encourages firms to develop innovative products in tune with the need of patients.[9] In other words, marketing is a channel through which firms get information about the pattern of R&D that they have to undertake (see Catherine 1999; Calfee 2002) for theoretical

---

[8] We have also considered different lag length in our model. However, there are no qualitative differences in our estimated result.

[9] Insights about the marketing and R&D strategy of the firms were gained during our field survey.

justification. Thus, here marketing moderates the effect of R&D and R&D also moderates the effect of marketing.

R&D-Export Interaction

Let us now explain the export and the R&D interaction of firms. The benefit that a firm gets from its R&D effort will be more with increased export earnings because of the following reasons: First, R&D expenditure is a sunk cost of a firm. A firm's sunk cost decision may be made taking into consideration the global market size because greater access in the global market allows firms to transfer the risk and the cost of R&D expenditure across the borders. Secondly, the results or the benefits of R&D are relatively easily transferable across the national borders. Once an innovation is made, it can be exploited anywhere in the world, although some modifications or additional testing of the new products might be necessary to confirm to local regulations. Additionally, the rise in the share of the OTC and the generic products in the global market have also encouraged Indian pharmaceutical companies to further enhance its age long capacity in process engineering and come out with high value generics.

6.4.1.3 Firm Specific Variables

The study also considers other firm specific determinants of profits viz., the market share, extent of diversification, technology import and the efficiency of firms.

Measured in terms of the output share of a firm in the total industry output, the variable market share captures the relative size of firms in the market and a proxy for their market power in the industry (Brozen 1971; Demsetz 1973, 1974).

Pharmaceutical companies produce multiple outputs. Thus, an *index for diversification* based on the Herfindahl index of diversification has also been included to examine its impact on the profitability of firms (see Table 6.1). There are many reasons due to which firms can diversify their product basket. An important reason might be the transaction cost in the marketization of joint product (see Teece 1980, 1982; Williamson 1967 for theoretical justification). Firms may also diversify due to the presence of certain 'competencies', 'know-how' and 'complementary-assets' in areas of marketing, management and product design (see Stimpert and Dunhaime 1997; Scott 1999).

We have also included the overall technical efficiency scores of a firm in the profitability equation. The technical (input as well as the output) efficiency score can also be interpreted as the overall measure of capability of a firm to manage its resources.

Additionally, the study also considers the imported stock of technology (see Chap. 3 for a measurement of this variable) and the imported raw material as an additional variable in the profitability model. We have seen that imported technology improves the efficiency and the technological growth of firms. Here also we would also like to examine its effect on the profitability of firms.

Lastly, a time dummy has also been introduced which takes a value one from 1995 onwards and zero for the rest of the year to examine the impact of policy reform on the profitability of firms (see also Fig. 6.1).

6.4.2 Econometric Specification

The final equation that is used to estimate the determinants of profits of firms is given by[10]

$$\begin{aligned}\Pi_{it} = {} & \beta_0 + \beta_1(MES)_t + \beta_2(HI)_t + \beta_3(AMI)_t + \beta_4(MS)_{it} + \beta_5(IT)_{it} + \beta_6(DI)_{it} \\ & + \beta_7(TD)_{it} + \beta_8(IRW)_{it} + \beta_9(R\&D\_1)_{it} + \beta_{10}(EXP)_{it} + \beta_{11}(MK)_{it} \\ & + \beta_{12}(R\&D\_1^{*}MK)_{it} + \beta_{13}(R\&D\_1^{*}EXP) + \beta_{14}(EFF)_{it} \\ & + \beta_{15}(\mathrm{MT}) + \mu_i + v_{it}, \qquad (6.2)\end{aligned}$$

$$v_{it} \sim IID(0, \sigma_v^2)$$

Here 'μ_i' are unobserved firm specific effects like, firm specific entrepreneurial or managerial skills, which are assumed to be fixed. 'v_{it}' are a stochastic term which are assumed to be identically and independently distributed, IID(0, σ^2). It is assumed that the independent variables are independent of v_{it} for all i and t. The above econometric model is a panel data model and has been estimated following the appropriate method devised for panel estimation.

[10] While conducting profitability analysis, it is necessary to check for the possible presence of simultaneity among the dependent and the independent variables. The presence of simultaneity may arise specifically for the firm specific strategic variables and the profit margin of firms, because optimum-spending R&D, marketing and the profit margin of firms are derived simultaneously as a profit maximization exercise of firms. Further, there can bi-directional causality between the profitability in an industry and the structure of the industry (see, Martin 2002; Hay and Morris 1991 for a theoretical discussion on this issue) Disregarding such simultaneous relationship between the profit margin of firms and its R&D or advertisement or trade relationship may lead to the serious problem of simultaneity bias. In the context of our study, we have conducted the Hausman test for simultaneity taking into consideration all industry specific structural variables as well as firm specific strategic variables like marketing intensity, R&D intensity, export intensity. The result of the Hausman test, however, rules out any simultaneity among the variables considered in our model. Therefore, given the data point and the time framework for which we are conducting our analysis we do not notice any presence of endogenity among variables.

6.5 Empirical Results And Findings

The Hausman (1978) specification test (Table 6.2) statistic accepts the null hypothesis that individual invariant effects (u_i) are not correlated with the regressors i.e., $E(u_i/X_{it}) = 0$. This suggests that the model should be estimated using the fixed effect estimation technique.

An important component of panel data model (Fixed effect model) is the presence of firm specific effects. The available statistics (see Table 6.3) again indicate the presence of firm specific effects namely the managerial and entrepreneurial skill of managers.

Consider now the independent variables of the model. Table 6.4 summarizes the principle findings of the analysis.

6.5.1 Industry Specific Variables

It is noticed that the extent of concentration is significant at 5% level. However, contrary to the conventional wisdom, the coefficient attached with the degree of concentration is negative. In the Indian pharmaceutical industry, the value of the Herfindahl Index is quite low (see Chap. 2), signifying intense competition among firms. In our study period, the value of concentration has increased. However, such a rise in the value of concentration does not signify collusive behavior among firms. Instead, many small sized firms have left the market because they are unable to withstand the rising competition in this sector. Among the existing firms, the intensity of competition has increased because new firms have entered the market with new products.[11] Thus, we find that, with the rise in the value of concentration measured in terms of the H-index, the profitability of firms fall.

The MES also do not have any statistically significant impact on the profitability of firms because the scale economy is present at a very low level of output production (see Chap. 2). Hence, it does not put large or medium sized firms at a cost disadvantageous position. This again indicates that there is no entry barrier in this industry due to economies of scale in production.

Our studies also indicate that the degree of product differentiation in this industry is significant at 5 % level. This implies that, with the rise in the degree of overall product differentiation in this industry the profitability of firms fall. This implies that unlike a consumer goods industry where product differentiation creates entry barriers, in the Indian pharmaceutical industry increased advertisement expenditure at the *industry level increases the market demand and encourages entry of generics and close substitutes* with similar efficacy with existing products.

[11] While calculating the age of the firms, we noticed that 27 new companies have entered the market between 1995 and 2002.

Table 6.2 Hausman specification test results

Chi^2	Probability
84.24	0.000

Table 6.3 'F' test that all u_i = 0 to check for the presence of individual effects

F statistic	21.43
Probability	0.0000

Table 6.4 Determinants of firm's profitability[a]

Variables	Coefficients	t-values	Prob> | t|>0
Herfindahl index for concentration	−4.850546**	−2.47	0.014
MES	−0.0289183	1.38	0.167
Degree of product differentiation in the industry	−4.21872**	−2.14	0.032
Market share	2.172511**	2.01	0.044
Efficiency	.1571723**	2.41	0.016
Diversification index	.0580754**	2.27	0.023
Time dummy	−.0543197***	−1.75	0.081
Research and development (RD)	−.8041128***	−1.03	0.074
RD*MK	17.04699*	3.22	0.001
RD*EXP	0.4355746	0.35	0.725
Export intensity(EXP)	.3886145*	3.83	0.000
Marketing intensity(MKT)	−2.21490*	−4.44	0.000
Marketing over time	0.1201663	0.8	0.424
Imported raw-material	−.8525721*	−3.69	0.000
Imported technology	.4398827**	2.54	0.011
R square (overall)	0.1434		
F statistic	104.54*		

*** Significant at 10 per cent level, ** significant at five per cent level, *significant at one per cent

[a]We have also computed the correlation of the determinants and the profitability of firms. We did not notice any discrepancy in the sign of the correlation and coefficient that is obtained from regression analysis. Thus for example the correlation with profitability and marketing is negative

6.5.2 Strategic Variables

Among strategic variables considered in this study, the marketing intensity of firms is statistically significant at 1 % level but it has a negative coefficient attached with it. In the presence of R&D interaction, the coefficient β_{11} captures the marketing effort of firms when its expenditure for R&D is zero. In other words, it captures the marketing effort of firms for the existing products (not new product). We have argued that if firms just pursue to market their old products then they may not be successful in their efforts if their rivals also spend on an equal scale. Hence their profitability will fall. Our analysis establishes that the increased marketing for the existing product on the part of the firms is futile to increase market demand for the product and leads to wasteful competition.

Our analysis also indicates that marketing efforts of firms are also unable to build any brand name for the products. In other words, the effect of marketing efforts of

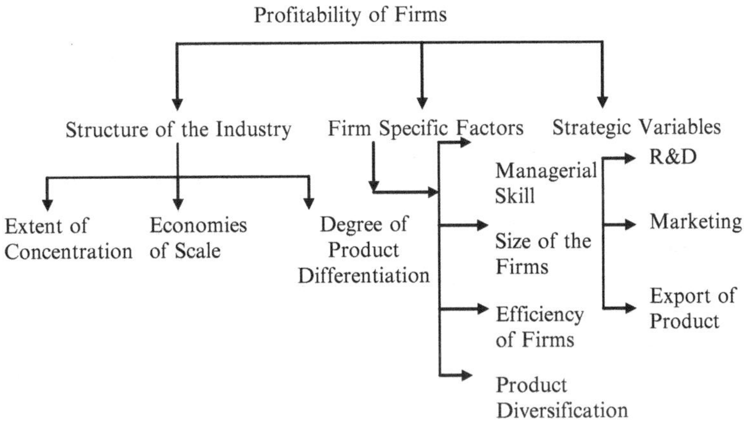

Fig. 6.1 Conceptual framework to examine the determinants of a firm's profitability

firms is short-lived. One reason is that many Indian firms have competence in process engineering. In the absence of product-patent, firms could easily imitate and come out with a generic version of the product of a rival within years of introduction of a new product in the market. Thus, unlike the market for the developed country, here we find that firms are unable to build any brand name for the product.

R&D intensity is statistically significant at a 10 % level. However, the negative coefficient with the R&D intensity also implies that higher spending for R&D reduces the profitability of firms. There can be two possible reasons for such an effect viz., first, the lagged effect in R&D. We have considered a 1-year lag in our econometric specification.[12] This time lag may not be sufficient to capture the successes in R&D. Second, in the presence of marketing interaction, the coefficient β_9 captures the effect of R&D when the expense for marketing is zero. This, therefore, captures the inability of firms to market its new product (if firms are successful in their R&D effort), generates adequate demand for the product to recoup expenses incurred for R&D, and hence leads to a fall in profitability.

The coefficient attached with the joint effort of marketing and R&D in Table 6.4, however, suggests that it is one of the most effective strategies of firms to earn high profit. It indicates that firms can get sufficient returns from R&D and earn high profit only if they have a vast marketing network. It also indicates that, if firms, instead of marketing their existing product, market the newly invented product, they can earn higher profit.

The regression analysis also confirms that, by exporting its product in the international market, firms can earn higher profit.

[12] We have mentioned that we have tried different lag lengths like 2, 3, 4 and even 5 years lag length. However, there are no qualitative differences in our estimated results.

6.5.3 Firm Specific Variables

From our profitability analysis, we also notice that by installing imported technology, firms can earn higher profit.

We, however, find that by importing raw materials and intermediaries the profitability of firms regresses. We have reiterated that in recent years, many pharmaceutical firms started importing cheap bulk drugs from China. While by importing low cost raw materials, firms are able to cut down their cost of raw material, it has also escalated the costs of process synthesis and other manufacturing related costs. Further, many pharmaceutical firms have failed to fulfill the regulatory requirements of the international standard by importing raw materials from China. Altogether, our analysis indicates that these have an adverse effect on the profitability of firms.

The positive sign for market share variable indicates that firms with a larger market share earn a higher profit in this industry, which is intuitively obvious.

However, a positive relation with the Herfindahl index for diversification and the profitability of firms implies that 'specialized firms' that have niche products under their command are more profitable. It also indicates that instead of producing too many products, Indian pharmaceutics must identify its areas of competence for various therapeutic segments and specialize in the production of such products. We also note from our previous efficiency analysis that firms that integrate with up-stream raw-material industry are more efficient. Together this implies that by integrating with raw-material industry, firms can cut their costs at various stages of production, achieve higher technical efficiency in producing the specialized product and earn higher profit.

Contrary to the general perception, it is also noticed that changes in the policy environment captured by the dummy variable have a negative impact on the profitability of firms. This implies that the liberalization policy and the regulatory changes related to quality control and good manufacturing practice have adversely affected the profitability of firms. We noted from our efficiency and productivity analysis (see Chaps. 3 and 5) that due to policy changes, only few firms have appropriated the benefit from technology changes, but the rest of the firms the distance from the frontier has magnified or their total value of output per unit of input employed has decreased in a relative sense. The profitability analysis reinforces that to comply with the new regulatory requirement due to policy changes, either there has been a fall in total revenue or the cost of production must have soared up. Together these have reduced the profitability of firms.

Lastly, our study also shows that the most efficient firms are also the most profitable ones in this industry. In other words, one of the important sources for high profit earning for firms lies in efficiency in the production process. Thus, by achieving higher efficiency, a firm can also earn a high profit margin.

6.6 Conclusion and Direction for Further Research

Earning high profit is an important objective of Indian pharmaceutical firms in the era of liberalization and patent regime. Having argued that remaining efficient does not necessarily imply that a firm can also remain profitable, in this chapter, we have examined the determinants of the profitability of Indian pharmaceutical firms.

Our study indicates that industrial structure does not favorably create any entry barrier for firms to insulate its high profit earning from incumbents. The analysis also indicates that firm-specific strategies like marketing intensity or R&D intensity do not have any favorable impact on the profitability of firms. However, the interaction between R&D and marketing is one of the most successful strategies for firms. In other words, if firms can come out with new products that have some therapeutic qualities and *successfully market the product,* they can earn higher profit. This implies that neither R&D nor marketing by itself is sufficient for firms to earn high profit. It clearly establishes that firms should expend its marketing effort mainly for disseminating information about its new product, which is possible only when it does serious R&D. Another interesting finding is that firms that have more niche products under their commands are more profitable. We have cross-checked from the balance sheet of companies that on an average the more specialized firms are small sized. This implies that small sized firms that have a more dispersed product basket should try to identify their niche products and specialize in the production and promotion of such products.

Lastly, our study also indicates that the import of raw material has reduced the profitability of Indian pharmaceutical firms. India already has a well-established globally reputed raw-material industry. Thus, instead of purchasing cheap and low quality products from China, it is better to rely on its domestic supplier. Since Indian pharmaceutical products have a reputation in the international market, in the coming years, it is expected that international demand for Indian pharmaceutical products will increase (see KPMG report 2006). If domestic producers for final products purchase their raw material from indigenous firms, such increased demand for final products will also have a positive spill over effect on the domestic raw-material bulk drug industry. This will have an expansionary effect on the growth and development of the raw-material bulk industry and will be beneficial for the country in the long run.

6.6.1 Directions for Further Research

There are a few possible extensions of the present analysis. First, instead of examining the profitability of pharmaceutical firms, one can also examine the persistence of profit of firms over the years (by applying panel autoregressive model) and its determinants. Second, one can also characterize firms based on the nature of R&D and marketing and examine how profitable the firms are for undertaking different forms or types of R&D or marketing. The prowess database, however, does not provide such detailed information regarding R&D or the marketing activities of firms. Hence, it is beyond the scope of our analysis. Third, based on our empirical findings one can also theoretically model R&D and marketing decisions of firms and show how both the strategies together enable firms to earn a higher profit instead of focusing exclusively on any one of them. Fourth, we have not attempted to examine the impact of R&D spillover on the profit earning of firms. One can construct indices to capture the spillover due to public or even private spending for R&D and capture its impact on profitability. Fifth, using a more comprehensive ORG Marco data-base, one can also analyze how the timing and the successes in the innovative efforts of firms help them earn higher profit.

Finally, in the context of our study, we did not notice any problem of simultaneity. However, one can extend the time framework for the study and check for simultaneity and in its presence develop a simultaneous equation econometric specification by considering the firm-specific strategic variables and the profit that a firm earns. Again, due to non-availability of data, we have not measured the profit efficiency of firms. One can, however, construct a price index and measure the profit efficiency of firms.

Chapter 7
The Problem of Availability of Patented Drugs Due to Product Patent and Parallel Trade: A Theoretical Approach

7.1 Introduction

In the introductory chapter of our book, we have argued that pharmaceutical firms produce drugs that have high social value. Consequently, debates surrounding the amendment of the patent law are also intimately linked with the problem of availability of patented drugs for the consumers of India. This chapter therefore takes up an important issue viz., to examine the problem of availability of drugs that might arise due to product patents. Since product patents are of recent origin, and there is lack of availability of adequate empirical data to assess this *'problem of availability of patented drugs'* empirically we have addressed this issue theoretically. As it will be evident, the conclusions arrived at by doing such theoretical analysis can also be valid for other developing countries and are relevant not only for the welfare of the Indian population but also for other developing countries that have also recognized "Product-Patents" due to WTO compulsion.

The rest of the chapter unfolds in the following manner. The next section motivates the present problem followed by the section that develops the analytical model of our study. In this section, we have introduced and compared two important pricing strategies viz., uniform pricing and discriminatory pricing strategy. We have compared the results and have drawn implication for the availability of drugs that might arise due to product patents for developing nations. Section 7.4 considers a situation where an innovating firm located in the developed nation shifts its production unit to a developing country due to a low cost of production and looks at its implication. Finally, the problem of arbitrage (also popularly know in the patent literature as the problem of parallel trade) is taken up in the fifth section. A concluding section follows thereafter.

M. Mazumdar, *Performance of Pharmaceutical Companies in India*, Contributions to Economics, DOI 10.1007/978-3-7908-2876-4_7,

7.2 The Background

The availability of drugs in a country depends on two sets of factors arising from the supply side and the demand side. Supply side factors are primarily determined by the endowment of technology and the cost of production, whereas the demand side factor is the price that a consumer is willing to pay for the product. A profit-maximizing producer is primarily driven by the profit that it earns while it takes its decision to supply the product in a country.

The profit of a firm depends on both the supply side as well as demand side factors and also on market conditions. The market conditions are mainly determined by the strategic behavior of rival firms and the extent of competition in the market. Among supply side factors, the availability of technology is one of the most fundamental criteria to ensure the accessibility of drugs in a country. Technology in economics is defined as the production relationship between inputs and the output. It refers to 'the process by which the production system transforms its inputs into its output'. Thus apart from the engineering relation between inputs and the output, it also refers to the set of other factors like, for example the institutional set up, environmental constraints, the employer and the employee relation, all of which can have an important bearing on the final production of the product.

In the introductory chapters and the section for policy review, we have discussed how the dearth of technology among the domestic producers in the early 1970s and the recognition of product patents resulted in the concentration of the industry in the hands of few multinational companies. This gave rise to serious problems in the availability of essential medicines for the consumers of India. However, subsequently due to government policies, the lack of technology was not a serious problem and Indian pharmaceutical firms could produce almost all varieties of products at a much cheaper price (see Chap. 2). Such was not the case for other developing and even developed nations, which did not recognize product patents for a long period. In terms of its product quality today India stands much ahead of China and Brazil for producing and supplying generic products in international markets.

Realizing the transition, Indian pharmaceutical firms are undergoing due to policy changes, in the efficiency and productivity analysis we have examined technological aspects of the pharmaceutical industry in detail. In a sense, the above analysis therefore looks at supply side factors and in turn brings out certain important issues relating to the availability of off-patented generic drugs for the consumers of India. Combining our research findings from the efficiency and productivity analysis, we can conclude that the frontier firms have experienced technological progress and therefore they are producing larger volumes of the product using the same set of inputs (see Chap. 5 and also Chap. 3). Our study also indicates that the inefficiency that is noticed arises mainly due to technological change or due to an outward shift in the frontier (see Chap. 3). Put otherwise, in an aggregative sense the output produced per unit of the inputs employed is not declining for this sector. Therefore, the production of drugs may not be hampered due to the inefficiency of firms that we notice; instead, the technological progress that is noticed for this sector indicates the drug market in India is getting flooded either with the larger volume of the same product or with new products. This also implies that the consumers of India may get access to new varieties of generic products. Another interesting finding from our analysis is that R&D initiatives of firms are beneficial if it is undertaken on a large scale and targeted for advanced product or processes. A crucial point to understand here is that Indian pharmaceutical firms have ventured into R&D quite recently. From the primary survey with pharmaceutical firms (see Sect. 7.5.1) and from a number of other secondary sources, we find that most of the Indian firms undertake either process R&D, or imitative R&D which do not require heavy investment although large firms that have ventured into high end R&D have come out with some successes. In the presence of product patents, this implies that most Indian firms do not have enough capacity to compensate for the loss in patented products that might arise in the long run if innovative foreign firms depart from the Indian market. This may have serious implications for the availability of new novel drugs for the consumers of India in the long run.

This brings an important question to the fore. Do Indian firms have the capability to cater to the needs of the consumer for novel innovative products? The answer is 'no' because most Indian firms do process R&D. Few firms that have ventured in product R&D have come out with new products but do not have enough financial strength to carry out product R&D up to the end. We therefore find that a number of technological collaborations are taking place between innovative foreign and Indian firms.

This again strengthens our arguments that the dearth of availability of patented drugs may become a chronic problem in the long run if innovative foreign firms do not supply their product and also if Indian pharmaceutical firms cannot imitate the patented product of foreign MNCs (Chaudhuri 2003, 2005; Lanjouw 1997; Watal 1999, 2000) due to the product patent regime. Nevertheless, it can also be argued that if patent law is properly implemented, then the threat of imitation will be reduced and with its low cost of production and age long competency in process engineering the country can be an attractive hub for foreign multi-national companies to shift their production base.[1] Foreign multi-national companies can bring in new technology for the country and therefore new drugs will be available to the Indian consumer which Indian companies are unable to produce.

Additional market opportunity or low cost of production, however, may not provide sufficient incentives for MNCs to establish their production units or even to

[1] The British Government Department for International Development (Grace 2004) documented that the cost of the manufacturing facility in India that complies with international regulatory norms is about one –fourth of the cost of setting up a similar plant in the US or Europe. Further Civil construction is about US $8–12 per square foot in India compared to US $75 in the US. The cost of an Indian based laboratory analyst/chemist is only one fifth to one eighth of that of a US personnel. In addition, Indian scientists are well trained and equally knowledgeable but earn about one third of the Western counterpart's salaries.

supply their products to a country like India. This is because the decision of an MNC to supply its product is also driven by the level of demand for the product in that country. If a firm charges uniform price for its product across the globe, then it may not be optimal for it to supply the product in a developing country if the level of demand and correspondingly the demand price for the product is low. Further, the problem of availability of the patented drug also becomes more acute when local producers cannot imitate and produce the product due to the existence of Patent Act. Marjit and Beladi (1998) in their paper have derived this result under the assumption of uniform price charged by firms. But in reality firms discriminate prices for their products for different markets across the globe if the demand elasticities differ. A number of empirical studies conducted to compare prices of pharmaceutical products across the world also bear testimony to this fact. To mention a few, in 1998 the U.S. House of Representatives Minority Staff International Report indicated the US prices of medicine to be 72 % higher than those in Canada and 102 % higher than those in Mexico. The study by Danzon and Kim (1998), Danzon and Chao (2000), Danzon and Furukawa (2003) also indicate that price differences of the medicine are generally consistent with income differences of the countries concerned. In the context of developing countries the study by Pérez-Casas (2000) indicates that prices of the HIV AIDS drug in developing countries is as low as an order of about one-fifth of the US prices. A more recent study by Scherer and Watal (2000) also indicate that the effect of income on the prices of the medicine is gradually increasing over time.

A comparative scenario of Indian drug prices vis-à-vis other nations have not been explored much by researchers. In this context Table A.1 (see Appendix A) attempts to compare the prices of selected Indian products with two developed and two developing nations. It is evident from the figures in the table, that the prices of the medicine in developing countries are less than the developed world indicating the existence of some correlation in the income and the prices of the medicines concerned. The fact that Indian prices are comparatively lower has been revealed by the figures (see Table A.1, Appendix A)

In the case of India however, low drug prices may not be entirely due to the income effect. Historically, a lack of product patent led to a highly competitive, vibrant pharma industry in India that has been involved in various cost reducing innovative activities. Consequently, Indian prices are seen to be lower than other developing nations such as Pakistan that has indeed lower per-capita income compared to India.

Given such empirical evidences, we have introduced the option of price discrimination for a multinational firm opting to supply a drug both in the developed as well as in developing nations and examined the problem of non-availability of a drug (see Marjit and Beladi 1998). We have proved that the possibility of non-availability of a drug with product patent reduces with a price discrimination strategy. Additionally, the paper also examines the possibilities of establishing a production unit in a developing country, which provides a production facility at a low cost.

However, successful price discrimination is possible only when the possibility of arbitrage opportunities across nations is controlled. This problem is popularly known as the problem of "Parallel Trade" (Gallus 2004; Maskus 2000, 2001; Fink 2000) in the patent literature and the possibility emerges when a *trader* from a low priced market for the drug resells it in another market at a high price. One way to control such practices is through legal measures. However, legal treatment for parallel trade varies from country to country, for example, Australia, Hong-Kong and India allows parallel trade whereas in the US and Japan it is legally banned (Ganslandt and Maskus 2007). Given the wide differences in the legal structure of countries to deal with parallel-trade, it is sometimes difficult for a company to control cross-border trade in goods through legal routes. Clearly even in the presence of parallel trade an MNC can supply a medicine at a comparatively lower price in the developing country if the profit it realizes under such circumstances is higher than the profit it earns by solely operating in the developed country. The question that arises is under what condition can this happen. We have shown in our model that this can happen only if the relative market size of the developing nation is more than half the size of the developed nation.

7.3 The Analytical Model

This chapter begins with a simple model of Marjit and Beladi (1998) but modifies substantially to arrive at various possibilities. There are two possible markets in the economy viz. a developed country market denoted by M_d and a developing country market denoted by M_{dl}. Manufacturer "F" located in the developed country market produces a patented life saving drug, which is an outcome of the R&D undertaken by it. The manufacturer has the option of selling the product only in M_d or of selling the product both in M_d as well as in M_{dl}. As with Marjit and Beladi (1998) let us consider the following simple demand functions for the product,

$$q = (a_1 - p) \text{ for } M_d \tag{7.1}$$

and,

$$q = (a_2 - p) \text{ for } M_{dl} \tag{7.2}$$

where $a_1 > a_2$ are the intercepts of demand curves, and $q =$ quantity demanded and $p =$ price of the product.

For simplicity we assume that the cost of production is represented by constant marginal cost (=average cost)c_m. For simplicity, we also assume that there is no fixed cost of production in our model. The manufacturer "F" has two options before her, to supply the product in the market of M_{dl} by charging a uniform price (P_U) in M_d and M_{dl} or to supply the product with price discrimination (P_d). It is likely that a profit-maximizing manufacturer would adopt a price discrimination strategy if faced with different elasticities of demand in two separate markets.

7.3.1 Options of Price Discrimination

Manufacturer "*F*" while maximizing her profit under price discrimination takes into account two different demand functions, one for M_d and another for M_{dl}, separately. With price discrimination, let us assume that the manufacturer "*F*" faces the profit functions Π_d and Π_{dl} by serving the market of M_d and M_{dl}. At this stage we assume away any arbitrage from the low cost to the high cost market. Maximization of Π_d and Π_{dl} then results in the following proposition.

Proposition 1. *If* $a_2 > c_m$ *then the manufacturer "F" will always serve the market of* M_{dl} *with price discrimination.*

Proof. We have,

$$\Pi_{dl} = \left[a_2 q - q^2 - c_m q\right] \tag{7.3}$$

From the *First order condition (F.O.C.)* $\frac{d\Pi_{dl}}{dq} = 0$ we get the following equilibrium price and quantity,

$$q_{dl} = \frac{a_2 - c_m}{2}, \text{ where } q_{dl} = \text{quantity served in } M_{dl} \tag{7.4}$$

and

$$p_{dl} = \frac{a_2 + c_m}{2}, \text{ where } p_{dl} = \text{price charged in } M_{dl} \tag{7.5}$$

And, $\prod_{dl}^{0} = \frac{(a_2 - c_m)^2}{4}$ where Π_{dl}^{0} = profit earned by serving the market of M_{dl}

$$\prod_{dl}^{0} > 0 \Rightarrow a_2 > c_m \tag{7.6}$$

Because of similar demand structure, we can also argue that the profit "*F*" earns from the market of M_d will be $\prod_{d}^{0} = \frac{(a_1 - c_m)^2}{4}$. Therefore, the total profit the manufacturer earns with price discrimination strategy ($\equiv \Pi^{Pd}$) by serving both the market is

$$\prod^{Pd} = \frac{(a_2 - c_m)^2}{4} + \frac{(a_1 - c_m)^2}{4} \tag{7.7}$$

If however, the manufacturer charges a uniform price for her product in M_d and M_{dl}it faces a combined demand functions for both the countries. Maximizing her profit function under the strategy of uniform pricing then results in the following proposition.

Note 1: Clearly if $a_2 < c_m$, no drug can be sold in the developing country, the price discrimination exercise loses meaning and we arrive at a trivial case. In order to examine non-trivial cases, we have attempted in this paper to derive conditions under which an MNC will serve both the markets.

Proposition 2. *Let A be the set of values of a_2 for which positive profit is earned when uniform price is charged in both the markets and B be the set of values of a_2 for which positive profit is earned under price discrimination, then $A \subseteq B$.*

Proof. When uniform price is charged the relevant demand curves faced by the manufacturer is as follows

$$q = (a_1 - p) \text{ for } p > a_2$$

$$q = a_1 + a_2 - 2p \text{ for } p < a_2 \tag{7.8}$$

And $\prod_U = \left[\frac{a_1 + a_2}{2} q - \frac{1}{2} q^2 - c_m q\right]$

F.O.C. requires $\frac{d\Pi_U}{dq} = 0, \ \Rightarrow q^o = \frac{a_1+a_2}{2} - c_m$ where q^o = profit maximizing quantity produced by charging the uniform price in M_d and M_{dl}.

$$\therefore \Pi_U^O = \frac{1}{2}\left(\frac{a_1 + a_2}{2} - c_m\right)^2, \text{ where } \prod_U^O \text{ is the profit earned by charging uniform price in } M_d \text{ and } M_{dl} \tag{7.9}$$

If the manufacturer serves, only M_d she will enjoy profit of

$$\Pi_d^0 = \frac{(a_1 - c_m)^2}{4} \text{ (see proposition 1)} \tag{7.10}$$

Now the condition under which the "*F*" will serve M_{dl} can be derived (see Marjit and Beladi 1998) as

$$\frac{(a_1 - c_m)^2}{4} < \frac{1}{2}\left(\frac{a_1 + a_2}{2} - c_m\right)^2 \tag{7.11}$$

$$\Rightarrow \left[\frac{a_1(\sqrt{2} - 1) - a_2}{\sqrt{2}} + (\sqrt{2} - 1)c_m\right] < 0 \tag{7.12}$$

With further manipulation we get

$$a_2 > (2 - \sqrt{2})c_m + a_1(\sqrt{2} - 1) \tag{7.13}$$

Therefore $A = \{a_2 : a_2 >; \ (2 - \sqrt{2})c_m + a_1(\sqrt{2} - 1)\}$
From Proposition 1 we have $B = \{a_2 : a_2 > c_m\}$
To prove $A \subseteq B$ we need to prove that

$$\left(2 - \sqrt{2}\right)c_m + a_1\left(\sqrt{2} - 1\right) > c_m \text{ or } \sqrt{2}(a_1 - c_m) - (a_1 - c_m) > 0 \tag{7.14}$$

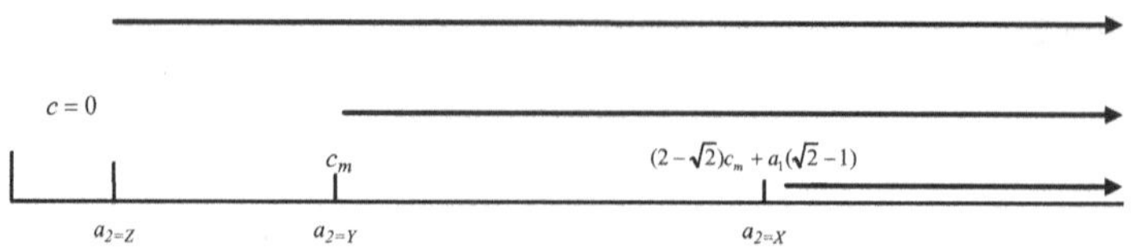

Fig. 7.1 Range of values of a_2 for which the manufacturer serves the market M_{dl} with price discrimination and uniform pricing strategy

which is always true

Hence $A \subseteq B$ *Q.E.D.*

Proposition 2 can also be visualized with the help of a line diagram (see Majumdar and Rajeev 2010) depicted in Fig. 7.1. The figure plots the different values of a_2 for which "*F*" serves the market of M_{dl} with her patented product for alternative pricing strategies. Under the strategy of uniform pricing when $a_2 = (2-\sqrt{2})c_m + a_1(\sqrt{2}-1)$ the manufacturer is indifferent between serving and not serving the market of M_{dl}. Let us denote this value of a_2 as *X*.

For all points to the left of *X*, the manufacturer will not serve M_{dl} with uniform pricing. When $a_2 = c_m$, the manufacturer is indifferent between serving and not serving the market of M_{dl} with price discrimination. Let us denote this value by of a_2 by *Y*. At all points to the right of *Y*, $a_2 > c_m$ and the manufacturer serves M_{dl} with price discrimination. On the line diagram, it also includes all the points to the left of *X*. Therefore, with price discrimination the manufacturer serves the market of M_{dl} for a greater range of values of a_2. This is precisely what we have derived mathematically.

Based on our analysis, we can then infer that the possibility of non-availability of the patented drug in the developing country reduces under price discrimination. The problem persists even if after product patent the condition $a_2 < c_m$ *holds.*

7.4 Production in the Developing Country

Until now in the model, we have assumed that the manufacturer "*F*" produces the drug in the developed country. Suppose due to a low cost of production in the developing country, it establishes its production plant there. What will then be the possible consequences?

Let us assume that the cost of producing a product in a developing country is *c* and $c < c_m$. A lower value of *c* can be mainly due to low cost of factors of production like labor, raw material, or capital. Manufacturer "*F*" can then produce the product from the developing country and supply it in M_d and M_{dl} with price discrimination. Let Π_F^C be the total profit the manufacturer "*F*" earns by serving the market of M_d

and M_{dl} when the cost of production is c; and $\Pi_F{}^{C_m}$ is the profit earned when the cost of production is c_m. Then

$$\Pi_F^C = \left[\frac{(a_1 - c)^2}{4} + \frac{(a_2 - c)^2}{4}\right] > \Pi_F{}^{C_m}$$
$$= \left[\frac{(a_1 - c_m)^2}{4} + \frac{(a_2 - c_m)^2}{4}\right] \text{ as } c < c_m \tag{7.15}$$

It can then be argued that due to locational advantage, manufacturer "*F*" may have the incentive to set up its production unit in the developing country and the developing country in turn can also benefit from the product patent. However, even if the condition $c < c_m$ holds true, manufacturer "*F*" may not always produce and supply the product in the developing country if $a_2 < c$. Assume now the cost of production in the developing country, $c = 0$. The problem of non-availability of patented drugs still persists even when $c = 0$ with uniform pricing policy if the following condition $a_2 > a_1(\sqrt{2} - 1)$does not hold (see Marjit and Beladi 1998). In our model if $c = 0$, we have the following corollary which follows from proposition 2.

Corollary 1. *If the cost of production $c = 0$ manufacturer "F" will always produce and supply the drug in the market of M_{dl} under the strategy of price discrimination.*

Proof. Let $C = \{a_2 : a_2 > a_1(\sqrt{2} - 1)\}$ be the set of values of a_2 at which "*F*" supplies the drug in M_{dl} with uniform pricing policy and zero cost of production $(c = 0)$. Similarly, let $D = (a_2 : a_2 > 0)$ be the set of values of a_2 at which "*F*" supplies the product in M_{dl} with price discrimination. Since $a_1(\sqrt{2} - 1) > 0, C \subseteq D$ always hold true.

The result can also be explained with the help of Fig. 7.1. With $c = 0$, $a_2 = a_1 (\sqrt{2} - 1)$ lies somewhere in between *X* and *Y* or in other word $Y < a_2 = a_1(\sqrt{2} - 1) < X$. However, it lies to the left of the point $a_2 = z$ at which the manufacturer "*F*" supplies the drug to the developing country with price discrimination strategy and zero cost of production. From the above line diagram it is then evident that $A \subseteq B \subseteq C \subseteq D$. Thus we can argue that with zero cost of production and price discrimination strategy, MNCs will always supply the drug in the developing country.

Note 2: It is optimal for the manufacturer to produce in the developing country and even to sell there if $a_2 > c$. If this condition holds, by not selling in the developing country the manufacturer will lose a part of her profit.[2]

---

[2] The absence of strict patent regulation always brings the risk of imitation. Historically, Indian imitators are observed to be more cost efficient. This is seen to deter the flow of new technology to India in the process patent regime. With product patent in force, it is expected that MNCs may explore Indian markets with new technology and more technological collaboration can be conjectured.

7.5 Parallel Trade

Up to this stage of the model, we have assumed that the manufacturer is directly involved in selling the product. However, in reality, we observe that, instead of selling the product directly, the manufacturer sells the product through distributors or traders. When the marketing of the product is done through distributors, an interesting case emerges whereby the manufacturer fails to perfectly discriminate the prices for the product across markets. Such circumstance arises when the distributor engages in arbitrage trading. The incentive for such arbitrage opportunity arises, if there is sufficient price difference between the developed and the developing nation to cover the transaction cost and still offer gains to distributors. The problem is cited in the literature as the problem of "parallel-trade" (see West and Mahon 2003; Kanavos et al. 2004) and is an outcome of the "Principle of exhaustion" upheld in legal regimes of the countries. "Principle of exhaustion", means that the Intellectual Property Right (IPR) holders' exclusive rights over the products are lost upon first sale of a product within national borders and thus "parallel trade" cannot be excluded through legal routes. In other words with the exhaustion principle in force, an IPR holder's right to control the resale of the patented good from one market to another is lost.[3]

7.5.1 Consequences of Parallel Trade in Developing Countries: Some Findings from Field Survey

The important question that arises at this juncture is, in the presence of arbitrage opportunities, will the manufacturer sell drugs at a lower price in a developing country? To understand the situation a survey of limited size was conducted by

[3] Treatment for exhaustion policies varies from country to country. The European Union pursues regional exhaustion, which means that goods, once purchased, may be freely resold within its frontiers, but parallel imports from non-member countries are excluded. In the US the first sale doctrine is up-held (i.e. rights are exhausted when purchased outside the vertical distribution chain). Parallel Import of pharmaceutical products is permissible in the US provided it satisfies regulatory norms. The International forum on the TRIPS related WTO agreement is however, silent about the issue of parallel trade. Article 7 of the TRIPS agreement clearly emphasizes that its objective is to "contribute to the promotion of technological innovation and to the transfer and dissemination of technology, to the mutual advantage of producers and users of technological knowledge and *in a manner conducive to social and economic welfare, and to a balance of rights and obligations*". TRIPS also address, or rather withholds from addressing the issue of parallel imports: none of its provisions, except those pertaining to national treatment and most-favoured-nation treatment is "used to address the issue of intellectual property rights" (Art. 6). In other words, parallel trade remains essentially a matter of national interest.

selecting a few MNCs and trading bodies[4] belonging to this sector. It is revealed by all the companies that the strength and the extent of parallel trade to reduce the profitability of a company depend largely on the market size in the source country i.e., from where the parallel trade originates. If the source country is substantially small compared to the country for which parallel trade is destined, then the price differential can be quite large. The flow of the product from the low priced nation can then greatly reduce the profit that the company earns in the high priced market. Further because the size of the source-country market is small (in most cases), the profit that the company earns from that country may not be enough to compensate for the loss that the company incurs in the large (developed) country. As reported by GlaxoSmithKline Company the most glaring example of parallel trade occurred in 2002 when HIV-AIDS drugs meant for the poor patient in African nations were resold in Europe. This led to a loss of about US $18 million dollar in sales for the company.[5]

Legal treatment for parallel trade differs from country to country and therefore it is often difficult to file a legal suit against parallel trade. International trading blocks also agreed that if parallel trade is legally permitted, then it is difficult for multinational companies to control it because the traders can always earn higher profit by engaging in such activities. Further, in recent years cross-border trade in medicine has also increased due to internet-based trading and a rise in sale in over the counter medicines. Under such circumstances, MNCs might not reduce the price significantly for developing countries. The companies surveyed therefore apprehend that a large number of developing countries with small market size (like Guatemala, Bolivia, Argentina, Malaysia, Srilanka etc.) might be deprived of new patented medicines at *affordable prices* if the "exhaustion principle" is recognized in those countries. Clearly, these possibilities can arise even in the presence of product patents in an importing nation.

The companies also revealed that if the market for the source country is substantially large then the problem of parallel trade might not be that serious. To substantiate their arguments, the companies stated that the extent of cross-border trade in medicine is much higher in European countries because the European Union (EU) upheld parallel trade among member countries. However, the widespread prevalence of parallel trade, may not affect profits of companies significantly. This is because the relative differences of the market (and hence prices) for medicines among member countries are not large. This therefore, does not

[4] Namely Astra-Zeneca, GlaxoSmithKline and Wyeth Lederle and international trading bodies such as Chemo, Hexal and Mitsui.

[5] The incident is widely quoted in a number of sources and is one of the most vivid evidences of parallel trade in the pharmaceutical sector. GlaxoSmithKline sued several participants engaged in parallel trade including the legal parallel trader partner in pharmaceuticals, Dowelhurst Ltd., for trade mark infringement see Gautam Nair 2002; Sarah and Rory 2003; Graham Dukes 2004, Also see case *Glaxo Group Ltd* vs. *Dowelhurst Ltd, [2004]* E.T.M.R. 39 (July 31, 2003) *available at* 2003 WL 21729286 and EWCACiv290 http://www.bailii.org/ew/cases/EWCA/Civ/2004/290.html.

adversely affect the total earning of companies. It is worth mentioning here that empirical studies conducted by Ganslandt and Maskus (2003, 2004), Kanavos and Costa-Front (2005), on parallel trade, the survey report by the National Economic Research Associates (NERA 1999) and the famous verdict by the European Court of Justice for Merck versus Prime crown and Merck versus Stephar cases[6] also indicate the wide spread prevalence of parallel trade among European Union nations. However, in spite of having such incidences of parallel trade, companies have not withdrawn the supply of medicines to EU nations even though companies are not happy about the incidence and want to introduce quota system (McConaghie 2002).

Based upon insights from the primary survey, we next attempt to introduce parallel trade in our model. In particular, we try to understand how the relative market sizes can make an impact on the availability of the drug even in the presence of parallel trade.

To this end, we proceed sequentially by first considering two distributors, one serving the market of the developed nation and the other that of the developing nation, but without the opportunity of engaging themselves in parallel trade. We next bring in the opportunity of parallel trade and examine the strategic moves of the manufacturer under such a scenario.

7.5.2 Case1: No Opportunity for Parallel Trade

Following what is observed in reality, let us assume that the manufacturer "F" instead of selling the product by itself sells it through independent distributors A and B for M_d and M_{dl} respectively. When distributors are incorporated in the model two sets of prices prevail in the market viz., the wholesale prices at which distributor purchases the medicine from the manufacturer and the retail prices which the final consumers pay. In the first stage, the manufacturer sets a wholesale price P_B^W for distributor B and P_A^W for distributor A. Because of a similar demand structure, we can either model the problem of distributor A or, distributor B. Let us take the case of B. The distributor's problem is then

$$\text{Max } \Pi^B = \left(P^{dl} - P_B^W\right) D\left(P^{dl}\right) \tag{7.16}$$

$$= \left(a_2 - q^{dl} - P_B^W\right) q^{dl} \tag{7.17}$$

[6] The references relate to cases to those of ECJ. See Case C −187/80 *Merck & Co. Inc.* versus *Stephar B.V. and Petrus Stephanus Exler* and Joined case C-267-268/95 *Merck and Co. Inc. and others* versus *Princecrown Limited and others.*

where q^{dl} is the quantity the distributor sells in the market of M_{dl}, p^{dl} is the retail price for the product in country M_{dl} and P_B^W is the wholesale price at which the distributor purchases the product from the manufacturer. The distributor treats P_B^W as his marginal cost and tries to maximize its profit.

From the F.O.C. we get

$$q^{dl} = \frac{a_2 - P_B^W}{2},\ p^{dl} = \frac{a_2 + P_B^W}{2} \text{ and } \Pi^B = \left(\frac{a_2 - P_B^W}{2}\right)^2 \tag{7.18}$$

7.5.2.1 Manufacturer's Problem

Let Π_M^B be the profit the manufacturer earns by selling its product to distributor B in country M_{dl}.

$$\therefore \Pi_M^B = (p_B^W - c)\left(\frac{a_2 - P_B^W}{2}\right) \tag{7.19}$$

We assume that $a_2 > P_B^W > c$ for the manufacturer to earn profit

The manufacturer selects p_B^W to maximize its profit. From the F.O.C. we therefore get

$$p_B^W = \frac{a_2 + c}{2} \tag{7.20}$$

Substituting this value in (7.18) for retail price and the equilibrium quantity of medicine, we get

$$q^{dl} = \frac{a_2 - c}{4} \text{ and } p^{dl} = \frac{3a_2 + c}{4} \tag{7.21}$$

The profit that the manufacturer and the distributor B earn in country M_{dl} is $\frac{(a_2-c)^2}{8}$ and $\frac{(a_2-c)^2}{16}$ respectively.

Due to having identical demand structures, we can similarly argue that the profit from the market M_d for the manufacturer and the distributor will be $\frac{(a_1-c)^2}{8}$ and $\frac{(a_1-c)^2}{16}$ respectively.

Therefore the total profit the manufacturer earns by serving both the market is

$$\prod_M = \frac{(a_2 - c)^2}{8} + \frac{(a_1 - c)^2}{8} \tag{7.22}$$

Remark 1. It is easy to check that $\left[\frac{(a_2-c)^2}{8}+\frac{(a_2-c)^2}{16}\right]<\left[\frac{(a_2-c)^2}{4}\right]$ or in other words the total profit that is earned by the manufacturer and the distributor in country M_{dl} is less than the profit that the manufacturer could earn by selling the product itself.

Further the price that the consumer pays in the presence of distributors i.e. $\frac{3a_2+c}{4}>\frac{a_2+c}{2}$ ($\equiv$ price that the consumer pays when the manufacturer itself sells the commodity) or in other words the consumer also ends up paying higher price for the product. Differences in the result arise because under the distributorship there are two forms of discrimination: one due to the markup set by the manufacturer and the other due to the distributor. The net outcome is a rise in the final price of the product for the consumer over and the above the monopoly price and a fall in the quantity of the good demanded. There is thus a welfare loss to the society.

7.5.3 *Existence of Parallel Trade*

From the above exercise, it is obvious that differences in the prices of the medicine that prevail at the retail level lead to opportunities for parallel trade. In the presence of parallel trade, the manufacturer cannot enforce differential pricing and earn monopoly profit from the markets of M_d and M_{dl}. The re-selling of the cheap product from developing countries in the market of developed nations reduces its profit in the developed nation. Under such circumstances the manufacturer is left with three strategic options (1) to deter parallel trade by charging the lower price of the developing country in the developed nation or as well (2) to accommodate a certain volume of parallel trade by the trader or (3) to confine its operation in the developed country. However, it can be proved that the manufacturer will always earn higher profit by accommodating parallel trade then by deterring it through charging the lower uniform price of developing nations (see Appendix A). The manufacturer is then left with the last two strategic options. In the next section, we have compared pay-offs for the manufacturer under these two strategic options.

7.5.3.1 Optimal Strategy for the Manufacturer

Let us assume that due to differences in the price of the medicine between the developing and the developed countries at the retail level, it is profitable for distributor B to engage in parallel trade. The one-way trade from the developing to the developed country arises in this model due to retail price difference of the medicine between countries. As documented by Maskus and Chen (2002), Danzon and Towse (2003) and Bale (1998) the one way trade between the country may arise due to various economic and legal factors such as smallness in the size of the market of the developing country (which we have explicitly considered in our model), product asymmetry, differences in legal treatment for parallel trade etc.

Without parallel trade the demand function that distributor A faces in the developed country M_d is $p^d = (a_1 - q^d)$

With parallel trade the demand function is

$$P^d = (a_1 - q^d - q^d_B) \tag{7.23}$$

Where q^d_B= quantity the distributor B sells in M_d or the volume of parallel trade.

Therefore, the profit functions that the distributors A and B face for M_d are as follows:

$$\Pi^{M_d}_A = \{a_1 - (q^d + q^d_B) - P^W_A\}q^d \tag{7.24}$$

$$\Pi^{M_d}_B = \{a_1 - (q^d + q^d_B)\}q^d_B - P^W_B q^d_B \tag{7.25}$$

We also assume that distributors compete in *Cournot fashion* in M_d and maximize their profits.

Therefore, F.O.C. requires $\frac{\partial \Pi^{M_d}_A}{\partial q^d} = \frac{\partial \Pi^{M_d}_B}{\partial q^d_B} = 0$

Now,

$$\frac{\partial \Pi^{M_d}_A}{\partial q^d} = 0 \Rightarrow a_1 - 2q^d - q^d_B - P^W_A = 0 \tag{7.26}$$

and

$$\frac{\partial \Pi^{M_d}_B}{\partial q^d_B} = 0 \Rightarrow a_1 - q^d - 2q^d_B - P^W_B = 0 \tag{7.27}$$

Solving (7.26) and (7.27) the equilibrium quantities q^d_B and q^d are as follows:

$$q^d_B = \frac{a_1 + P^W_A - 2P^W_B}{3}, \; q^d = \frac{a_1 + P^W_B - 2P^W_A}{3}$$

With the following equilibrium quantities (in the presence of parallel trade), the manufacturer faces the following profit function Π^M_P

$$\begin{aligned} \therefore \Pi^M_P &= P^W_B q^d_B + P^W_B q^{dl} + P^W_A q^d - c\left(q^d_B + q^{dl} + q^d\right) \\ &= P^W_B \frac{a_1 + P^W_A - 2P^W_B}{3} + P^W_B \frac{a_2 - P^W_B}{2} + P^W_A \frac{a_1 + P^W_B - 2P^W_A}{3} \\ &- c\left\{\frac{a_1 + P^W_A - 2P^W_B}{3} + \frac{a_2 - P^W_B}{2} + \frac{a_1 + P^W_B - 2P^W_A}{3}\right\} \end{aligned} \tag{7.28}$$

The manufacturer maximizes Π_P^M with respect to P_B^W and P_A^W.

$$\therefore \frac{\partial \Pi_P^M}{\partial P_B^W} = \frac{a_2}{2} - P_B^W + \frac{a_1}{2} + \frac{P_A^W}{3} - \frac{4}{3}P_B^W + \frac{1}{3}P_A^W + \frac{c}{2} + \frac{2}{3}c - \frac{c}{3} = 0 \tag{7.29}$$

and

$$\frac{\partial \Pi_P^M}{\partial P_A^W} = \frac{a_1}{3} + 2\frac{P_B^W}{3} - \frac{4}{3}P_A^W + \frac{1}{3}P_A^W + \frac{2}{3}c - \frac{c}{3} = 0 \tag{7.30}$$

Simplifying the terms in (7.29) and (7.30) we get the following expressions.

$$\frac{\partial \Pi_P^M}{\partial P_B^W} = 3a_2 + 2a_1 - 14P_B^W + 4P_A^W + 5c = 0 \tag{7.31}$$

$$\frac{\partial \Pi_P^M}{\partial P_A^W} = 2P_B^W + a_1 - 4P_A^W + c = 0 \tag{7.32}$$

Substituting the value of P_A^W from (7.32) in (7.31) and solving for equilibrium P_B^W & P_A^W we get

$$P_B^W = \frac{a_2 + 2c + a_1}{4} \tag{7.33}$$

$$P_A^W = \frac{a_2 + 4c + 3a_1}{8}$$

Substituting the values for p_A^W and p_B^W in expression (7.31) and (7.32) we get:

$$q^d = \frac{a_1 - c}{6}, q^{dl} = \frac{3a_2 - a_1 - 2c}{8}, q_B^d = \frac{7a_1 - 3a_2 - 4c}{24} \tag{7.34}$$

It is interesting to note that q_B^d, the volume of parallel trade, is a decreasing function of a_2 and c and the increasing function of a_1. In other words, a rise in the willingness to pay for the medicine by the consumers in the developing country or a rise the cost of production reduces the volume of parallel trade. Alternatively, if the consumer in the developed country pays high for the medicine, it increases the volume of parallel trade from the developing to the developed country. Also note that the volume of medicine supplied in the developing country, q^{dl}, is a falling function of a_1 and c and rising function of a_2. At, $a_2 = \frac{a_1+2c}{3}$ the quantity of medicine sold by the distributor in the developing country is zero.

Thus in the presence of a huge income differential between the developed and the developing nation, the emergence of parallel trade may substantially reduce the availability of medicine for consumers of the developing country.

The retail prices that prevail in the developed and the developing country in the presence of parallel trade are

$$p_p^d = a_1 - \frac{a_1 - c}{6} - \frac{7a_1 - 3a_2 - 4c}{24} = \frac{13a_1 + 3a_2 + 8c}{24} \tag{7.35}$$

$$p_p^{dl} = a_2 - \frac{3a_2 - a_1 - 2c}{8} = \frac{5a_2 + a_1 + 2c}{8} \tag{7.36}$$

Finally, the profit that the manufacturer earns by accommodating parallel trade is

$$\begin{aligned}\Pi_P^M =& \left(\frac{a_1 - c}{6}\right)\left(\frac{a_2 + 4c + 3a_1}{2}\right) + \left(\frac{3a_2 - a_1 - 2c}{8}\right)\left(\frac{a_2 + 2c + a_1}{2}\right) \\ &+ \left(\frac{7a_1 - 3a_2 - 4c}{24}\right)\left(\frac{a_2 + 2c + a_1}{2}\right) \\ &- c\left\{\frac{a_1 - c}{6} + \frac{3a_2 - a_1 - 2c}{8} + \frac{7a_1 - 3a_2 - 4c}{24}\right\}\end{aligned} \tag{7.37}$$

Further simplification of the above terms results in the following expression

$$\Pi_P^M = \left(\frac{a_1 - c}{6}\right)\left(\frac{3a_1 + a_2 - 4c}{8}\right) + \left(\frac{a_1 + a_2 - 2c}{4}\right)\left(\frac{3a_2 + 2a_1 - 5c}{12}\right) \tag{7.38}$$

In the presence of parallel trade, multinational firms can limit its operation in the market of the developed country when it earns higher profit by doing so. Therefore, we need to examine the condition under which the multinational firm earns higher profit by shifting its production base to the developing country and accommodating parallel trade instead of just confining its operation in the developed country. Comparison of profits yields the following proposition.

Proposition 3. *If $\sqrt{3}a_2 > a_1 > 2c$, the manufacturer earns higher profit by shifting its production base in the developing country even in the presence of parallel trade.*

Proof. We know that

$$\Pi_P^M = \left(\frac{a_1 - c}{6}\right)\left(\frac{3a_1 + a_2 - 4c}{8}\right) + \left(\frac{a_1 + a_2 - 2c}{4}\right)\left(\frac{3a_2 + 2a_1 - 5c}{12}\right)$$

is the profit that the manufacturer earns from M_{dl} and M_d, in the presence of parallel trade. Let $\Pi_M^{M_d}$ be the profit the manufacturer earns by confining its operation in the developed country M_d.

Now

$$\Pi_M^{M_d} = \frac{(a_1 - c_m)^2}{8} \text{ \{compare with equation (6.22)\}} \tag{7.39}$$

If $\Pi_P^M > \Pi_M^{M_d}$, the manufacturer earns higher profit by shifting its production base in the developing country even in the presence of parallel trade.

Cross-multiplying the terms of Π_P^M & $\Pi_M^{M_d}$ we get the following inequalities

$$5a_1^2 + 6a_1a_2 - 12a_1c - 12a_2c + 14c^2 + 3a_2^2 > 6a_1^2 - 12a_1c_m + 6c_m^2 \tag{7.40}$$

$$\Rightarrow 5a_1^2 + 6a_1(a_2 - c) - 12c(a_2 - c) + 2c^2 + 3a_2^2 - 6a_1c > 6a_1^2 - 12a_1c_m + 6c_m^2$$

$$\Rightarrow 6(a_1 - 2c)(a_2 - c) + 2c^2 + 3a_2^2 - a_1^2 - 6a_1c > - 12a_1c_m + 6c_m^2$$

$$\Rightarrow 6(a_1 - 2c)(a_2 - c) + 2c^2 + \left(\sqrt{3}a_2\right)^2 - a_1^2 + 6c_m(a_1 - c_m) + 6a_1(c_m - c) > 0$$

$$\Rightarrow [6(a_1 - 2c)(a_2 + c)] + \left(\sqrt{3}a_2 + a_1\right)\left(\sqrt{3}a_2 - a_1\right) + 6c_m(a_1 - c_m) + 6a_1(c_m - c) + 2c^2 > 0 \tag{7.41}$$

But $a_2 > c$,$a_1 > c_m$ and $c_m > c$.

$\therefore \sqrt{3}a_2 > a_1 > 2c$ provides a sufficient condition for allowing parallel trade *Q.E.D.*

Remark 2. We have proved that (see Proposition 3) in the presence of parallel trade the developing country can still be an attractive location for multinational companies to shift their production base. However, for that to materialize the relative market size of the developing country (measured in terms ofa_2) should be more than half the size of the developed nation. The economic intuition behind the proposition is simple. When the relative market size of the developing country is large, then the manufacturer can compensate for the loss in the revenue in the developed country by earning higher from the developing country. It turns out that a small developing country should not allow parallel exports of the drug if it wants to ensure a foreign manufacturer to establish its production plant there; one alternative is to legally ban parallel exports of drugs.

In this context, it will be an interesting and worthwhile exercise to compare the profit that a manufacturer earns in the presence of parallel trade with the profit it earns when there is no parallel trade from the developing to the developed country. Comparing the profit given by (7.39) and (7.22) we arrive at the following proposition:

Proposition 4. *If $a_2 > \frac{1}{3}a_1$ and the cost of production is moderately low, the profit that the manufacturer earns by accommodating parallel trade is higher than the profit it earns when there is no parallel trade.*

Proof. We know that

$$\Pi_P^M = (\frac{a_1 - c}{6})(\frac{3a_1 + a_2 - 4c}{8}) + (\frac{a_1 + a_2 - 2c}{4})(\frac{3a_2 + 2a_1 - 5c}{12})$$

and $\prod_M = \frac{(a_2-c)^2}{8} + \frac{(a_1-c)^2}{8}$

Cross-multiplying the terms of Π_P^M & $\Pi_M$we get the following expressions $5a_1^2 + 6a_1a_2 - 12a_1c - 12a_2c + 14c^2 + 3a_2^2$ and $6a_1^2 - 12a_1c + 6a_2^2 - 12a_2c + 12c^2$

$$\therefore \Pi_P^M > \Pi_M \Rightarrow$$

$$5a_1^2 + 6a_1a_2 - 12a_1c - 12a_2c + 14c^2 + 3a_2^2 > 6a_1^2 - 12a_1c + 6a_2^2 - 12a_2c + 12c^2 \tag{7.42}$$

$$\Rightarrow a_1(3a_2 - a_1) + 3a_2(a_1 - a_2) + 2c^2 > 0 \tag{7.43}$$

Now, $a_1 > a_2$ therefore a sufficient condition for expression (A.1) to hold true is $a_2 > \frac{1}{3}a_1$ *Q.E.D.*

Remark 3. The economic intuition behind the proposition is simple. Keeping in view real-life situations, we have assumed that the manufacturer, instead of selling the product directly, sells it through distributors by charging different wholesale prices. It is widely known in economic literature that in the presence of distributors the problem of 'double-monopoly distortion' (see, Oz shy 1995) arises. However, the manufacturer can mitigate the problem of 'double-monopoly distortion' if it can introduce competition at the retail level. Because of competition from distributor *B*, distributor *A* sells the medicine at a price lower than that of the developed country when it had a monopoly market. This, therefore, brings prices and quantities of the medicine sold in the developed country close to the profit maximizing level of the manufacturer when he was also the sole seller of the product. In other words because of competition from distributor *B* the problem of 'double-monopoly distortion' is eliminated to an extent in developed nations. In addition, due to the presence of parallel trade, the manufacturer while maximizing profits, sets a high price for distributor *B* and a low price for distributor *A*. The quantity that is sold by distributor *B* also increases with parallel trade. When the relative market size of the developing country is large (condition provided in Proposition 4), the manufacturer can charge a higher wholesale price from distributor *B* (see Eq. 7.35). Therefore, this enables the manufacturer to earn even higher revenue from distributor *B* and in turn allows the manufacturer to earn higher profit.

7.6 Concluding Remarks and Direction for Further Research

In this paper, we have theoretically examined two important issues; first, the problem of non-availability of a patented drug in developing countries due to product patent has been examined by introducing the option of price discrimination strategy by an MNC. It is proved that, if an MNC, can discriminate the price for its product across the globe the problem of non-availability of the drug is reduced. Further, if local cost of production is sufficiently low, a developing country can be an attractive location for an MNC to shift its production base. The problem of the non-availability of the drug then gets further reduced. It can also be argued that after relocating its production plant in the developing country, an MNC can charge lower price and can supply drugs to other poor countries as well where the level of demand is even lower (at each price level) due to low purchasing power. This in turn can generate additional employment opportunities in the developing country where the production facility is located. Consequently, the welfare level in the country concerned will increase.

Second, we have examined the problem of parallel trade by incorporating distributors explicitly in the model. From the results of the model, it can be concluded that if the relative market size of the developing country is sufficiently large, then even in the presence of parallel trade, an MNC can supply a drug at a lower price in the developing country. Also by accommodating parallel trade, a firm can earn higher profit than operating only in the developed country market. This is because in the presence of parallel-trade the manufacturer can vertically limit the operation of distributors by charging two different sets of wholesale prices.

This paper also throws light on the pros and cons of recognizing product patent in a developing country. In the absence of product patent, an MNC that invents a new drug may not come and establish its production unit in a developing country that has high imitative and reverse-engineering capability. Our survey findings in this regard reveal that imitation is not an easy exercise. However, imitation is comparatively easier (though not instantaneous) if the foreign firm brings the technological know-how to the developing country. This may happen due to greater spill-over effect, information leakage and attrition among the technical personnel. In other words, just on the basis of knowledge that is made available in the public domain by an MNC due to patent disclosure, it is rather difficult to come up with an imitation. The large number of technological collaboration that has been seen to take place in India after recognition of product patent is probably a testimony to this fact.

A small developing country on the other hand, with cheaper resources can attract foreign direct investment and can benefit from the product patent regime only if it can limit parallel trade. Otherwise, a mere recognition of product patent may not ensure access to patented medicines for its own consumers. It can also be inferred from our results that, because of parallel trade, the retail price of the medicine in the developing country increases. Therefore, even though the problem of availability of drug might not arise for a large developing country, people from the low-income strata might be deprived of a patented medicine. If the objective of the government is to maximize access to a medicine then limiting parallel trade would be beneficial.

It should be kept in mind that recognition of product patent will create a monopoly market structure for a newly invented product and, in the process, the consumer may suffer in terms of paying high prices for the medicines. If, on the other hand, imitation is allowed and the developing country concerned has strong capacity in imitation, then competition amongst domestic firms may bring down the prices of medicines during the course of time.

Thus, the analysis highlights that the impact of product patent are not uniform across all developing countries. It depends upon the purchasing power of its consumer, size of the market, imitative capacity of the country and other such factors.

7.6.1 Directions for Further Research

There are a few possible theoretical extensions to this model. First, in our analysis we have considered the case of a single product market. However, pharmaceutical companies produce multiple products. One can thus consider a multiple product case and model how the production decision of a firm is different for the decision to sell for different varieties of medicine. One can also model how parallel trade affects such decisions. Second, in our model, we have considered only the production decision of the MNC at the cost of R&D. An interesting extension would be to incorporate R&D in our model and examine R&D outsourcing decisions of firms and how such decisions are affected by parallel trade.

The model is also useful for undertaking empirical research. One can generate data to test how MNCs sell different types of drugs in different countries. How differences in relative market sizes compel MNCs to sell drugs only in some developed countries. A qualitative study based on case studies and interview data analysis would generate greater theoretical and empirical insights. However, such an analysis is beyond the scope of the present research work.

Appendix A

Deterring Parallel Trade

MNCs can also counter parallel trade by strategically pricing its product. In fact, the potential for parallel trade emerges when there is a large price differential for the medicine between the two markets. The manufacturer can however, "choke off" the potential for parallel trade by charging a price in a way such that the lower uniform price of the developing country prevails in the developed market. The manufacturer then sets p_A^W in such a way that the retail price of the medicine are the same in the market of M_{dl} and M_d or in other words $p^B = p^A$. With $p^B = p^A$ however the incentive for parallel trade is curbed. To set the same retail price for both the countries $p^A = \frac{a_1 + P_A^W}{2}$ should be equal to $\frac{3a_2 + c}{4}$ or in other word

$$\frac{a_1 + P_A^W}{2} = \frac{3a_2 + c}{4} \tag{A.1}$$

$$\Rightarrow P_A^W = \frac{3a_2 + c - 2a_1}{2} \tag{A.2}$$

At price, $P_A^W = \frac{3a_2 + c - 2a_1}{2}$ the retail price for the medicine in country M_d is $\frac{3a_2+c}{4}$ and there is no scope for parallel trade. The quantity that is demanded

$$q^A = \frac{4a_1 - 3a_2 - c}{4} \tag{A.3}$$

By charging the low price of the developing country, the profit that the manufacturer earns from the country M_d

$$\Pi_{Md} = \frac{(3a_2 - c - 2a_1)(4a_1 - 3a_2 - c)}{8} \tag{A.4}$$

Let Π_U^M be the total profit the manufacturer earns (from the developed and the developing market) by charging the lower uniform price of the developing country in the developed world. Therefore

$$\Pi_U^M = \left[\Pi_{Md} = \left\{ \frac{(3a_2 - c - 2a_1)(4a_1 - 3a_2 - c)}{8} \right\} + \Pi_M^{M_{dl}} = \frac{(a_2 - c)^2}{8} \right] \tag{A.5}$$

If $\Pi_P^M > \Pi_U^M$, the manufacturer earns higher profit by accommodating parallel trade than by deterring it by charging the lower uniform price of M_{dl}.

Cross-multiplying and simplifying the terms of Π_P^M and Π_U^M we get the following expressions $5a_1^2 + 6a_1a_2 - 12a_1c - 12a_2c + 14c^2 + 3a_2^2$ and $108a_1a_2 - 48a_1^2 - 12a_1c - 12a_2c + 12c^2 - 48a_2^2$

$$\therefore \Pi_P^M - \Pi_U^M = 53a_1^2 + 51a_2^2 + 8c^2 - 102a_1a_2 \tag{A.6}$$

For $\Pi_P^M > \Pi_U^M$, we need to show that

$$\begin{aligned} &53a_1^2 + 51a_2^2 + 8c^2 > 102a_1a_2 \\ &\Rightarrow 53a_1^2 + 51a_2^2 - 102a_1a_2 + 8c^2 > 0 \\ &\Rightarrow 2a_1^2 + 8c^2 + (\sqrt{51}a_1 - \sqrt{51}a_1)^2 > 0 \end{aligned} \tag{A.7}$$

which is always true. From the above result, we therefore conclude that *for all values of* a_1 *and* a_2 *the strategy of accommodating parallel trade dominates the strategy of deterring parallel trade.*

Table A.1 Comparison of retail prices of selected generic products across countries in the year 2002–2003 (prices converted into Indian rupees, conversion rate of exchange considered 1USD = Rs 45.50,1 GBP = Rs 83.51 1 PAK Rs = Rs .84 and 1 Indonesian Rp = Rs .005)

Drug dosage and pack	Prices in India (Rs)	Prices in Pakistan (Rs)	Prices in Indonesia (Rs)	Prices in UK (Rs)	Prices in US (Rs)
Ciproflaxin HCL 500 mg 10s tabs	29	423	393	1,185.7	2,352.35
Norflaxin 400 mg 10s tabs	21	168	130.63	304.78	1,843.66
Anti-ulcerant					
Rantidine 150 mg 10s tabs	6.2	74.09	178.35	247.16	863.59
Omeprazole 30 mg 10s tabs	23	578	290	870.91	2,047.5
Cardiovascular					
Atenolol 50 mg 10s tabs	7.5	71.82	119.7	NA	753.94
Simvastatin 10 mg 10s tabs	35	283.1	187	537.74	1,149.79
Amlodipine Besylate 5 mg 10s tabs	7.8	200.3	78.42	338.28	660.12
Anti-viral fungal					
Zidovudine 100 mg 10s tabs	77	313.5	331.57	996.16	895.5
Anti-histamine					
Cetirizine 10 mg 10s tabs	6	35.71	57.5	262.19	927.29
Anti-anxiolotics/psychotics					
Alpramazoo 0.5 mg 10s tabs	7	161	31.05	NA	446.81
Anti Cancer					
Boposide 100 mg 10s tabs	190	554.7	242.9	1,217.43	6,210.3
Antiasthmatic					
Fluticasone 50 mcg inhaler	210	NA	782.65	1,628.25	NA
Urology					
Sildenafil Citrate 50 mg 4s tabs	48	NA	135.69	1,614.89	1,744.93

Source: Centre for Trade and Development (CENTAD) study presented in the workshop "Trade and Barrier to Access to Medicines in Hyderabad, 9–12 October 2007." Also available at http://population.developmentgateway.org/uploads/media/population/IPRs_and_Indian_Pharmaceuticals.doc

Chapter 8
Conclusions and Policy Suggestions

8.1 Overview of the Study

The Indian pharmaceutical industry is at the crossroads due to the recognition of the product patent in the amended Patent Act of 2005 and the gradual liberalization policy of the government of India. While the recognition of product patents is a big challenge for Indian pharmaceutical companies that have hitherto relied on imitation for their growth, the liberalization of the market economy has also opened up new opportunities for Indian pharmaceutical firms. In response to policy changes and growing competition, firms started adopting new strategies like increased outlays in R&D related activities, endeavors to sell their product in the global market and investment in plant and machinery. However, the benefit from such change may not be immediate. Also, when access to resources and technology differs across firms, the process of liberalization may create winners and losers and performance differences may widen between firms.

While a number of studies have looked into various aspects of the Indian pharmaceutical industry, there are however, a limited number of studies that has examined the performance of Indian pharmaceutical firms using firm level data in the post reform period. Given the relevance of the issue, our study has filled this research gap by examining the performance of Indian pharmaceutical firms. The analysis has been conducted by utilizing the firm level data that is provided by the CMIE prowess database. Performance of firms has been analyzed by examining their productivity and profitability.

The productivity of a firm is defined as the output produced per unit of the inputs used. An important component of the productivity of the firms is its efficiency. A fundamental criterion for firms to remain competitive and face current challenges is to use its resources for production most efficiently. In order to estimate the efficiency of firms, we have constructed a frontier by taking into account the input and the output set of the best performing firms in the sample and examined how best the firms are managing their inputs vis-à-vis firms that produce the same level of output. Alternatively, we have also examined whether a firm is producing

M. Mazumdar, *Performance of Pharmaceutical Companies in India*,
Contributions to Economics, DOI 10.1007/978-3-7908-2876-4_8,

the maximum possible output that is achievable with the inputs that they are employing compared to firms that employ a similar level of inputs. Firms that lie below the frontier are inefficient firms and firms that lie on the frontier are efficient firms. The output and the input distance of firms from the frontier measures the extent of output and input efficiency of a firm. In a sense in efficiency analysis, we have therefore analyzed how best firms are performing compared to other firms in the sample in a relative sense. While measuring the efficiency of firms, we have also applied a model that has enabled us to estimate the input specific efficiencies for inputs that a firm employs and also the output efficiency of the firms. There are a limited number of studies that have examined both the output and the input efficiency of the firms. In this respect, the findings from the current study are a new contribution to the literature. After estimating the efficiency of firms, we have regressed the efficiency scores on a set of firm specific variables like its size, strategies that they are adopting and others. The database that we have used to examine the determinants of the efficiency of the firms allows us to consider a number of firm specific variables that previous studies have not covered.

Besides, we have also classified firms in different groups based on the strategies that they are adopting and compared the efficiency of the firms at two levels viz., first, with respect to their own group members by constructing a local frontier and second by considering all firms in the sample by constructing a global frontier. Also known as the Meta-frontier approach to efficiency analysis in literature, we have analyzed the following questions by applying such techniques viz., who are the most efficient firms in the industry? To which strategic group do they belong? and how do they influence the efficiency of other firms within a group? Groups have been formed based on the following criterion. We have assumed that firms from the same group face similar production opportunities, whereas firms from diverse groups have diverse characteristics and opportunities. We have argued that differences in production opportunities amongst firms may arise due to R&D related spending, due to export earning and also due to differences in product varieties produced by firms. A cross comparison of the efficiency of firms at two different levels adds robustness to the analysis and gives a clear direction to correct efficiency at various levels. If, on an average, firms from a group suffer from low levels of efficiency mainly because the group as a whole is inefficient, then policies should be directed to bridge the gap between local and global frontiers by removing constraints from which firms from a group suffer. If, on the other hand, the low level of efficiency arises because, on an average, distances of firms are high from both the group specific local as well as global frontiers, it implies that, on a whole, the efficiency of firms from a group are also low and hence there are only few efficient firms from that group. One can then identify the characteristic features of group specific efficient firms and locate the sources of such differences. By classifying firms into various strategic groups, this study therefore adds a new dimension to the applied empirical work relating to the Meta-Frontier analysis, which the earlier applications have not considered.

After examining the efficiency of firms, we have also analyzed how far the productivity changes of a firm are driven by the efficiency of firms and the shift in the production frontier for the sector or technical change. While estimating the productivity of the firms, we have also constructed frontiers at different points in time. The frontier approach to productivity analysis locates how far the productivity of a firm arises due to its efficiency and also due to an outward shift in the production frontier or technological progress. Additionally, like the meta-frontier approach to efficiency analysis here also we have classified firms into two groups. The first one is based on R&D related expenditure and the second one is on export earning. This has enabled us to check whether firms with R&D related expenditure have experienced an outward shift in their production frontier for a greater number of times compared to firms without any R&D related outlays. Similarly, whether the shift in the production frontier for firms selling their product in the international market is higher compared to firms that sell their product only in the domestic market have also been checked and analyzed. Finally, using an appropriate econometric model, we have also estimated the determinants of the technical shift of the sector.

Apart from calculating the productivity and efficiency of firms, we have also examined the profitability of firms. It is of paramount importance for firms to retain profitability in the post reform scenario in order to carry out its investment in R&D related activities or to invest in new plants and machinery. Thus, using firm level data and appropriate panel data econometric techniques, we have analyzed the effectiveness of strategies of the firm to determine the profit that a firm earns. Apart from strategies, we have also identified a number of firm specific variables that may also determine the profitability of the firms.

Finally, in the post product scenario an important concern arises regarding the problem of the availability of patented drugs. Because Indian firms with their age long capacity in imitation could easily 'reverse-engineer' the patented product of foreign firms, the availability of drugs was not a serious problem for consumers of India. But with product patents in force, neither Indian firms can 'reverse-engineer' the patented product of foreign firms, nor do Indian firms have the capacity to carry out product R&D and compete with innovative foreign companies in product innovation. Thus, in the post product-patent regime, whether foreign firms will supply their innovative drugs is an important and controversial question. In this study, we have also analyzed this problem. Since product patents are of recent origin, and there is a lack of availability of adequate empirical data to assess this *'problem of availability of patented drugs'* empirically we have addressed this issue theoretically.

8.2 Major Findings

The growth and development of the Indian pharmaceutical industry challenge the conventional IPR wisdom that upheld the view to recognize 'product patents' for a knowledge intensive sector like the pharmaceutical sector. It clearly brings out the fact that, in the absence of technology, the adherence for such policies can be detrimental for the growth of the industry. On the other hand, we noticed that certain supportive policies of the government like the recognition of only process patents and protection from foreign competition played a pivotal role for the development of this sector. We also noticed that positive externalities from the public sector and the research units enabled firms to gain competency in process engineering and maintain a competitive edge in the international market.

From the review of important policies, we however, noticed a shift in public policies from protection to competition. Analysis of the aggregate data at the industry level also revealed that, in recent years, the industry has persistently grown at a rate of about 16 %. We also noticed that in spite of high competition, the pharmaceutical industry is one of the most profitable industries. We traced the largeness in the size of the firm, R&D, marketing and export intensity as the main sources for better performance of firms.

After analyzing general trends on various aggregates of the Indian pharmaceutical industry, we have undertaken an in-depth analysis on the performance of firms. We have analyzed efficiency, productivity and profitability by using appropriate mathematical and econometric techniques. The empirical analysis reveals many interesting facts. Major findings from the analysis are presented briefly herein.

8.2.1 Major Findings from the Output and the Input Efficiency of Firms

The efficiency analysis undertaken for Indian pharmaceutical firms reveals that, over the years, on an average the output efficiency of Indian pharmaceutical firms are declining over the years. We have argued (and also shown by undertaking a productivity analysis in Chap. 5) that such decline is an outcome of an outward shift of the production frontier leading to a rise in the distance of firms that lie below the frontier. Such shift in the frontier for the sector is possible either due to increased competition or due to new investment in plant and machinery, or due to increased process and product innovation or it might be an outcome of the combination of all three factors.

Our analysis also reveals that among the inputs used by firms, labor and raw material are most efficiently used, whereas capital, power, and fuel show some sign of inefficiency in its use. We have argued that underutilization of capital stock and the use of coal-based technology by a large number of small firms leads to capital and power and fuel inefficiency. An interesting finding from our analysis is that even though firm are, on an average, using their inputs efficiently, there has been a persistent fall in the output efficiency of firms. Such circumstances arise because a large proportion of firms lie in the increasing returns to scale (IRS) zone of the production possibility set. Generally, firms that have low scale of operation and limited market reach lie in the IRS zone of the production frontier. Thus lower price realization coupled with the presence of economies of scale in production has resulted in a low level of efficiency for the sector.

A look into the determinants of efficiency reveals that the recent spurt in R&D activity is beneficial to increase the efficiency of firms only when it is targeted for high value products and done in a large scale. In other words, instead of spending 3–4 % of their revenue on R&D related outlays, firms should spend around tento 15 % of their revenue in R&D related output. However, in contrast to popular belief, the efficiency of firms falls with the rise in the export intensity of firms. It is also interesting to note that firms that produce both bulk drugs and formulations and are integrated vertically with the raw-material industry are more efficient compared to firms that produce only bulk drugs and formulations. As expected, the use of imported raw material and imported capital improves the efficiency of firms.

8.2.2 Major Findings from the Group-Wise Comparison of the Efficiency of Firms

In the next step, we have estimated and compared the efficiency of firms at two levels viz., at the group level and also at the global level. A group wise analysis of the efficiency of firms reveals that the benefit from doing R&D is marginal. We calculated by comparing the production possibility ratio (PPR) that, on average, firms without any R&D investment could gain an additional benefit of only 8 % (over the years) in their efficiency by investing in R&D.

We next considered firms that sell their product in the international and domestic market. Comparing the efficiency scores for firms that sell their product only in the domestic market with firms that also sell their product in the international market, we notice that firms that sell their product in the international market have higher efficiency scores. We computed that inefficient firms that target only the domestic market could, on an average, gain an efficiency of around 13 % (over the years) by just selling their product in the international market.

We however, noticed that when we estimate the efficiency of firms against global frontiers, firms with higher export intensity (i.e., more than 25 %) are less efficient compared to firms with low export intensity(i.e., less than 25 %). However, when estimated against their own local frontier, this group of firms is most efficient. We argued that efficiency for firms with higher export earning might be less compared to firms with low export earning mainly because an overwhelming proportion of firms from the high export intensive group sell their products in the unregulated markets of less developed countries where there is low price realization. Second, few firms from this group that have also targeted the regulated and the semi-regulated market are the efficient ones. While the entry into such markets is difficult because of various regulatory barriers, returns are also higher. The firms that target the semi-regulated or the regulated markets are the efficient ones. By comparing the PPR of high and low exporting firms, we computed that, if firms from the high export intensive group maintain a balance between the global and domestic market, they can, on an average, gain an efficiency of around 33 %.

Lastly, by comparing the efficiency of firms across product groups, we noticed that firms producing both bulk drugs and formulations are the most efficient ones. This also implies that integrating vertically with the downstream intermediary industry reduces the cost of transaction and, hence, a higher efficiency gain is possible. The value of PPR for firms producing bulk drugs and formulations also indicates that if firms, producing only formulations or bulk drugs, re-orient their production strategies in order to produce both categories of product, a significant gain in the efficiency level can be achieved with respect to the global frontier. This can be as high as 30 % for firms producing formulations and 10–20 % for firms producing bulk drugs.

8.2.3 Major Finding from the Productivity of Firms

After analyzing the efficiency of firms, we have examined the productivity of firms. There are two main sources of the productivity growth of a firm viz., one is the change in efficiency and the other is the shift in the production frontier or technical change. The productivity analysis of Indian pharmaceutical firms revealed that the sector has experienced an outward shift in the production frontier a significant number of times. In other words, the process liberalization and competition has opened up new production possibilities that were unavailable previously. However, only few firms enjoy benefits of the technical change. Consequently, we notice that inefficiency of the sector has magnified whenever there is technological progress.

Just like the previous chapter where we have compared the efficiency of firms at the group level and with respect to all the firms in the sample, here also, we have compared the productivity and its components for different groups of firms. To undertake such analysis we have extended the Malmquist Productivity Index. By extending the Malmquist Productivity, we get an additional component for the productivity change of firms, which is the change in the production possibility ratio. The change in the production possibility ratio captures the catching up effect of firms with respect to its own group member and also with respect to all the firms in the sample. By measuring the productivity change at the group level, we can also capture the shift in the production frontier or technical change for a group of firms.

We noticed that both firms with R&D related outlays and firms without any R&D related outlays have experienced an outward shift in their production possibility frontier. In other words, both these groups of firms have experienced technical progress. The analysis also revealed that, compared to firms with high export intensity and firms selling their product in the domestic market, firms with low export intensity have experienced technical change a larger number of times.

By examining the characteristics of frontier firms, we find that, generally frontier firms spend on R&D on a large scale. They also use capital-intensive techniques for their production process and have also upgraded their technology by installing imported plant and machinery. We also notice that almost all the frontier firms have some technological collaboration with foreign or domestic multi-national companies either in the form of contract R&D or in contract manufacturing.

From the regression analysis undertaken to determine the technical change of the sector, we notice that the sources of technical change lies in the use of imported technology and capital-intensive techniques. The analysis also indicates that the technological progress for the sector is driven by R&D initiatives of large sized firms. Generally, large sized firms do advanced process R&D in which they have competency. This has favorably affected the technical change for the sector. However, our study also indicates that the use of importing raw material regresses technology. We have argued that the root cause for such technological regress lies in the import of low quality bulk drugs from China. We here reiterate that India already has an excellent raw material bulk drug industry. Firms should therefore continue to purchase their raw material from the domestic market. Increased demand in the domestic market will further propel growth in the domestic bulk drug industry and benefit firms by strengthening their presence in the global market. We also notice that the liberalization policy of the government and the changes in regulation have favorably affected the technical change for the sector. However, the size of the firm or increased export earning has no effect on the technical change for the sector.

8.2.4 Major Findings from the Profitability Analysis of Indian Pharmaceutical Firms

Finally, we have also identified the determinants of the profitability of firms by using appropriate panel data models. In our regression analysis we have considered industry specific variables, certain firm specific variables and also few important strategic variables of firms. Our study indicates that changes in the structure of the industry do not favorably create any entry barrier for firms to insulate its profit earning from incumbents. In other words, new firms can always enter the market and drive down the profit of incumbents at competitive levels. This however, does not happen in the Indian pharmaceutical sector. Therefore, firms can consistently earn high profit mainly because of firm specific factors. As expected, among firm specific factors, we noticed that the rise in the size of firms increases the profitability of firms. We also noticed that firms that are more efficient are also more profitable.

We noticed that spending more on marketing and R&D related outlays reduces the profitability of firms. However, our analysis reveals that the joint effort of marketing and R&D is an effective strategy of firms to earn high profit. It indicates that firms can get sufficient returns from R&D and earn high profit only if they have a vast marketing network. It also indicates that if firms, instead of marketing their existing products, market the newly invented products they can earn higher profit. A positive relation with the Herfindahl index for diversification and the profitability of firms implies that 'specialized firms' that have niche products under their command are more profitable. We also noticed that the use of imported raw material and capital improves the profitability of firms.

8.2.5 Findings from the Theoretical Analysis of the Problem of Availability of Patented Drugs

Lastly, we have also theoretically addressed the problem of availability of patented drugs that may arise due to product patents. The main findings from the analysis are as follows. First, it is proved that if an innovative foreign company can discriminate the price for its product across the globe the problem of non-availability of the drug is reduced. Further, if local cost of production is sufficiently low, a developing country can be an attractive location for the foreign firm to shift its production base. The problem of non–availability of the drug is then further reduced. For that to happen the maximum price that consumers are willing to pay must cover the unit cost of production. Therefore a low cost of production by itself is not sufficient to attract firms to relocate their production. There must be sufficient demand for the product.

However, firms can successfully discriminate prices for the drug only when 'parallel-trade' a the form of arbitrage activities among traders does not arise. In the next step, we have therefore incorporated traders or distributors in our model to model the problem of arbitrage or parallel trade. It is well known in economic theory that firms earn higher profit when they can successfully discriminate the prices for their products. However, we have proved that compared to the profit that a firm earns when it successfully discriminates prices for its product across the globe, the profit that it earns even in the presence of 'parallel-trade' (or when it cannot fully discriminate the prices for its product due to arbitrage) can be higher provided that the relative market size of the developing country is sufficiently large.This arises because, in the presence of distributors, the problem of 'double-monopoly distortion' arises. The problem of 'double-monopoly distortion' is reduced in the developed nation due to competition between traders or distributors. This therefore brings the prices and quantities of the medicine sold in the developed country close to the profit maximizing level of the manufacturer when he was also the sole seller of the product. In addition, due to the presence of parallel trade, the manufacturer while maximizing its profit sets a higher price for the distributor of the developing nation. When the relative market size of the developing country is large, the manufacturer earns even higher revenue from the distributor of the developing nation and this, in turn, allows the manufacturer to earn higher profit.

8.3 Policy Implications

Based on the empirical and theoretical analysis of the study, various policy implications can also be drawn for the Indian pharmaceutical industry.

From the efficiency analysis, it is evident that small firms can gain efficiency in output if they grow in size. Majumdar and Rajeev (2009b) estimated that small firms can gain output efficiency by about 20 % if they expand their scale of operation and grow in size. However, large-sized firms cannot gain efficiency if they simply merge in size. Significant gain in efficiency is possible if firms integrate vertically with down-stream firms that produce raw-material for this industry. We also notice that the use of imported technology is an effective means of attaining higher output efficiency. With the use of imported technology, firms can maintain quality standard at par with the global norm. This will enable firms to expand their size and scope of operation in the global market. As far as firm-specific strategic variables are concerned, we noticed that R&D is not enough for firms to do R&D but firms must undertake R&D at an appropriate scale. It can be argued that due to the recognition of product patents and increased competition in the domestic and global market, firms must invest in R&D to come out with new products or processes. In a related study, Mazumdar and Rajeev (2007) also noted the presence of scale economies in R&D related activities. This provides an additional incentive to firms to merge and grow in size. We also notice that firms selling their products in the domestic market should try more for the global market. In the short run, they can target the semi-regulated market or even the unregulated market where the entry cost is minimal but the returns are higher compared to the domestic market. After acquiring repute in the international market they can, however, target the global regulated market in the long run. Additionally, by capturing the global market, firms can expand their scale of operation in production. This will, therefore, increase the un-used capacity utilization in plants and machinery and help firms to increase their capital efficiency. Thus, the benefit of exporting products in the global market is twofold, namely, first, by gaining higher output efficiency and second it will also indirectly help firms to gain higher capital efficiency. With regard to input-specific efficiencies, we noted that firms could cut down their cost of energy if they replace the coal-based energy generating technology with the ones that use gas and diesel as the source of fuel. Thus, there should be an effort on the part of firms to replace the old technology with modern ones.

We also noticed that the use of imported technology and capital-intensive technique open up new production possibilities for firms. In other words, firms that use advanced capital-intensive techniques mainly drive the technical shift for the sector. Thus, firms should make efforts to upgrade their production base by installing advanced plants and machinery and benefit from the technological progress or an outward shift in the production frontier. By using advanced technology, firms can also tap the growing opportunity in contract manufacturing market. MNCs are also keen to outsource their manufacturing related activities to cut down their cost of production. We also noticed that R&D undertaken by large sized firms also shifts the production frontier for firms. We reiterate that large sized firms mainly do advanced R&D and also on a large scale. This again establishes that R&D is beneficial if it is done on a large scale. One possible route for Indian pharmaceutical firms to do more R&D will be to engage in contract R&D with foreign innovative companies and gain competence in R&D. Foreign innovative firms may also enter R&D contracts because the cost of R&D is less in India. Moreover, India has a large pool of diverse population, which is favorable for undertaking various forms of clinical testing for the invented product.

Our analysis also establishes that increased marketing reduces the profitability of firms. However, if firms come out with new product or process and do marketing then it is one of the most effective strategies to earn high profit. This again establishes the importance of R&D. From the point of view of profitability analysis, we also noticed that instead of producing too many products, firms should specialize in product varieties for which they have core competence. With specialized products, firms can also enter easily into collaboration with MNCs in production and benefit from knowledge sharing.

8.3.1 Implications for Public Policies

Reforms pursued by the Indian government pertaining to the Indian pharmaceutical sector has opened up new production opportunities that was hitherto unavailable to Indian pharmaceutical firms. This has led to an outward shift in its production frontier. However, the efficiency of the firms has also reduced in the post-reform era and firms fail to produce the maximum-targeted output that is offered by the sector. Thus, merely following policies to promote competition may not be enough to improve the performance of firms. Public policies must be designed in a way that firms also appropriate benefit of the competition.

In this regard, we noticed that the use of imported plant and machinery improves the efficiency of firms. However, many small and medium sized firms may not have enough resources to carry out such expensive investment activities. Thus, a possible route to assist firms will be to provide finance at a reasonable cost to upgrade their production system. The government can also purchase medicines from these firms for public hospitals at a cheaper rate. Such assured market from public agencies will also help firms withstand the uncertainties of the market, get a fair price for their product. This in turn will also help them to recover costs involved in the investment they made.

We also noticed that firms gain efficiency by exporting their product in the international market. Setting up the export promotion cell is of importance to give appropriate training to firms to export their product. Given the importance of the use of imported technology to perform better, the government may also set up technological promotion cell to impart appropriate training regarding the use of imported technology.

Our study also establishes that R&D is useful only when it is done on a large scale (that is firms invest say around 10–15 % of their revenue for R&D) and directed for advanced process and product development. Few firms however, have the capacity to undertake such risky R&D related activity. Thus, public-private technological collaboration is indispensable to boost up the R&D endowment of the country. In recent years, the bio-technological revolution has changed the nature of pharmaceutical R&D. The impact of biotechnology can be best appropriated when firms cluster in one geographical region because of knowledge spillover.

As a facilitator, the government should, therefore, set up Biotech Park in appropriate locations of the country in close knit collaboration with public research institutes.

Our study also indicates that, in recent years there has been a spurt of R&D activities among firms. Also, the use of advanced plant and machinery is noticed among firms. To continue with such knowledge-intensive activities, firms need skilled labor with appropriate knowledge in pharmaceuticals. One way to promote such activities will be to encourage advanced studies in pharmaceutical engineering, microbiology and others. The government should therefore set up such institutes to impart specialized knowledge to avoid any bottleneck in the supply of skilled labor for this sector.

Results from theoretical modeling imply that neither *product-patent nor parallel trade is a serious threat to a large developing country like India. If product patent is* **properly enforced,** *then large developing countries can be an attractive destination for the foreign companies to shift their production base. However, recognizing product patent does not ensure the availability of patented drugs for small developing nations like Nepal, Bhutan or Bangladesh. Medium sized nations must control parallel trade.* One should, however, remember that mere availability of drugs might not ensure accessibility of drugs among the common mass in a country like India because of a wide disparity in the income level. Thus, one cannot rule out the importance of the role of the public sector and public hospitals and health care centers to distribute drugs at appropriate prices.

'Using Data Envelopment Analysis.': **Property Rights, Control, and the Performance of Firms in Indian Industry Discovery in pharmaceutical research regulation on the launch delay of new drugs-evidence from twenty-five major markets in the 1990s in Drug Discovery** efficiency of Australian dairy farms using alternative frontier methodologies **Affects Global Market Entry Exports** for bootstrapping in non-parametric frontier models differentials An application to milk production in Nordic countries **industry development: unpacking the advantages of size advertising, and generic entry in the US pharmaceutical** processes.

M. Mazumdar, *Performance of Pharmaceutical Companies in India*, Contributions to Economics, DOI 10.1007/978-3-7908-2876-4,

References

Acemoglu, D, J Linn (2004) Market size in innovation: theory and evidence from the pharmaceutical industry, Working Paper, MIT, Department of Economics, Massachusetts

Aghion P, Howitt P (1992) A model of growth through creative destruction. Econometrica 60(2):323–351

Ahluwalia IJ (1991) Productivity growth in Indian manufacturing. Oxford University Press, Delhi

Althin R (2001) Measurement of productivity changes: two Malmquist index approaches. J Prod Anal 16(2):107–128.

Amel D, Froeb L (1991) Do firms differ much? J Ind Econ 39(3):323–331

Apte PG, Vaidynathan R (1982) Concentration, controls and performance in 29 manufacturing industries in India. Indian Econ Rev 17:241–264

Aradhana (2007) The Indian pharmaceutical industry. In: Kumar N, Joseph KJ (eds) International competitiveness and knowledge based industries in India. Oxford University Press, New Delhi

Assaf A (2009) Accounting for size in efficiency comparisons of airports. J Air Trans Manage 15(5):256–258

Assaf A, Matawie KM (2008) A bootstrapped metafrontier model. Appl Econ Lett 2:1466–4291

Audretsch DB (1999) Small firms and efficiency. In: Zoltan J Acs (ed) Are small firms important? their role and impact. Springer, Berlin, Heidelberg, pp 241–272

Aw BY, Hwang AR (1995) Productivity and the export market: a firm-level analysis. J Dev Econ 47:313–332

Bain J (1956) Barrier to new competition. Harvard University Press, Cambridge, MA

Bain J (1951) Relation of profit rate to industry concentration: American manufacturing, 1936–1940. Quat J Econ 65:293–324

Balakrishnan P, Pushpangadan K (1994) TFPG in manufacturing industry: a fresh look. Econ Pol Wkly 30:2028–2032

Balakrishnan P, Pushpangadan K, Suresh BM (2000) Trade liberalization and productivity growth in manufacturing: evidence from firm-level panel data. Econ Pol Wkly 7:3679–3682

Baldwin JR, Gorecki PK (1985) The determinants of small plant market share in Canadian manufacturing industries in the 1970s. Rev Econ Stat 67:156–161

Bale HE Jr (1998) The conflicts between parallel trade and product access and innovation: the case of pharmaceuticals. J Int Econ Law 1(4):637–653

Balk BM (2001) Scale efficiency and productivity change. J Prod Anal 15:159–183

Baltagi BH (2003) Econometric analysis of panel data, 3rd edn. Wiley, New York

Banker RD, Natarajan R (2008) Evaluating contextual variables affecting productivity using data envelopment analysis. Oper Res 56:48–58

Banker RD (1993) Maximum likelihood, consistency and data envelopment analysis: a statistical foundation. Manage Sci 10(39):1265–1273

M. Mazumdar, *Performance of Pharmaceutical Companies in India*,
Contributions to Economics, DOI 10.1007/978-3-7908-2876-4,

Banker RD, Cooper WW (1994) Validation and generalization of DEA and its uses. Top 2(2):249–314

Bardburd RM, Caves RE (1982) A closer look at the effect of market growth on industries' profits. Rev Econ Stat 64:635–642

Barney JB (1991) Firm resources and sustained competitive advantage. J Manage 17(1):99–120

Bartelsman EJ, Doms ME (2000) Understanding productivity: lessons from longitudinal microdata. J Econ Lit 28:569–594

Battese GE, Rao DSP (2002) Technology gap, efficiency and a stochastic metafrontier function. Int J Bus Econ 1:87–93

Battese GE, Rao DSP, O'Donnell CJ (2004) A metafrontier production function for estimation of technical efficiencies and technology gaps for firms operating under different technologies. J Prod Anal 21:91–103

BCPW (1941) The pioneer Indian house of chemical & pharmaceutical industries. Bengal Chemical and Pharmaceutical Works, Calcutta

Berg SA, Førsund FR, Jansen ES (1992) Malmquist indices of productivity growth during the deregulation of Norwegian banking 1980–89. Scand J Econ 94:211–228

Bhadhuri S, Ray AS (2001) R&D and technological learning in Indian industry: econometric estimation of the research production function. Oxford Dev Stud 29(2):101–123

Bhandari AK, Maiti P (2007) Efficiency of Indian manufacturing firms: textile industry as a case study, international. J Bus Econ 6(1):71–88

Bhandari AK, Ray SC (2007) Technical efficiency in the Indian textiles industry: a nonparametric analysis of firm-level data. University of Connecticut Department of Economics Working Paper Series 2007-49

Bhavani T (1991) Technical efficiency of Indian modern small scale sector: an application of frontier production function. Indian Econ Rev 26(2):149–166

Biman JN, Gockowski J, Nkamleu GB (2008) Technical efficiency and productivity potential of cocoa farmers in West African countries. Dev Econ 46(3):242–263

Bos J, Schmiedel H (2007) Comparing efficiency in European banking: a meta-frontier approach. J Bank Finance 31(7):2081–2102

Boshrabadi HM, Villano R, Fleming E (2007) Technical efficiency and environmental-technological gaps in wheat production in Kerman province of Iran. Agric Econ 38(1):67–76

Bottazzi G, Dosi G, Lippi M, Pammolli F, Riccaboni M (2002) Innovation and corporate growth in the evolution of the drug industry. Int J Ind Organ 19:1161–1187

Breusch TS, Pagan AR (1980) The lagrange multiplier test and its applications to model specification in econometrics. Rev Econ 47:239–253

Brozen Y (1971) Bain's concentration and rates of return revisited. J Law Econ 14:351–369

Calfee JE (2002) Public policy issues in direct-to-consumer advertising of prescription drugs. J Public Policy Market 21:174–193

Carter J (1977) In search of synergy: a structure-performance test. Rev Econ Stat 59:279–289

Catherine M (1999) Market structure, R&D and advertisement in the pharmaceutical industry. J Ind Econ 12(2):169–194

Caves DW, Christensen LR, Diewert WE (1982) The economic theory of index numbers and the measurement of input, output, and productivity. Econometrica 50(6):1393–1414

Caves RE, Khalizadeh-Shirazi J, Porter ME (1975) Scale economies in statistical analyses of market power. Rev Econ Stat 57:133–140

Caves RE (1992) Determinants of technical efficiency in Australia. In: Caves RE (ed) Industrial efficiency in six nations. MIT Press, Cambridge, pp 241–272

Caves RE, Barton DR (1990) Efficiency in U.S. manufacturing industries. MIT Press, Cambridge

Chakroborty S (1995) Issues in industrial economics. Avebury Publishing, Brookfield

Charnes A, Cooper WW, Lewin AY, Seiford LM (eds) (1994) Data envelopment analysis: theory, methodology and applications. Kluwer Academic, Boston

Chaudhuri S (1984) Indigenous firms in relation to the transnational corporation in the drug industry in India, unpublished thesis, Jawaharlal Nehru University, New Delhi

Chaudhuri K, Das S (2006) WTO, the TRIPS and Indian pharmaceutical industry. J Quant Econ 4(1):97–110

Chaudhuri S (1997) The evolution of the Indian pharmaceutical industry. In: Felker G et al (eds) The pharmaceutical industry in India and Hungary: policies, institutions and technological development, World Bank, N.W. Washington, D.C. 20433, U.S.A., Technical Paper, 392, pp 42–86

Chaudhuri S (1999) Growth and structural changes in the pharmaceutical industries in India, Working paper series No. 356, IIM: Indian Institute of Management, Calcutta

Chaudhuri S (2004) The pharmaceutical industry. In: Sen A, Gokarn S, Vaidya R (eds) The structure of Indian industry. Oxford University Press, New Delhi

Chaudhuri S (2005) The WTO and the India's pharmaceuticals industry. Oxford University Press, New Delhi

Chaudhuri S, Goldberg P, Jha P (2006) Estimating the effect of global patent protection in pharmaceuticals: a case study of quinolones in India. Am Econ Rev 96(5):1477–1514

Chaudhuri S (2003) Generic competition, price control and affordability of drugs in India, Working Paper, 478, Indian Institute of Management, Calcutta

Chen Z, Shunfeng S (2008) Efficiency and technology gap in China's agriculture: a regional meta-frontier analysis. China Econ Rev 19(2):287–296.

Chen KHM (2007) The impact of agglomerative industrial dynamic externalities on regional technology gaps: a case of the ICT industry in Taiwan. Aust J Reg Stud 13(3):261–287

Chhibber PK, Majumdar SK (1999) Foreign ownership and profitability. J Law Econ, University of Chicago Press, 42(1):209–38

Chilingerian JA, Sherman HD (2004) Health care applications: from hospitals to physicians from productive efficiency to quality frontiers. In: Cooper WW, Seiford LM, Zhu J (eds) Handbook on data envelopment analysis. Kluwer Academic, Boston, pp 265–298

Chou TC (1986) Concentration, profitability and trade in a simultaneous equation analysis: the case of Taiwan. J Ind Econ 34:429–443

Church J, Ware R (2000) Industrial organization: a strategic approach. McGraw Hill, New York

Clerides KS, Lach S, Tybout RJ (1998) Is learning by exporting important? Micro-dynamics evidence from Colombia, Mexico and Morocco. Quart J Econ 113:903–947

Cleveland WS (1979) Robust locally weighted regression and smoothing scattersplots. J Am Stat Assoc 74(368):829–836

Coase RH (1937) The nature of the firm. Economica 4:386–405

Cockburn I, Henderson R (1996) Public-private interaction in pharmaceutical research. In: Proceeding of the national academy of sciences, 93/23, Irvine CA, pp 12725–12730

Cockburn I, Henderson RM (2000) Publicly funded science and the productivity of the pharmaceutical industry. In: Jaffe A, Lerner J, Stern S (eds) Innovation policy and the economy, vol I. MIT Press, Cambridge, MA, pp 1–34

Cockburn IM, Henderson RM (1998) Absorptive capacity, coauthoring behavior, and the organization of research in drug. J Ind Econ 46(2):157–182

Cockburn IM, Henderson R (1997) Public-private Interaction and the productivity of pharmaceutical research, NBER Working Paper No. 6018, Cambridge, MA, Apr 1997

Coelli T (1996) A guide to Frontier version 4.1: a computer program for stochastic frontier production and cost function estimation. CEPA Working Paper 96/07, Centre for Efficiency and Productivity Analysis, University of New England, Armidale

Collins NR, Preston LE (1968) Concentration and price-cost margins in manufacturing industries. University of California Press, Berkeley

Collins NR, Preston LE (1969) Price-cost margins and industry structure. Rev Econ Stat 51:271–286

Comanor WS (1967) Market structure, product differentiation and industrial research. Quart J Econ 81:639–651

Comanor WS, Wilson TA (1967) Advertising, market structure and performance. Rev Econ Stat 49:423–440

Commanor WS (1986) The political economy of the pharmaceutical industry. J Econ Lit 24:1187–1217

Cook WD, Seiford LM (2009) Data envelopment analysis (DEA) – thirty years on. Eur J Oper Res, Elsevier, 192(1):1–17

Cooper WW, Park KS, Pastor JT (1999) RAM: a range adjusted measure of efficiency for use with additive models, and relations to other models and measures in DEA. J Prod Anal 11:5–42

Cornwell CP, Schmidt P, Sickles RC (1990) Production frontiers with cross-sectional and time series variation in efficiency levels. J Econometrics 46:185–200

Coscelli A (2000) The importance of doctor's and patient's preference in the prescription decision

Cowling K (1976) On the theoretical specification of industrial structure-performance relationships. Eur Econ Rev 8:1–14

Cowling K, Waterson M (1976) Price-cost margins and market structure. Economica 43:267–274

Cubbin J, Geroski PA (1987) The convergence of profits in the long run: inter-firm and inter-industry comparisons. J Ind Econ 35:427–442

Danzon PM, Wang YR, Wang L (2005) The impact of price. Health Econ 14(3):269–292

Danzon PM (1997) Price discrimination for pharmaceuticals: welfare effects in the US and the EU. Int J Econ Bus 4(3):301–321

Danzon P, Kim J (1998) International price comparisons for pharmaceuticals: measurement and policy issues. Pharmacoeconomics 14(1):15–25

Danzon PM, Towse A (2003) Differential pricing for pharmaceuticals: reconciling access, R&D and patents. Int J Health Care Finance Econ 3:183–205

Danzon PM, Furukawa MF (2003) Prices and availability of pharmaceuticals: evidence from nine countries, Health Affairs Web Exclusive 29 Oct 2003

Danzon PM, Chao LW (2000) Does regulation drive out competition in pharmaceutical markets? J Law Econ 43(2):311–357

Das A, Ray SC, Nag A (2007) Labor-use efficiency in Indian banking: a branch level analysis. Omega 37(2):411–425

Debreu G (1951) The coefficient of resource utilisation. Econometrica 19:273–292

Demsetz H (1973a) The market concentration doctrine. American Enterprises Institution, Washington, DC

Demsetz H (1973b) Industry structure, market rivalry and public policy. J Law Econ 16:1–10

Demsetz H (1974) Two systems of belief about monopoly. In: Goldschmid HJ, Mann HM, Weston JF (eds) Industrial concentration: the new learning. Little-Brown, Boston, pp 74–85

Demsetz H (1973c) Industrial structure, market rivalry, and public policy. J Law Econ 16:1–3

DiMasi J, Hansen R, Grabowski H (2003b) The price of innovation: new estimates of new drug developments cost. J Health Econ 23:151–185

DiMasi JA, Hansen RW, Grabowski HG, Lasagna L (2003a) The price of innovation: new estimates of drug development costs. J Health Econ 22:151–185

DiMasi JA, Hansen RW, Grabowski HG, Lasagna L (1991) Cost of innovation in the pharmaceutical industry. J Health Econ 10:107–142

Duncombe W, Miner J, Ruggiero J (1997) Empirical evaluation of bureaucratic models of inefficiency. Public Choice 93:1–18

Dutta A (2006) Intellectual property rights, market structure and social welfare: three essays in industrial organisation. Unpublished thesis, MIT University

Eaton BC, Lipsey RG (1978) Freedom of entry and the existence of pure profit. Econ J 88:455–456

Ellison SF, Cockburn I, Griliches Z, Hausman J (1997) Characteristics of demand for Pharmaceutical products: an examination of four cephalosporins. Rand J Econ 28(3):426–446

Emrouznejad A (2001) An extensive bibliography of data envelopment analysis (DEA), vol I: working papers, Business School, University of Warwick, Coventry CV4 7AL, England

Ernst and Young Report (2005) Unveiling India's pharmaceutical future

Färe R, Grosskopf S, Lindgren B, Roos P (1989, 1994) Productivity developments in Swedish hospitals; a malmquist output index approach. In: Charnes A, Cooper W, Lewin AY, Seiford L

(eds) Data envelopment analysis: theory, methodology and applications. Kluwer Academic, Boston, pp 253–272
Färe R, Lovell CAK (1978) Measuring technical efficiency of production. J Econ Theory 19:150–162
Farrell MJ (1957) The measurement of productive efficiency. J Roy Stat Soc Ser A Gen 120(3):253–281
Federation of Indian Chambers of Commerce and Industry (FICCI) (2005) Competitiveness of the Indian pharmaceutical industry in the new product patent regime. FICCI Report for national manufacturing competitiveness council (NMCC), New Delhi. Available at www.ficci.com/studies/pharma.pdf
Feinberg SE, Majumdar SK (2001) Technology spillovers from foreign direct investment in the Indian pharmaceutical industry. J Int Bus Stud 32(3):421–437
Ferrantino MJ, Ferrier GD (1995) The technical efficiency of vacuum pan sugar industry of India: an application of a stochastic frontier production function using panel data. Eur J Oper Res 80(3):639–653
Findlay SD (2001) Direct-to-consumer promotion of prescription drugs. Economic implication for patient, payers and providers. Pharmacoeconomics 19(2):109–119
Fink C (2002) How stronger patent protection in India might affect the behavior or transnational pharmaceutical industries. Development Research Group no. 219, The World Bank
Fink C (2000) Entering the Jungle of Intellectual Property Rights Exhaustion and Parallel Importation'. In: Fink Carsten et al (eds) Intellectual Property and Development Lessons From Recent Economic Research. World Bank and Oxford University Press, Oxford, pp 165–200
Førsund F (1999) The malmquist productivity index, TFP and Scale. Memorandum No. 233, School of Economics and Commercial Law, University of Göteborg, Sweden
Gallus N (2004) The mystery of pharmaceutical parallel trade and developing countries. J World Intell Prop 7(2):169–183
Gambardella A (1992) Competitive advantages from in-house scientific research: the US pharmaceutical industry in the 1980s. Res Policy 21:391–407
Gambardella A (1995) Science and innovation. Cambridge University Press, Cambridge, UK
Ganslandt M, Maskus KE (2007) Vertical distribution, parallel trade, and price divergence in integrated markets. Eur Econ Rev 51(4):943–970
Ganslandt M, Maskus KE (2004) The price impact of parallel trade in pharmaceuticals: evidence from the European Union. J Health Econ 23:1035–1057
Ganslandt M, Maskus KE (2001) Parallel trade in pharmaceutical products: implications for procuring medicines for poor countries. In: Granville B (ed) The economics of essential medicines. Royal Institute of International Affairs, London
Gattoufi S, Oral M, Reisman A (2004) Data envelopment analysis literature: a bibliography update (1951–2001). Socioecon Plann Sci 38:159–229
Gautam N (2002) Profiteers divert to Europe AIDS drugs meant for Africa. Asian Wall Street J. 7 Oct 2002, at A9
George J. Stigler (1968) "**Price and non-price competition**". *J Pol Economy,* University of Chicago Press, 76:149–165
Geroski P, van Reenen J, Walters CF (1997) How persistently do firms innovate? Res Policy 26(1):33–48
Goldar B, Ranganathan VS, Banga RR (2004) Ownership and efficiency in engineering firms: 1990–91 to 1999–2000. Econ Pol Wkly 39(5):441–447
Goldar B (1985) Unit size and economic efficiency of small scale washing soap industries in India. Artha Vijnana 27(1):21–40
Goldar B (1986) Productivity growth in Indian industry. Allied Publishers, Delhi
González E, Gascón F (2004) Sources of productivity growth in the Spanish pharmaceutical industry (1994–2000). Res Policy 33(5):735–745

Govindaraj R, Chellaraj G (2002) The Indian pharmaceutical sector: issues and options for health sector reform. World Bank Discussion Paper No. 437
Grabowski H, Vernon JM (1992) Brand loyalty, entry, and price competition in pharmaceuticals after the 1984 drug Act. J Law Econ 35:331–340
Grabowski HG, Vernon JM (1981) The determinants of R&D expenditures. In: Helms RB (ed) Drugs and health. AEI Press, Washington
Grabowski H, Vernon J (1987) Pioneers, imitators, and generics: a simulation model of Schumpeterian competition. Quart J Econ 102(3):491–525
Grabowski HG, Mueller DC (1978) Industrial research and development, intangible capital stocks, and firm profit rates. Bell J Econ 9:328–343
Grace C (2004) The effect of changing intellectual property on pharmaceutical industry prospect for India and China, technological transfer and access to medicine. Department for International Development (DFID), Health System Resource Centre, London
Graham D (2004) Interim report of task force 5 working group on access to essential medicines 32 UN Millennium Project, 1 Feb 2004
Greer DF (1971) Advertising and market concentration. South Econ J 38:19–32
Grosskopf S (1996) Statistical Inference and non-parametric efficiency: a selective survey. J Prod Anal 7(2–3):161–176
Grosskopf S (1993) Efficiency and productivity. In: Fried HO, Lovell CAK, Schmidt SS (eds) The measurement of productive efficiency. Techniques and applications. Oxford University Press, Oxford, pp 160–194
Grosskopf S (2003) Some remarks on productivity and its decompositions. J Prod Anal 20:459–474
Grossman G, Helpman E (1991) Quality ladders in the theory of growth. Rev Econ Stud 58:43–61
Gunaratne LH, Leung PS (2001) Asian black tiger shrimp industry: a productivity analysis. In: Economics and management of shrimp and carp farming in Asia: a collection of research papers based on the ADB/NACA farm performance survey, Hongkong
Gupta V (1983) A simultaneous determination of structure conduct and performance in Canadian manufacturing. Oxford Econ Pap 35:281–301
Härdle W, Simar L (1999) Applied multivariate statistical analysis. Springer, Berlin and Hiedelberg
Hathi Committee Report (1974) Ministry of petroleum and chemicals. Report of the committee on drugs and pharmaceutical industry popularly known as "Hathi Committee Report (H.C.R)"
Hausman JA (1978) Specification tests in econometrics. Econometrica 46:1251–1271
Hay DA, Morris D (1991) Industrial economics and organization. Oxford University Press, New York
Hayami Y (1969) Sources of agricultural productivity gap among selected countries. Am J Agric Econ 51(3):564–575
Hayami Y, Ruttan VW (1970) Agricultural productivity differences among countries. Am Econ Rev 60(5):895–911
Hayami Y, Ruttan VW (1971) Agricultural development: an international perspective. Johns Hopkins University Press, Baltimore, p 82
Helpman E (1992) Endogenous macroeconomic growth theory. Eur Econ Rev 36:237–276
Henderson R, Cockburn I (1996a) Scale, scope and spillovers: the determinants of research productivity in drug discovery. Rand J Econ 27(1):32–59
Henderson R, Cockburn I (1996b) Scale, scope, and spillovers: the determinants of research productivity. RAND J Econ RAND Corp 27(1):32–59, Spring
Hess J (1983) The economics of organisation, (2–3). Elsevier, Amsterdam
Hurwitz MA, Caves RE (1988) Persuasion or information? Promotion and the shares of brand name and generic pharmaceuticals. J Law Econ 31(2):299–320
Iyer K, Rambaldi A, Tang KK (2006) Globalisation and the technology gap: regional and time evidence. In: Leading economic and managerial issues involving globalisation. Chapter 15. Nova Scotia, New York

Jacquemin A, de Ghellinck E, Huveneers C (1980) Concentration and profitability in a small, open economy. J Ind Econ 29:131–144

Jayadevan CM (1996) Inter-state variation in total factor productivity growth rates: a case study of organised manufacturing industry in India. Man Dev December 18:97–108

Jordan DC (1999) Drug politics: dirty money and democracies. University of Okhalama, Okhalama

Kalirajan K, Bhide S (2005) The post-reform performance of the manufacturing sector in India. Asian Econ Pap 3(2):126–157

Kalirajan KP, Obwona MB (1994) Frontier production function: the stochastic coefficients approach. Oxford Bull Econ Stat 56:87–96

Kalirajan KP, Shand RT (1997) Sources of growth in Indian agriculture. Indian J Agric Econ 52:693–706

Kanavos P (2001) Overview of pharmaceutical pricing and reimbursement regulation. London School of Economics, London

Kanavos P, Costa-i-Font J (2005) Pharmaceutical parallel trade in Europe: stakeholder and competition effects. Econ Policy 20(44):751–798

Kanavos P, Costa-i-Font J, Merkur S, Gemmill M (2004) The economic impact of pharmaceutical parallel distribution in the European Union member studies: a stakeholder analysis. London School of Economics (LSE) Health and Social Care, London

Katayama H, Shihua L, Tybout JR (2009) Firm-level productivity studies: illusions and a solution. Int J Ind Organ 27:403–413

Kaul KV (2007) Chemical industry. In: Kumar N, Joseph KJ (eds) International competitiveness & knowledge-based industries in India. Oxford University Press, New Delhi

Kawagoe T, Hayami Y (1985) An intercountry comparison of agricultural production efficiency. Am J Agric Econ 67:87–92

Kennedy P (1998) A guide to econometrics. Blackwell, Oxford

Kessides IN (1986) Advertising, sunk costs, and barriers to entry. Rev Econ Stat 68:84–95

Kessides IN (1987) Do firms differ much? Some additional evidence, mimeo. Working paper, Department of Economics, University of Maryland

Kneip A, Park BU, Simar L (1998) A note on the convergence of nonparametric DEA estimators for production efficiency scores. Econ Theory 14:783–793

Koopmans TC (1951) An analysis of production as an efficient combination of activities. In: Koopmans TC (ed) Activity analysis of production and allocation, vol 13, Cowles commission for research in economics, monograph. Wiley, New York

KPMG (2006) The Indian pharmaceutical industry: collaboration for growth, www.in.kpmg.com/pdf/Indian%20Pharma%20Outlook.pdf

Krishna P, Mitra D (1998) Trade liberalisation, market discipline and productivity growth: new evidence from India. J Dev Econ 56:447–462

Krugman P (1991) Geography and trade. MIT-Press, Cambridge

Kudaligama VP, Yanagida JF (2000) A comparison of intercountry agricultural production functions: a frontier function approach. J Econ Dev 25(1):57–74

Kumar N (1990) Mobility barriers and profitability of multinational and local enterprises in Indian manufacturing. J Ind Econ 38(4):449–463

Kumar N, Siddhartan NS (1994) Technology, firm size and export behaviour in developing countries: the case of Indian enterprises. J Dev Stud 16(2):13–38

Kumar, J (2003) Ownership structure and corporate firm performance. Technical report 0304004, Econ WPA Indira Gandhi Institute of Development Research

Kumar S (2001) Regional variation in technical efficiency of Indian manufacturing sector: a stochastic frontier approach. Indian Econ J 48(2):82–91

Kumar N, Pradhan JP (2004) Economic reforms, WTO and Indian drugs and pharmaceutical industry, vol 42, CMDR monograph series. Centre For Multi-Disciplinary Development Research, Dharwad

Kuosmanen T (2008) Representation theorem for convex nonparametric least squares. Econ J 11(2):308–325 (to appear)
Kuosmanen T (2006) Stochastic nonparametric envelopment of data: combining virtues of SFA and DEA in unified framework. MTT Discussion Paper 3:51 s
Kwoka JE Jr (1978) The effect of market share distribution on industry performance. Rev Econ Stat 61(1):101–109
Kwoka JE Jr (1981) Does the choice of concentration measure really matter? J Ind Econ 29:445–453
Kwong WJ, Norton E (2007) The effect of advertising on pharmaceutical innovation. Rev Ind Organ 31(3):221–236
Kyle MK (2003) Pharmaceutical price controls and entry strategies, Working Paper, Fuqua School of Business, Duke University
Kyle MK (2004) The role of firm characteristics in pharmaceutical product launches, Working Paper, Fuqua School of Business, Duke University
Lalitha N (2002) Indian pharmaceutical industry in WTO regime: a SWOT analysis. Econ Pol Wkly 37:3542–3555
Lall S (2000) The technological structure and performance of developing country manufacturing exports, 1985–1998. Queen Elizabeth House, University of Oxford Working paper series
Lall SV, Rodrigo GC (2001) Perspective on the sources of heterogeneity in Indian industry. World Dev 29(12):2127–2143
Lanjouw JO (2005) Patents, price controls, and access to new drugs: how policy. NBER Working Papers 11321, National Bureau of Economic Research
Lanjouw JO (1997) The introduction of product patents in India: heartless exploitation of the poor and suffering?, Economic Growth Center Discussion Paper, no 775, Yale University. pp 1–56
Lau LT, Yotopoulos PA (1989) The metaproduction function approach to technological change in world agriculture. J Dev Econ 31:241–269
Leffler KB (1981) Persuasion or information? The economics of prescription drugs advertising. J Law Econ 24(1):45–74
Leibenstein H (1966) Allocative efficiency vs. "x-efficiency". American Economic Review 56(3):392–415
Liu L (1993) Entry-exit, learning and productivity changes: evidence from Chile. J Dev Econ 42:447–462
Liu L, Tybout JR (1996) Productivity growth in Chile and Colombia: the role of entry, exit and learning. In: Roberts MJ, Tybout JR (eds) Industrial evolution in developing countries: micro patterns of turnover, productivity and market structure. Oxford University Press, New York
Lovell CAK (1993) Production frontier and productive efficiency. In: Fried HO, Lovell CAK, Schmidt SS (eds) The measurement of productive efficiency-techniques and applications. Oxford University Press, London, pp 3–67
Lovell CAK (2003) The decomposition of malmquist productivity indexes. J Prod Anal 20:437–458
Lustgarten SH (1975) The impact of buyer concentration in manufacturing industry. Rev Econ Stat 57:125–132
Majumdar SK (1994) Assessing firms capabilities – theory and measurement – a study of Indian pharmaceutical-industry. Econ Pol Wkly 29(22):M83–M89
Mazumdar M, Rajeev M (2009a) Input and output efficiency of manufacturing firms in India: a case of the Indian pharmaceutical sector. ISEC Working paper 219
Majumdar M, Rajeev M (2009) Comparing the efficiency and productivity of the Indian pharmaceutical firms: a malmquist–meta-frontier approach. Int J Bus Econ 8(2):159–181
Majumdar M, Rajeev M (2010) Efficiency of manufacturing firms in India: a non-radial approach. Centre de Sciences Humaines, Occasional paper, (Forthcoming)
Mazumdar M, Rajeev M (2010) Product patent, the problem of availability of drug and parallel trade: a theoretical approach. J World Intellect Prop Right, (Blackwell) 13(4):581–604, July 2010

Mazumdar M, Rajeev M (2007) TRIPS agreement and the emerging in-house R&D activity of the Indian pharmaceutical companies: a panel data analysis of the firm level data. PES Bus Rev 3(1):3–23

Malmquist S (1953) Index numbers and indifference surfaces. Trabajos de Estadistica 4:209–242

Manjappa DH, Mahesha M (2008) Measurement of productivity growth, efficiency change and technical progress of selected capital-intensive and labour-intensive industries during reform period in India. Indian J Econ Bus 7(1):167–178

Mansfield E (1968) Industrial research and development expenditure: determinants, prospects, and relation of size of firm and inventive output. J Polit Econ 72(4):290–311

Mansfield E (1983) Technological change and Market Structure: an empirical study. Am Econ Rev 73:205–209

Mansfield E (1985) How rapidly does new industrial technology leak out? J Ind Econ 34(2):217–223

Mansfield E (1986) Technological change and international diffusion of technology: a survey of findings. In: McFtriedge D (ed) Technological change in Canadian industry. University of Toronto Press, Toronto, pp 77–99

Mariani M (2007) Firm and regional determinants in innovation models: evidence from biotechnology and traditional chemicals. In: Mazzucato M, Dosi G (eds) Knowledge accumulation and industry evolution: the case of pharma-biotech. Cambridge University Press, Cambridge

Marjit S, Beladi H (1998) Product versus process patents. J Policy Model 20(2):193–199

Marshall A (1920) Principles of economics: an introductory volume. Cambridge University Press, Cambridge

Martin S (1979a) Advertising, concentration and profitability: the simultaneity problem. Bell J Econ 10:639–647

Martin S (1979b) Entry barriers, concentration and profit. South Econ J 46:471–488

Martin S (2002) Advanced industrial economics. Blackwell, Oxford

Maskus KE (2000) Parallel imports: global trade policy. World Econ 23(9):1269–1284

Maskus KE (2001) Parallel imports in pharmaceutical: implications for competition and prices in developing countries. Final Report to World Intellectual Property Organization

Maskus KE, Chen Y (2002) Parallel imports in a model of vertical distribution: theory, evidence, and policy. Pac Econ Rev 7:319–334

Mason E (1939) Price and production policies of large-scale enterprises. Am Econ Rev 29 (Suppl 29):61–74

Mathur S (2007) Indian IT and ICT industry: a performance analysis using data envelopment analysis and malmquist index. Glob Econ J 7(2):1553–5304

McCarty TA, Yaisawarng S (1993) Technical efficiency in New Jersey school districts. In: Fried HO, Lovell CA, Schmidt SS (eds) The measurement of productive efficiency: techniques and applications. Oxford University Press, New York

McConaghie A (2002) Parallel trade: is Pharma fighting a losing battle? Pharma Focus. Volume 5, 5 July 2002

McGahan AM (1999) The performance of U.S. corporations: 1981–1994. J Ind Econ 47:373–398

Milner C, Vencappa D, Wright P (2007) Trade policy and productivity growth in Indian manufacturing. World Econ 30(2):249–266

Minority Staff International Report (1998) Prescription drug prices in the 1st congressional district in Maine: an international price comparison. Committee on government reform and oversight, US, 24 Oct 1998

Mitra A, Varoudakis A, Veganzones MA (2002a) Productivity and technical efficiency in Indian states' manufacturing: the role of infrastructure. Econ Dev Cult Change 50(2):78–96

Mitra A, Goldar B, Minhas BS (2002b) Total factor productivity growth in Indian industries: a review of studies' national income accounts and data systems. Oxford University Press, New Delhi

Mitra A (1999) Total factor productivity growth and technical efficiency in Indian industries: a study of panel data for fifteen major states. Working Paper No. E/203/99, Institute of Economic Growth, New Delhi

Mitra A, Varoudakis A, Veganzones-Voroudakis M-A (2002c) Productivity and technical efficiency in Indian states' manufacturing: the role of infrastructure. Econ Dev Cult Change 50(2):395–426

Mueller D (1986) Profits in the long run. Oxford University Press, New York

Mueller D (1990) The dynamics of company profits. Cambridge University Press, Cambridge

Mukherjee K, Ray SC (2004) Technical efficiency and its dynamics in Indian manufacturing: an inter-state analysis. Indian Econ Rev 40(2):101–125

Nakao T (1979) Profit rates and market share of leading industrial firms in Japan. J Ind Econ 2:371–383

Narayana PL (1984) The Indian pharmaceutical industry: problems and prospects. National Council of Applied Economic Research (NCEAR), New Delhi

Narayana and Joseph (1993) Industry and Trade Liberalisation: Performance of Motor Vehicles and Electronics Industries, 1981–91, Economic and Political Weekly (EPW), Vol. 28 No. 8/9, Feb. 20–27, pp. M13–M20.

Natarajan R, Duraisamy SM (2008) Efficiency and productivity in the Indian unorganized manufacturing sector: did reforms matter? Int Rev Econ 55(4):373–399

National Economic Research Associates (1999) The economic consequences of the choice of regime of exhaustion in the area of trademarks. NERA, London

Neogi C, Ghosh B (1994) Intertemporal efficiency variation in Indian manufacturing industries. J Prod Anal 5:301–324

Nerlove M, Arrow KJ (1962a) Optimal advertisement policy under dynamic condition. Economica 29:129–142

Nerlove M, Arrow KJ (1962b) Optimal advertisement and policy under dynamic conditions. Economica 29:129–142

Neumann M, Bobel I, Haid A (1979) Profitability, risk and market structure in West German industries. J Ind Econ 27:227–242

Neumann M, Bobel I, Haid A (1985) Domestic concentration, foreign trade and economic performance. Int J Ind Organ 3:1–19

NIHCM (2000) Prescription drugs and intellectual property protection. Issue briefs August, National Institute for Health Care Management Research and Educational Foundation, Washington, DC. Available at www.nihcm.org/pdf/HITIssueBrief.org

NIHCM (2002) Changing pattern of pharmaceutical innovation. National Institute for Health Care Management Research and Educational Foundation, Washington, DC. Available at www.nihcm.org/pdf/HITIssueBrief.org

Nikaido Y (2004) Technical efficiency of small scale industry: application of stochastic frontier model. Econ Pol Wkly 39(6):592–597

Parameswarn M (2002) Economic reform and technical efficiency: firm level evidence from selected industries in India, Working Paper 339, Centre of Development Studies, Kerala. Available at http://www.cds.edu/download_files/339.pdf

Pastor JT, Ruiz JL, Sirvent I (1999) An enhanced DEA Russell graph efficiency measures. Eur J Oper Res 115:596–607

Pavcnik N (2002) Trade liberalization, exit, and productivity improvements: evidence from Chilean plants. Rev Econ Stud 69:245–276

Peltzman S (1973) An evaluation of consumer protection legislation: the 1962 drug amendments. J Polit Econ 81(5):1049–1091

Peltzman S (1974) Regulation of pharmaceutical innovation: the 1962 amendments. American Enterprise Institute, Washington, DC

Pérez-Casas C (2000) HIV/AIDS medicines pricing report, setting objectives: is there a political will? Update: December, [online]. Available at www.accessmed-msf.org

Pharma Review (2005) The Indian pharma reference guide. Konsposh Publication, New Delhi

Pharmaceutical Enquiry Committee (1954) Report of the pharmaceutical enquiry committee. Government of India, Ministry of Commerce and Industry, GOI, New Delhi, pp 17–18
Porter M (1980) Competitive strategies: technique for analyzing industries and companies. Free school, New York
Porter M (1985) Competitive advantage: creating and sustaining superior performance. Free school, New York
Porter ME (2003) The economic performance of regions. Reg Stud 37:549–578
Pradhan JP (2007a) Strengthening intellectual property rights globally: impact on India's pharmaceutical. Singapore Econ Rev 52(2):233–250
Pradhan JP, Kumar N (2007) Knowledge based export in India: a firm level analysis of determinants. In: Kumar N, Joseph KJ (eds) International competitiveness & knowledge based industry. Routledge, New Delhi, pp 53–96
Pradhan JP, Sahu P (2009) Transnational of Indian pharmaceutical SMEs. Bookwell Press, New Delhi
Pradhan JP (2002a) FDI spillover and local productivity growth: evidence from Indian pharmaceutical industry. Artha-vijanana 64(3–4):21–34
Pradhan JP (2002b) Liberalization firm size and R&D performance. A firm level study of Indian pharmaceutical industry. J Indian Sch Polit Econ 14(2):54–79
Pradhan JP (2006a) Global competitiveness of Indian pharmaceutical industry: trends and strategies. ISID Working Paper Series 2006/05
Pradhan JP, Abhinav A (2006b) Overseas acquisition versus greenfield foreign investment: which internationalization strategy is better for Indian pharmaceutical enterprises? ISID Working Paper Series 2006/05
Raizada B (2002) Intellectual property, technology and policy framework – experience of India in the pharmaceutical sector. Document prepared for the WIPO national Seminar on Industrial Property and the Patent Cooperation Treaty (PCT)
Ramani SV (2002) Who is interested in biotech? R&D strategies, knowledge base and market sales of Indian biopharmaceutical firms. Res Policy 31:381–398
Ramaswamy VK (1994) Technical efficiency in modern small scale firms in Indian industry: application of stochastic production frontier. J Quant Econ 10(2):309–324
Rao DSP, O'Donnell CJ, Battese GE (2003) Meta-frontier functions for the study of inter-regional productivity differences, CEPA Working Papers Series, WP012003, School of Economics, University of Queensland
Ray SC (2002a) Did India's economic reform improve efficiency and productivity? A non-parametric analysis of the initial evidence from manufacturing. Indian Econ Rev 37(1):23–57
Ray SC (2004) Data envelopment analysis. Cambridge University Press, Cambridge
Ray SC, Jeon Y (2007) Reputation and efficiency: a non-parametric assessment of America's top rated MBA programs. Eur J Oper Res 189(1):245–268
Ray SC (1988) Data envelopment analysis, non-discretionary inputs and efficiency: an alternative interpretation. Socioecon Plann Sci 22(4):167–176
Ray SC (1991) Resource-use efficiency in public schools: a study of Connecticut data. Manage Sci 37:1620–1628
Ray SC (1997) Regional variation in productivity growth in Indian manufacturing: a nonparametric analysis. J Quant Econ 13(1):73–94
Ray SC (2002b) Did India's economic reforms improve productivity and efficiency in manufacturing? Indian Econ Rev 37(1):23–57
Ray SC, Desli E (1997) Productivity growth, technical progress and efficiency change in industrialized countries: comment. Am Econ Rev 87(5):1033–1039
Reiffen D, Ward M (2005) Generic drug industry dynamics. Rev Econ Stat 87:37–49
Rey P (2003) The impact of parallel imports on prescription medicines, mimeo. Instiute for Industrial Development (IDEI), University of Toulouse, Toulouse
Rizzo AJ (1999) Advertising and competition in the ethical pharmaceutical industry: the case of antihypertensive drugs. J Law Econ 42(1):89–116

Robert JM, Tybout RJ (1997) The decision to export in Colombia: an empirical model of entry with sunk costs. Am Econ Rev 87(4):545–564

Robert JM, Tybout RJ (1996) Industrial evolution in developing countries: micro patterns of turnover, productivity and market structure. Oxford University Press, New York

Röller LH, Sinclair-Desgagné B (1996) On the heterogeneity of firms. Eur Econ Rev 40:531–539

Ruggiero J (2004) Performance evaluation in education: modeling educational production. In: Cooper WW, Seiford LM, Zhu J (eds) Handbook on data envelopment analysis. Kluwer Academic, Boston, pp 265–298 (Chapter 10)

Rumelt RP (1987) Theory, strategy and entrepreneurship. In: Teece DJ (ed) The competitive challenge. Harper & Row, New York, pp 137–158

Rumelt RP, Schendel D, Teece DJ (1991) Strategic management and economics. Strateg Manage J 12(Winter Special Issue):5–29

Russell RR (1985) Measures of technical efficiency. J Econ Theory 35:109–126

Ruttan VW, Binswanger HP, Hayami Y, Wade WW, Weber A (1978) Factor productivity and growth: a historical interpretation. In: Binswanger HP, Ruttan VW et al (eds) Induced innovation: technology, institution, and developments. John Hopkins University Press, Baltimore

Sachverständigenrat Gesundheit (2005), des Sachverständigenrates zur Begutachtung der Entwicklung im Gesundheitswesen: Koordination und Qualität im Gesundheitswesen, Berlin

Sahu SK (1998) Technological transfer dependence and self reliant development in the third world: the pharmaceutical and machine tool industries in India. Praeger, Westport

Santerre RE, Stephen PN (2004) Health economies: theories, insights and industry studies, 3rd edn. South-Western, Mason

Sarangi H, Phani BV (2008) Determinants of operational efficiencies in the Indian pharmaceutical industry. Int Trans Oper Res 16(1):109–130

Saving TR (1970) Concentration ratios and the degree of monopoly. Int Econ Rev 11:139–146

Sawhney PK, Sawhney BL (1973) Capacity utilization, concentration and price cost margins: results on Indian industries. J Ind Econ 21(2):145–153

Scherer FM, Ross D (1990) Industrial market structure and economic performance, 3rd edn. Huognton Mifflin, Boston

Scherer FM (1993) Pricing, profits, and technological progress in the pharmaceutical industry. J Econ Perspect 7(3):95–115

Schmalensee R (1989) Inter-industry studies of structure and performance. In: Schmalensee R, Willig R (eds) Handbook of industrial organization, vol 2. North-Holland, Amsterdam, pp 951–1009

Schwatrzman D (1976a) Innovations in the pharmaceutical industry. John Hopkins University, Baltimore

Schwatrzman D (1976b) Pharmaceutical R&D expenditure and rates of returns. In: Helms RB (ed) Drugs development and marketing. American Enterprise Institute, Washington, DC

Schweitzer SO (1997) Pharmaceutical economics and policy. Oxford University Press, New York, University Press

Scott M, Fiona M (2000) Barriers to entry, brand. Int J Ind Organ 18(7):1085–1104

Scott JT, Pascoe G (1986) Beyond firm and industry effects on profitability in imperfect markets. Rev Econ Stat 68:284–292

Scott-Morton F (1999) Entry decision in the generic drug industry. Rand J Econ 30:421–440

Sen G (1992) Margin, costs and competition: the tyre industry in 1974–83. In: Ghosh A, Subrahmaniam KK, Eapen M, Drabu HA (eds) Indian industralization: structure and policy issues. Oxford University Press, Delhi

Sharma KR, Leung PS (2000) Technical efficiency of carp pond culture in South Asia: an application of stochastic metaproduction frontier function model. Aquacult Econ Manage 4:169–189

Shepherd WG (1974) The treatment of market power. Columbia University Press, New York

Shy O (1995) Industrial organization: theory and application. The MIT Press, Cambridge, MA

Siddharthan NS (2004) Globalisation: productivity, efficiency and growth, an overview. Econ Pol Wkly 39(5):420–422
Siddharthan NS, Lal K (2004) Liberalization, MNE and productivity of Indian enterprises. Econ Pol Wkly 39(5):441–448
Silberston A (1972) Economies of scale in theory and practice. Econ J 82(325):369–391
Simar L, Wilson PW (2007) Estimation and inference in two-stage, semi-parametric models of production. J Econ 136(1):31–64
Simar L, Wilson PW (1998) A general methodology for bootstrapping in nonparametric frontier models, Papers 9811, Catholique de Louvain – Institut de statistique
Singh SP, Agarwal S (2006) Total factor productivity growth, technical progress and efficiency change in sugar industry of Uttar Pradesh. Indian Econ J 54(2):59–82
Sipilainen T, Kuosmanen T, Kumbhakar SC (2008) Measuring productivity, 2008 International Congress, August 26–29, 2008, Ghent, Belgium 44277, European Association of Agricultural Economists
Srivastava V (2001) The impact of India's economic reform on industrial productivity, efficiency and competitiveness. Draft of the report submitted to the National Council of Applied Economic Research, New Delhi
Srivastava V (1996) Liberalization, productivity and competition: a panel study of Indian manufacturing. Oxford University Press, Delhi
Statman M (1983) Competition in the pharmaceutical industry: the declining profitability of drug innovation. American Enterprise Institute, Washington, DC
Stephen D (1979) Choosing between concentration indexes: the Iso-concentration curves. Economica 46:67–75
Sticchcombe AL (1965) Social structure and organizations. In: March JG (ed) Handbook of organization. Martinus Nijhoff, Dordrecht
Stigler GJ (1964) A theory of oligopoly. J Polit Econ 72:44–61
Stimpert JL, Dunhaime IM (1997) Seeing the big picture: the influence of industry, diversification and business strategy on performance. Acad Manage J 40(3):560–583
Strickland AD, Weiss LW (1976) Advertising, concentration and price-cost margins. J Polit Econ 84:1109–1121
Swamy PAVB (1971) Statistical inference in random coefficient regression models. Springer, Berlin
Swamy PAVB, Mehta JS (1977) Estimation of linear models with time and cross-sectionally varying coefficients. J Am Stat Assoc 72:890–898
Tariff Commission (1968) Report of the fair selling prices of drugs and pharmaceuticals. Government of India, Bombay
Tavares G (2002) A bibliography of data envelopment analysis (1978–2001). Rutcor Research Report, Rutgers University, 640 Bartholmew Road, Piscataway
Teece DJ (1980) Economics of scope and scope of the enterprises. J Econ Behav Organ 1:223–247
Teece DJ (1982) Towards the economic theory of the multi-product firm. J Econ Behav Organ 3(1):39–63
Temin P (1979) Technology, regulation and market structure in modern pharmaceutical industry. Bell J Econ 10(2):67–89
Trivedi P (2003) Growth and productivity in selected manufacturing industries in India: a regional prospective # 375, Visiting Research Fellow Series, Institute for Developing Economics, Chiba
Tulkens H, van den Eeckaut P (1995) Non-parametric efficiency, progress, and regress measures for panel data: methodological aspects. Eur J Oper Res 80:474–499
Tybout J (2003) Plant- and firm-level evidence on 'New' trade theories. In: Harrigan J (ed) Handbook of international trade. Basil-Blackwell, Oxford
Tybout J (2000) Manufacturing firms in developing countries: how well do they do and why? J Econ Lit 38:11–44
Varian H (1984) The nonparametric approach to production analysis. Econometrica 54:579–594
Vinesh K (2002) Liberalisation, FDI and productivity spillover- an analysis of Indian manufacturing firms. Oxford Econ Pap 54:668–718

Viscusi WK, Vernon MJ, Harrington JE (2000) The economies and regulation and antitrust, 3rd edn. Mit Press, Cambridge

Watal J (1999) Introducing product patents in the Indian pharmaceutical sector: implications for prices and welfare. World Competition 20:5–21

Watal J (2000) Pharmaceutical patents, prices and welfare losses: policy options for India under the WTO TRIPS agreement. World Econ 23(5):733–752

Weiss LW (1969) Advertising, profits, and corporate taxes. Rev Econ Stat 51:421–430

Weiss LW (1976) Optimal plant size and the extent of suboptimal capacity. In: Masson RT, Qualls PE (eds) Essays in honor of Joe S. Bain. Ballinger, Cambridge

West P, Mahon J (2003) Benefits to payers and patients from parallel trade. York Health Economics Consortium, York

WHO Report (2004) The world health report 2004 – changing history. World Health Organization 2004, Geneva

Wiggins SN (1981) Product quality regulation and new drug introductions: some new evidence from the 1970s. Rev Econ Stat 63(4):615–619

Williamson OE (1967) The economics of discretionary behaviour. Chicago University Press, Chicago

Williamson OE (1981) The modern corporation: origins, evolution, attributes. J Econ Lit 19:1537–1568

Wooldridge JM (2004) Econometric analysis of cross section and panel data. Mit Press, Cambridge

World Bank (1997) The state in a changing world. Oxford University Press, New York

World Bank (1993) The east Asian miracle. Oxford University Press, New York

Zieschang K (1984) An extended farrell efficiency measure. J Econ Theory 33:387–396

Susan E Feinberg & Sumit K Majumdar, 2001. "Technology Spillovers from Foreign Direct Investment in the Indian Pharmaceutical Industry," Journal of International Business Studies, Palgrave Macmillan, vol. 32(3), pages 421–437, September.

Index

M. Mazumdar, *Performance of Pharmaceutical Companies in India*, Contributions to Economics, DOI 10.1007/978-3-7908-2876-4,

D

E

F

G

FSC
www.fsc.org
MIX
Papier | Fördert gute Waldnutzung
FSC® C083411

Kolibri 360 GmbH
Ferdinand-Jühlke-Straße 7
99095 Erfurt, Deutschland
produktsicherheit@kolibri360.de